# Benefits, Costs, and Cycles in Workers' Compensation

# Huebner International Series on Risk, Insurance, and Economic Security

**J. David Cummins, Editor**
The Wharton School
University of Pennsylvania
Philadelphia, Pennsylvania, U.S.A.

**Series Advisors:**

Dr. Phelim P. Boyle,
University of Waterloo, Canada
Dr. Jean Lemaire,
Universite Libre de Bruxelles, Belgium
Prof. Akohiko Tsuboi,
Kagawa University, Japan
Dr. Richard Zeckhauser,
Harvard University, U.S.A.

**Previously published books in the series:**

1. Cummins, J. D.; Smith, B.; Vance, R.;
   VanDerhei, J.: *Risk Classification in Life
   Insurance*
2. Mintel, J.: *Insurance Rate Litigation*
3. Cummins, J. D.: *Strategic Planning and
   Modeling in Property-Liability Insurance*
4. Lemaire, J.: *Automobile Insurance:
   Actuarial Models*
5. Rushing, W.: *Social Functions and
   Economic Aspects of Health Insurance*
6. Cummins, J. D. and Harrington, S.: *Fair Rate
   of Return in Property–Liability Insurance*
7. Appel, D. and Borba, P.: *Workers'
   Compensation Insurance Pricing*
8. Cummins, J. D. and Derrig, R.: *Classic
   Insurance Solvency Theory*
9. Cummins, J. D. and Derrig, R.: *Financial
   Model Insurance Solvency*

The objective of the series is to publish original research and advanced
textbooks dealing with all major aspects of risk bearing and economic
security. The emphasis is on books that will be of interest to an
international audience. Interdisciplinary topics as well as those from
traditional disciplines such as economics, risk and insurance, and
actuarial science are within the scope of the series. The goal is to
provide an outlet for imaginative approaches to problems in both the
theory and practice of risk and economic security.

# Benefits, Costs, and Cycles in Workers' Compensation

**Edited by**
**Philip S. Borba and David Appel**
Milliman & Robertson, Inc.

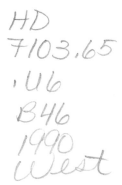

**Kluwer Academic Publishers**
Boston / Dordrecht / London

Distributors for North America:
Kluwer Academic Publishers
101 Philip Drive
Assinippi Park
Norwell, Massachusetts 02061, USA

Distributors for all other countries:
Kluwer Academic Publishers Group
Distribution Centre
Post Office Box 322
3300 AH Dordrecht, THE NETHERLANDS

**Library of Congress Cataloging-in-Publication Data**

Benefits, costs, and cycles in workers compensation / edited by Philip
    S. Borba and David Appel.
        p.      cm. — (Huebner international series on risk, insurance,
    and economic security)
    Papers from the proceedings of a National Council on Compensation
Insurance conference.
    Includes bibliographical references.
        ISBN 0-7923-9037-7
    1. Workers' compensation—United States—Congresses.  I.
Borba, Philip S.   II. Appel, David, 1950–.   III. National Council on
Compensation Insurance.   IV. Series.
HD7103.65.U6B46   1989
368.4′1′00973—dc20                                              89-15536
                                                                    CIP

Printed in the United States of America

# Contents

# Contributing Authors

**David Appel**
Milliman & Robertson, Inc.
Two Penn Plaza
New York, New York 10001

**Monroe Berkowitz**
Department of Economics
Rutgers University
New Brunswick, New Jersey 08903

**Philip S. Borba**
Milliman & Robertson, Inc.
Two Penn Plaza
New York, New York, 10001

**Richard J. Butler**
Department of Economics
Brigham Young University
Provo, Utah 84602

**J. David Cummins**
Department of Insurance
The Wharton School
University of Pennsylvania
Philadelphia, Pennsylvania
    19104-6218

**Michael J. Moore**
The Fuqua School of Business
Duke University
Durham, North Carolina 27706

**Robert S. Smith**
New York State School of Industrial and
    Labor Relations
Cornell University
Ithaca, New York 14853

**W. Kip Viscusi**
Department of Economics
Duke University
Durham, North Carolina 27706

**C. Arthur Williams, Jr.**
School of Management
University of Minnesota
Minneapolis, Minnesota 55455

**John D. Worrall**
Department of Economics
Rutgers University
Camden, New Jersey 08102

**Peter C. Young**
St. Cloud University
St. Cloud, Minnesota 56301

# Preface

Workers' compensation insurance presents a set of institutional characteristics that are unique. For every other form of insurance, both the insurer and the coverage provided under the policy are completely controlled either by the federal or a state government, or by an arrangement between the insured and a property–casualty insurer. Unemployment insurance, Social Security, and bank-deposit insurance are examples for which a legislative body sets the benefits and a government agency prescribes the insurance premium. By contrast, the coverage and premiums for automobile, homeowners, and fire insurance are individual contractual arrangements between a policyholder and one of the more than 1800 U.S. property–casualty insurance companies.

Workers' compensation insurance, however, is a hybrid in which state legislatures stipulate the terms of coverage, while *regulated competition* is the major determinant of prices. State legislatures enact statutes that prescribe the replacement rate and duration of indemnity benefits, as well as full reimbursement of medical expenses. And although the manual rates for workers' compensation insurance continue to be administered by a prior approval process in most states, the competitive-market price for coverage is achieved through a variety of price-modification plans (Appel and Borba, 1988).[1]

Given that most states enacted workers' compensation legislation over 70 years ago, that coverage is mandated by government and specified in a standard policy form, and that rates are typically reviewed by state insurance commissioners, it might be expected that compensation insurance would attract little public attention. However, during the 1980s, the workers' compensation line has become a less desirable market for property–casualty insurers. While the majority of the property–casualty insurance industry has recovered from the depths of the last underwriting cycle, workers' compensation has failed to show susbstantial improvement. This has given rise to a growing involuntary market and the need for large rate increases, which in turn have been the subject of considerable scrutiny.

Between 1980 and 1987, incurred losses as a percent of earned premium increased slightly from 65.4% to 66.6% for the property–casualty industry, while the loss ratio for the workers' compensation line increased from 67.6% to 85.4% in 1986 and 82.2% in 1987. Over the same eight-year period, the operating ratio, which includes expenses and investment income, remained virtually unchanged for the industry (1980, 95.9%; 1987, 95.6%) while the operating ratio for workers' compensation increased from 90.7% to 104.8%, after reaching a 107.4% peak in 1986. The implication of the operating result is that the investment income from the insurance transaction has failed to close the difference between premium revenues and losses and expense costs.

No single cause can completely explain the poor performance of the workers' compensation line. Nearly 20 years after the National Commission on State Workmen's Compensation Laws issued its 19 essential recommendations, benefit reform initiatives continue to be reviewed and refined by state legislatures. In addition to the costs of benefit reform, persistent medical care inflation has placed an upward pressure on rate levels that has attracted a great deal of attention from state attorneys-general, consumer advocates, employer associations, and other special-interest groups. And finally, the favorable investment income opportunities during the early 1980s set off a period of intense price competition from which compensation insurers have yet to recover.

The National Council on Compensation Insurance (NCCI) held a Conference on Economic Issues in Workers' Compensation Insurance to provide researchers and policymakers a forum for an intensive review of many important problems currently confronting the workers' compensation line of insurance. It would be imprudent to suggest that all important policy issues could be addressed at a single conference. Time constraints notwithstanding, the seven chapters in this volume are evidence of the diversity of topics of interest to policymakers and academic researchers.

The first five chapters address issues relating to workers' compensation benefits systems: the influence of workers' compensation benefits on compensating wage differentials, the effects of benefit increases on claim frequency and duration, the payment of workers' compensation benefits beyond retirement age, the costs and benefits of vocational rehabilitation, and evidence that workers' compensation insurance may be compensating off-the-job injuries. With respect to pricing issues, the last two chapters address the modeling of premium and loss cycles for workers' compensation insurance and the use of alternative financial models to evaluate the expected profitability of property–casualty insurance.

The concept of a compensating wage differential for a hazardous working condition has been part of the literature on labor markets for over 200 years (Smith, 1776). Recently, several authors have demonstrated that higher workers' compensation benefits will reduce compensating wage differentials by lowering the expected costs of job injury (Arnould and Nichols, 1983; Dorsey, 1983; Dorsey and Walzer, 1983). Michael Moore and W. Kip Viscusi extend this research with estimates of the aggregate savings to employers attributable to the availability of workers' compensation insurance benefits. Moore and Viscusi compare the reductions in compensating wage differentials to the workers' compensation premiums paid by employers and find that workers' compensation insurance is not an additional cost of doing business. In fact, the workers' compensation premiums are more than offset by the lower compensating wage differentials for hazardous working conditions.

It has been well established that increases in workers' compensation benefit provisions increase claim frequency and severity. The results from the *benefit utilization* analyses are consistant with a basic economic principle concerning opportunity costs: lowering the costs of not returning to work will increase the propensity to file a claim and will lengthen claim durations (Butler and Worrall, 1983; Chelius, 1982; Ruser, 1985; Worrall and Appel, 1982). With respect to the moral hazard problem, John D. Worrall and Richard J. Butler point out the need to distinguish between the effect of a benefit increase on *all* claims from the differential effect that the increase has on *specific* claims. Although a benefit increase will increase the propensity for all workers to file a claim or extend a disability spell, the effect for a specific worker will depend upon differences in workers' attitudes, among other factors that are difficult to observe. Worrall and Butler develop estimation procedures that isolate the general impact of a benefit increase while controlling for unobserved claimant characteristics. The empirical results find that 1) a 10% increase in benefits causes a 10% increase in claim frequency, and 2) a 10% increase in benefits increases claim duration by 2%.

Between 1980 and 2000, the number of individuals over the age of 65 is expected to increase faster than the number of individuals between 25 and 64 years of age. The demographic shift toward an older population implies that more workers may be eligible to receive workers' compensation benefits beyond the normal retirement age. C. Arthur Williams and Peter Young note that, in most workers' compensation benefit systems, benefits are not reduced after a disabled worker reaches the normal retirement age. The authors observe that, as the American workforce becomes older, the cost of providing disability benefits to retirement-age workers will increase, perhaps at the expense of providing benefits to other disabled workers. Williams and Young present several alternative approaches for compensating injured workers after the normal retirement age. Rather than a retirement-age benefit that continues to be based upon preretirement earnings, the authors recommend a system in which retirement-age disabled workers would receive a fraction of the retirement income and other postretirement employee benefits lost due to the disability.

Most students of workers' compensation benefit systems would agree that the first objective of a benefit system is to offset the economic losses arising from a workplace injury or death, and that a second objective is to minimize the nonworking spell and disruption caused by an injury (Rejda, 1976). A primary means for achieving the second objective is a rehabilitation program that shortens the disabled worker's recovery period or retrains the worker for alternative employment. Monroe Berkowitz reviews the historical role of rehabilitation programs for workers' compensation beneficiaries and the significant differences among the current workers' compensation statutes. Berkowitz reviews two important problems with the present rehabilitation programs. First, in spite of the fact that rehabilitation programs have been in existence since the earliest workers' compensation benefit statutes were enacted, there is no conclusive evidence that rehabilitation programs improve the disabled worker's return-to-work prospects or that rehabilitation programs can be justified on a cost–benefit evaluation. Second, in addition to the many significant changes in the coverage (e.g., mandatory versus optional) and responsibility for rehabilitation, there have been substantial changes in the nature of rehabilitation providers. In particular, the recent trend has been for public agencies to offer fewer rehabilitation services, while private providers have greatly increased the number and variety of rehabilitation programs. Berkowitz warns, however, that the shift toward private rehabilitation programs will require more careful supervision and control by the state industrial-accident boards and commissions. Without the close supervision, the costs for the rehabilitation programs may become unacceptably large.

The tremendous number of injuries covered under workers' compensation programs precludes employers, insurers, and industrial-accident boards from verifying the validity of every claim. Indeed, there can be little doubt that compensation is provided for many questionable disabilities and for disabilities caused by off-the-job injuries. Robert S. Smith addresses the latter question, estimating the proportion of disabilities that might be attributable to off-the-job injuries. The study compares the relative frequency of injuries that may be concealed or for which treatment may be delayed (e.g., sprains and strains) against the frequency of injuries that are difficult to conceal or require immediate medical treatment (e.g., fractures and lacerations). Smith finds strong circumstantial evidence to support the contention that workers' compensation is paying for some off-the-job injuries, even though the extent of the misrepresentation appears to be small.

The chapters by Richard J. Butler and John D. Worrall and by J. David Cummins address issues concerning the pricing and performance of the workers' compensation line of insurance. The increased amplitude of recent property–casualty underwriting cycles has increased the interest in the factors that influence premium and loss levels and that can be used to predict them. Butler and Worrall investigate premium and loss cycles separately, with special attention to premium and loss cycles at the state level. Butler and Worrall find that 1) workers' compensation premium and loss cycles have different lengths, and 2) there are substantial inter-state differences in the cycles. Butler and Worrall proceed to construct economic models in which interest rates, benefits, employment levels, and other variables are used to decompose the premium and loss cycles. Al-though the economic models explained part of the state-specific workers' compensation premium and loss cycles, substantial interstate differences continued to be observed. The authors suggest that, for further decom-position of the premium and loss cycles, good quantitative proxies are needed to measure the administrative characteristics of the state workers' compensation systems.

A highly controversial issue in insurance regulation is the profit margin to be allowed in the manual rates (Cummins and Harrington, 1987). J. David Cummins reviews and evaluates several of the models most frequently used to determine the profit margin in property–casualty rate-making formulas. In comparing the major classes of models, Cummins concludes that accounting models are flawed because 1) accounting models are retrospective rather than prospective, and 2) they use embedded yields to measure the rate of return on policyholder funds. By contrast, cash-flow models rely upon yields currently available in financial markets and produce a prospective rate of return. Cummins presents a succinct explanation of the technical differences between two cash-flow models that are most frequently used for property–casualty ratemaking, and finds that the two models are consistent with the principles of corporate finance and will produce correct results if applied properly.

In sum, the diversity of topics addressed in the present volume reflects the diversity of problems confronting workers' compensation insurance institutions. The chapters present important research findings and commentary that will be useful both for policy-setting decisions and as foundations for future research.

## Notes

1. An exception to the influence that market competition can have on the individual-risk pricing plans occurs when the manual rate is inadequate to cover the expenses and expected losses from a compensation insurance policy. In such cases, the risk is likely to be covered by the assigned risk pool and charged the manual rate.

## References

Appel, David, and Philip S. Borba, "Costs and Prices of Workers' Compensation Insurance." In David Appel and Philip S. Borba (eds.), *Workers' Compensation Insurance Pricing*. Boston: Kluwer Academic Publishers, 1988.

Arnould, Richard J., and Len M. Nichols. "Wage-Risk Premiums and Workers' Compensation: A Refinement of Estimates of Compensating Wage Differential." *Journal of Political Economy* 91, 2 (1983): 332–340.

Butler, Richard J., and John D. Worrall. "Workers' Compensation: Benefit and Injury Claims Rates in the Seventies." *Review of Economics and Statistics* 65, 4 (1983): 580–589.

Chelius, James R. "The Influence of Workers' Compensation on Safety Incentives." *Industrial and Labor Relations Review* 35 (1982): 235–242.

Cummins, J. David, and Scott A. Harrington (eds.). *Fair Rate of Return in Property–Liability Insurance*. Boston: Kluwer-Nijhoff Publishing, 1987.

Dorsey, Stuart. "Employment Hazards and Fringe Benefits: Further Tests for Compensating Differentials." In John D. Worrall (ed.), *Safety and the Workforce: Incentives and Disincentives in Workers' Compensation*. Ithaca, NY: ILR Press, 1983.

Dorsey, Stuart, and Norman Walzer. "Workers' Compensation, Job Hazards, and Wages." *Industrial and Labor Relations Review* 36, 4 (1983): 642–654.

Rejda, George E. *Social Insurance and Economic Security*. Englewood Cliffs, NJ: Prentice-Hall, Inc., 1976.

Ruser, John W. "Workers' Compensation Insurance, Experience Rating, and Occupational Injuries." *Rand Journal* 16, 4 (1985): 487–503.

Smith, Adam. *An Inquiry Into the Nature and Causes of the Wealth of Nations*. 1776.

Worrall, John D., and David Appel. "The Wage Replacement Rate and Benefit Utilization in Workers' Compensation Insurance." *Journal of Risk and Insurance* 49, 3 (1982): 361–371.

# Benefits, Costs, and Cycles in Workers' Compensation

# 1 HAVE INCREASES IN WORKERS' COMPENSATION BENEFITS PAID FOR THEMSELVES?

Michael J. Moore
W. Kip Viscusi

## The Rising Costs of Workers' Compensation

Since the early 1970s there has been a dramatic change in the market for hazardous jobs. The government began direct control of workplace technology through occupational safety and health regulations,[1] while the judicial system became an active player in the area of ex post compensation of job risks. This compensation for long-term health risks, particularly for asbestos workers, may run in the tens of billions of dollars.[2]

Much of the reason for the focus of public attention on these developments is that they represented a change in the role that these institutions played. Although the federal government has long had specific interests in particular areas of safety such as the working conditions for longshoremen and maritime workers, the advent of the Occupational Safety and Health Administration marked a sweeping expansion of these responsibilities. Similarly, the emergence of an important role for judicial compensation of job accidents in product liability suits did not represent an entirely new area of the law, but the advent of mass tort cases at the very least did represent a quantum leap in the degree of activity.

Perhaps because of these developments, there has not been sufficient

1

attention devoted to the equally important shift in the role of workers' compensation.[3] The state workers' compensation system has long been one of the principal sources of nonwage costs borne by employers. Although by no means as large a component of compensation as social security taxes, workers' compensation premiums have traditionally been of comparable importance to other nonwage costs. In the early 1970s workers' compensation premiums averaged around 1% of compensation,[4] which is comparable to the unemployment compensation tax share.[5]

In the early 1970s, the National Commission on State Workmen's Compensation Laws (1972) sought a somewhat more ambitious role for workers' compensation. In a series of recommendations, the Commission urged that benefits be raised in order to reduce the extent of wage loss. From 1973–1983 there has been a major shift in the level of workers' compensation premiums, which have risen from $6.8 billion in 1973 to $22.9 billion in 1983. As a percent of total compensation, workers' compensation increased its importance in that decade, since it constituted 1.73% of compensation in 1982, and 1.67% in 1983.

This dramatic increase in costs has not gone unnoticed by the employers who bear the costs. The rapid increase in the compensation burden in the late 1970s was a particular cause for alarm. Taking these cost increases at face value as a measure of the total cost of the system is not, however, appropriate from an economic standpoint.

A $16.1-billion increase in annual workers' compensation premiums is not tantamount to a general tax levy of $16.1 billion used to provide for contributions to the overall federal budget. The benefits to injured workers have also risen and, as a result, workers will view compensation for hazardous jobs as greater than before. From a conceptual standpoint, workers should willingly accept a reduction in wages for the added benefits and, if the level of benefits provided is not supra-optimal, workers will accept a wage reduction that exceeds the actuarial cost of the awards.[6]

There may be additional ramifications as well. More generous benefit levels may boost the number of injuries for which claims are filed and may lead workers to prolong the period of recovery. Although the magnitude of such influences remains controversial, the existence of some moral hazard problems of this type is suggested by existing research. These effects and existing evidence on their magnitude are discussed below.

In this chapter, we explore the extent to which the effect of higher workers' compensation costs is offset by these economic effects. The principal building block for our analysis is an estimate of the extent of wage reductions induced by higher benefit levels. To estimate this relationship, we employ three different sets of survey data for the years 1977 and 1982 that enable us to estimate not only the rate of tradeoff but also changes in the rate of tradeoff over time. The next section describes these data sets and the variables used.

The focus of the third section of the chapter is on the empirical model used in the estimation and on the regression results. There is indeed a substantial tradeoff between the base wage rate and workers' compensation benefits that greatly exceeds the actuarial cost of the benefits. These findings are used in the fourth section to calculate the cost of the increase in workers' compensation premiums after accounting for the wage reductions attributable to higher benefits. In all the cases considered, benefit increases have more than paid for themselves through wage reductions.

The cost of this economic "free lunch" is boosted, however, if higher benefit levels induce workers to collect benefits for a longer duration and for more injuries. The role of these factors is discussed in an exploratory analysis in the fifth section. As indicated in the concluding section, recognition of these offsets resulting from higher benefits greatly reduces the net-benefit impact of higher premium levels.

## Variable Descriptions and Characteristics of the Samples

The general approach we take is to estimate a wage equation in which we isolate the effects of worker characteristics, job characteristics (including job risks), and workers' compensation on wages. The estimated relationship then provides the basis for assessing the wage–workers'-compensation tradeoff.

This estimation relies on two large data sets pertaining to the labor market situation of individual workers. More specifically, the data used to estimate the parameters of interest are drawn from the University of Michigan Panel Study of Income Dynamics (PSID) and the 1977 Quality of Employment Survey (QES). Two years of the PSID are considered—1977 and 1982. We use the 1977 data to allow comparison of the results reported below with those of Viscusi and Moore (1987), and the 1982 data to capture the relationship between wages and workers' compensation of a more recent vintage.

Although it is possible to exploit the panel nature of the PSID, we do not do so here, choosing instead to treat each year as a distinct cross section. After exclusion of the nonrandom poverty subsample of the PSID, self-employed individuals, farmers, and individuals who are not heads of households and who experienced long-term unemployment in each year, 1329 and 1106 observations remain in the 1977 and 1982 waves. The QES sample used in Viscusi and Moore (1987) contained 485 observations.

As was the case in our previous work, the variables of primary interest in this study are the risk and insurance variables—INJURY and WCOMP. Since the PSID does not ascertain injury risks for individual workers, it is necessary to match injury-rate data to each worker by industry. Unfortunately, the detail afforded by three-digit industry data is not available in the PSID until 1981. Thus, the 1977 risk data in the PSID is more highly aggregated than the 1982 data, which causes more error to be introduced into the earlier measure.

The theoretical model developed in Viscusi and Moore (1987) defines risk as the probability of an injury. This suggests the use of the lost workday case rate as the empirical measure of risk, since the number of accidents is a better measure of frequency than the alternative, namely total lost workdays. Thus, INJURY is the lost-workday case rate reported by the Bureau of Labor Statistics and matched to individual workers by two-digit industry in the 1977 PSID and three-digit industry in the 1977 QES and 1982 PSID. As noted by Viscusi and Moore, use of INJURY ignores such issues as the duration and severity of wage loss. However, injury frequency data capture sufficiently the effects we wish to analyze here, and are more directly comparable to earlier results, so we abstract from duration issues.

We capture the ex post component of job-risk compensation by the workers' compensation wage replacement rate, REPRATE. This is an individual-specific measure of the fraction of weekly after-tax wages that is replaced by workers' compensation insurance. We compute the weekly benefit level for worker $i$, $b_i$, based on information on wages, marital status, number of dependents, and state of residence. We then construct the replacement rate by dividing $b_i$ by the worker's after-tax weekly wage, $GWAGE_i$ $(1\text{-}MTAX_i)$, where $GWAGE_i$ is the before-tax (gross) wage, and $MTAX_i$ is the marginal tax rate. The tax-rate variable used in our earlier study was computed based on reported earnings and tax-table information, assuming the worker took the standard deduction. This is not the case with the PSID data, however, since workers report their marginal tax rates there. To the extent that self-reporting improves the accuracy of $MTAX_i$, this represents an improvement over our computed measure.

The variable REPRATE measures the individual-specific rate at which wages are replaced by workers' compensation benefits in the event of an injury that qualifies for compensation:

$$REPRATE_i = \frac{b_i}{GWAGE_i \ (1\text{-}MTAX_i) \times 40}$$

As noted by Viscusi and Moore (1987), and by Topel (1984) for the analogous unemployment insurance replacement rate, the presence of GWAGE$_i$ and MTAX$_i$ in REPRATE$_i$ would lead to endogeneity bias in a wage equation if REPRATE$_i$ were inserted as a regressor. To address this endogeneity issue, we instrument REPRATE$_i$ using a first-stage regression of the after-tax wage on a vector of characteristics $Z_i$ that includes all of the exogenous variables in the model, second- and third-order terms for each

Table 1–1.   Variable Definitions for the PSID Sample

| Variable | Definition |
| --- | --- |
| EDUCATION | Grades completed.[a] |
| EXPERIENCE | Age—EDUCATION—6. |
| JOBTENURE | Years worked on current job. |
| BLACK | Race dummy variable (d.v.): BLACK = 1 if black, 0 otherwise. |
| FEMALE | Sex d.v.: FEMALE = 1 if female, 0 otherwise. |
| HEALTH | Health limitations d.v.: HEALTH = 1 if worker has a physical or nervous condition that limits the amount of work he can do, 0 otherwise. |
| UNION | Union status d.v.: UNION = 1 if worker's job is covered by a union contract, 0 otherwise. |
| INJURY | Incidence of cases involving a lost workday due to injury or illness by 3-digit industry, 1982, and by 2-digit industry, 1977. |
| WCOMP | Expected workers' compensation replacement rate: WCOMP = INJURY × REPHAT (predicted value). |
| BLUE | Collar color d.v.: BLUE = 1 if worker works in a blue-collar occupation, 0 otherwise. |
| WAGE | Workers' hourly wage after taxes. |
| REPRATE | Workers' compensation weekly wage replacement rate. |
| MTAX | Workers' marginal tax rate. |
| NEAST | Region d.v.: NEAST = 1 if worker lives in the northeastern United States, 0 otherwise. |
| NCENT | Region d.v.: NCENT = 1 if worker lives in the north central United States, 0 otherwise. |
| SOUTH | Region d.v.: SOUTH = 1 if worker lives in the southeastern United States, 0 otherwise. |
| WEST | Region d.v.: WEST = 1 if worker lives in the western United States, 0 otherwise. |
| CITY | Urban area d.v.: CITY = 1 if worker lives in an urban area with population in excess of 100,000, 0 otherwise. |

[a] Variable was coded differently in QES sample.

continuous exogenous variable, and state dummy variables. The predicted value of $REPRATE_i$, $REPHAT_i$, is then interacted with INJURY to reflect the fact that insurance benefits matter to workers only at positive risk levels, and that they matter more as risk levels increase. Workers facing zero risk will place no value on workers' compensation. Justification for utilizing this functional form is explored in greater detail in Viscusi and Moore (1987). We refer to the resulting variable as WCOMP.

A detailed list of the variables used in the empirical analysis is presented in Table 1–1. Worker characteristics include years of schooling (EDUCATION), years worked since completion of schooling (EXPERIENCE), years worked on the current job (JOBTENURE), race (BLACK dummy variable (d.v.)), sex (FEMALE d.v.), and health status (HEALTH d.v.). Job characteristics include whether or not the worker's job is covered by a union contract (UNION d.v.), the BLS injury risk (INJURY), the predicted expected replacement rate (WCOMP), and whether the job is a blue-collar occupation (BLUE d.v.).

The basic measure of pecuniary compensation is WAGE, the after-tax hourly wage. WAGE is computed from information on annual labor earnings and hours and the marginal tax rate, MTAX. Use of the after-tax wage or its natural logarithm is not widespread in the equalizing difference literature. With the exception of Viscusi and Moore (1987), pretax wages are always used as the dependent measure, despite the fact that the after-tax wage is theoretically appropriate. As was the case in this earlier study, use of the after-tax wage alters some of the results in terms of statistical significance.

Table 1–2 presents descriptive statistics for the PSID samples. Each sample appears representative of the U.S. working population. In addition, time-dependent measures such as EXPERIENCE, JOB TENURE, and EDUCATION are consistently large in 1982. Wages increase substantially, primarily due to inflation, since the average nominal wage for 1981, the year covered by the 1982 PSID, is approximately $7.29, compared with the 1976 average of $4.88. The 1981 wage in 1976 dollars is only $4.85. Finally, there is a substantial increase in the average risk level in the later sample.

The risk and workers' compensation variables reflect the experiences of a typical U.S. worker. The mean INJURY levels suggest that for these samples the average risk of a lost-workday injury ranged from 4–5 per 100 workers annually. These levels are comparable to figures for the average U.S. worker. The injury rate of 3.56 for the 1977 PSID subsample, which reflects working conditions in 1976, is very close to the 1976 private-sector average lost-workday rate of 3.5 per 100 workers. The 1982 PSID sample

Table 1-2. Descriptive Statistics

| Variable | PSID (Means (Standard Deviations)) | |
| | 1977 (N=1329) | 1982 (N=1106) |
| --- | --- | --- |
| EDUCATION[a] | 12.23 (3.03) | 12.75 (2.82) |
| EXPERIENCE | 19.71 (13.27) | 21.68 (11.84) |
| EXPERIENCE$^2$ | 5.64E+2 (6.24E+2) | 6.01E+2 (6.05E+2) |
| JOBTENURE | 5.44 (6.50) | 5.92 (6.81) |
| JOBTENURE$^2$ | 0.72E+2 (1.60E+2) | 0.79E+2 (1.85E+2) |
| BLACK | 0.07 (0.26) | 0.07 (0.26) |
| FEMALE | 0.17 (0.37) | 0.12 (0.32) |
| HEALTH | 0.06 (0.24) | 0.08 (0.28) |
| UNION | 0.30 (0.46) | 0.31 (0.46) |
| INJURY | 3.56 (1.72) | 4.56 (2.93) |
| WCOMP | 3.26 (2.47) | 4.28 (3.98) |
| REPRATE | 0.94 (0.54) | 0.92 (0.50) |
| WAGE | 4.88 (1.99) | 7.29 (2.42) |
| CITY | 0.53 (0.50) | 0.53 (0.50) |
| NEAST | 0.21 (0.41) | 0.20 (0.40) |
| NCENT | 0.32 (0.47) | 0.32 (0.47) |
| SOUTH | 0.29 (0.45) | 0.28 (0.45) |
| WEST | 0.18 (0.45) | 0.19 (0.46) |
| BLUE | 0.50 (0.50) | 0.49 (0.50) |

[a] Variable was coded differently in the QES sample.

rate of 4.56 for employment experiences in 1981 is somewhat greater than the 1981 national average of 3.8 injuries per 100 workers, but it is less than the manufacturing average lost-workday case rate of 5.1 per 100 workers.

The magnitudes of the workers' compensation variables suggest that the degree of coverage is quite extensive. Taking into account the favorable tax status of the benefits, workers' compensation replaces over 90% of the worker's wage in each of the sample years (REPRATE). The duration of these benefits is not, however, unlimited, so the effective replacement rate for injuries of long duration may be less. The expected replacement rate (WCOMP), which is the probability of suffering an injury times the replacement rate of wages, is 3.26 in 1977 and 4.28 in 1982.

The variable BLUE (i.e., blue-collar) is intended to capture important differences in job attributes other than risk that might influence the wage premium that a job commands. Thus, this variable is intended to act as a proxy for other job attributes, such as whether the job involves unpleasant working conditions. Inclusion of such nonpecuniary attributes has been the exception in the literature, since only a minority of compensating differential studies (e.g., Viscusi, 1979) include such measures. Since the PSID does not include such job attributes measures, we rely on the blue-collar dummy variable as a proxy for these concerns.

### Estimates of the Wage Equations

We estimated two equations for each PSID cross section, using posttax wages and their natural logarithms as the dependent variables. The principal variables of interest are INJURY and the WCOMP benefits. Higher INJURY levels should boost worker wages, since workers will demand a compensating differential for hazardous jobs. Similarly, higher expected replacement rates for injuries will lower the level of compensation, so that WCOMP, which reflects the interactive influence of the risk level and the replacement rate, should have a negative sign, based on theoretical considerations.

Table 1–3 summarizes estimates of the equation

$$\ln\text{WAGE}_i = \sum_k \beta_k X_{ik} + \gamma\text{INJURY}_i + \delta\text{WCOMP}_i + \varepsilon_i \qquad (1.1)$$

for each sample. Since the results were quite similar using the WAGE variable to those using lnWAGE as the dependent variable, only the semilogarithmic results are reported in detail. The characteristics $X_{ik}$ include EDUCATION, EXPERIENCE, EXPERIENCE$^2$, JOBTENURE, JOBTENURE$^2$, BLACK, FEMALE, HEALTH, UNION, BLUE, and

Table 1–3.   lnWAGE Regression Estimates (Standard Deviations in Parentheses)

| Variable | 1977 | 1982 |
|---|---|---|
| EDUCATION | 0.045 | 0.032 |
| | (0.004) | (0.004) |
| EXPERIENCE | 0.023 | 0.016 |
| | (0.003) | (0.004) |
| EXPERIENCE$^2$ | $-3.7E-4$ | $-2.5E-4$ |
| | $(0.7E-4)$ | $(0.7E-4)$ |
| JOBTENURE | 0.017 | 0.011 |
| | (0.005) | (0.003) |
| JOBTENURE$^2$ | $-4.5E-4$ | $-1.9E-4$ |
| | $(1.8E-4)$ | $(1.2E-4)$ |
| BLACK | $-0.130$ | $-0.135$ |
| | (0.040) | (0.036) |
| FEMALE | $-0.305$ | $-0.284$ |
| | (0.028) | (0.028) |
| HEALTH | $-0.098$ | $-0.094$ |
| | (0.042) | (0.032) |
| UNION | 0.169 | 0.153 |
| | (0.024) | (0.021) |
| BLUE | $-0.131$ | $-0.075$ |
| | (0.024) | (0.023) |
| INJURY | 0.034 | 0.023 |
| | (0.008) | (0.005) |
| WCOMP | $-0.010$ | $-0.015$ |
| | (0.006) | (0.004) |
| NEAST | $-0.4E-2$ | $-0.054$ |
| | $(3.1E-2)$ | (0.028) |
| NCENT | $1.6E-2$ | $-0.042$ |
| | $(2.9E-2)$ | (0.025) |
| SOUTH | $-6.7E-2$ | $-0.089$ |
| | $(3.0E-2)$ | (0.027) |
| CITY | 0.116 | 0.063 |
| | (0.021) | (0.019) |
| CONSTANT | 0.589 | 1.319 |
| | (0.080) | (0.079) |
| $\bar{R}^2$ | 0.38 | 0.31 |

the region and city size dummies NEAST, NCENT, SOUTH, and CITY. The variable INJURY is the nonfatal incidence rate for injuries and illnesses involving at least one last workday, and WCOMP is the measure of insurance described above. The injury frequency abstracts from differences in severity that may affect injury durations and the amount of benefits received. However, use of this variable makes a more precise theoretical interpretation possible, as discussed in Viscusi and Moore (1987).

In both the 1977 and 1982 samples, the equations perform as expected in terms of the usual components of an earnings equation. An additional year of education results in a 3%–4% increase in wages. Experience and job tenure both increase wages at a decreasing rate. Black and female workers earn substantially lower wages, as do workers with health limitations. Finally, the estimated wage premium for workers covered by a collective bargaining agreement is about 16%.

The variables of particular interest in table 1–3 are INJURY and WCOMP. In both samples, higher nonfatal injury risks increase wages significantly. Likewise, ex post compensation for injuries reduces wages, affecting the ex ante compensation for risk provided through the injury-risk compensating differential. In both years the WCOMP effect is statistically significant at the usual levels.

Table 1–4 summarizes the estimated risk and insurance effects. The results include the lnWAGE equations reported in table 1–3, estimates for equations with WAGE as the dependent variable, and results that we obtained with another set of data—the 1977 University of Michigan Quality of Employment Survey—that are described in Viscusi and Moore (1987). The evidence is consistent across the three sets of data and two dependent variables in terms of the nature of the influences. There is strong support for the prediction that risks increase wages and that

Table 1–4.    Elasticities (Coefficients and Standard Deviations)

| Wage Equations | After-tax WAGE | | After-tax lnWAGE | |
|---|---|---|---|---|
| | 1976[a] | 1981 | 1976[a] | 1981 |
| INJURY | 0.158 | 0.107 | 0.036 | 0.015 |
| | (0.035) | (0.037) | (0.008) | (0.005) |
| WCOMP | −0.140 | −0.185 | −0.031 | −0.031 |
| | (0.072) | (0.129) | (0.016) | (0.018) |
| RATE OF TRADEOFF | −.10 | −.11 | −.12 | −.15 |

[a] The source of the 1977 QES results is Viscusi and Moore (1987).

workers' compensation insurance reduces wages, conditional on the risk level. In each of the two models estimated with the 1982 data, the INJURY and WCOMP effects have the predicted signs and are significant at the .01 confidence level. The same is true of the INJURY coefficient in both 1977 samples. Likewise, WCOMP has the predicted sign and performs quite well in both the before-tax and after-tax lnWAGE equations. WCOMP is negative and significant in three of the four equations estimated using the 1977 samples. Furthermore, in every equation estimated, INJURY and WCOMP have the correct signs, and are jointly significant.

### Wage–Insurance Tradeoffs

The parameter of primary importance that can be calculated from these estimates is the implied rate of tradeoff between wages and workers' compensation. This estimate has interesting policy implications. In particular, the estimate makes it possible to establish the extent to which benefit increases are financed by workers through wage reductions. In addition, as shown in Viscusi and Moore (1987), estimation of this rate of tradeoff enables us to determine whether or not benefit levels are optimal by comparing the observed rate with that which would occur in an idealized world, recognizing the existence of administrative costs of the insurance program.

Calculation of the rate of tradeoff is straightforward. Equation (1.1) can be rewritten, dropping the $i$ subscript for convenience, as

$$\text{lnWAGE} = \sum_k \beta_k X_k + \gamma \text{INJURY} + \delta \frac{\text{INJURY} \times \text{BENEFIT}}{\text{WAGE} \times 40}$$

plus a random error term. The last term is the INJURY level multiplied by the weekly wage replacement rate. The weekly replacement rate is the value of BENEFIT, the weekly insurance payment, divided by 40 times WAGE, where WAGE is the after-tax hourly wage and 40 hours is the average full-time work week.

Multiplying both sides of the equation by WAGE $\times$ 40, we get

$$40 \times \text{WAGE} \times \text{lnWAGE} = \left[ \sum_k \beta_k X_k + \gamma \text{INJURY} \right] \times \text{WAGE} \times 40$$
$$+ \delta \text{INJURY} \times \text{BENEFIT}.$$

Totally differentiating the above expression and collecting terms, we get the expression for the rate of tradeoff between the weekly wage and weekly benefits,

$$40 \times \frac{\partial \text{WAGE}}{\partial \text{BENEFIT}} = \frac{\partial \text{INJURY}}{[1 + \ln\text{WAGE} - \Sigma \beta_k X_k - \gamma \text{INJURY}]}$$

The bottom row in Table 1–4 summarizes the estimated rates of tradeoff derived using this formula in conjunction with the estimated regression coefficients. The most striking result apparent in Table 1–4 is the size of the estimated rate of tradeoff in the 1977 QES and the 1982 PSID. These results are estimated with a less aggregative risk variable than are the 1977 PSID estimates and are consequently less subject to measurement error bias.

The results consistently indicate that benefit levels are too low relative to the rate of tradeoff that would be observed if the level of insurance were optimal. In Viscusi and Moore (1987), we show that the efficient rate of tradeoff (i.e., the relationship between wages and insurance if benefit levels are at their most preferred levels, given the actuarial constraint) is given by

$$\frac{\partial \text{WAGE}}{\partial \text{BENEFIT}} = \frac{-p(1 + a)}{1 - p}$$

where $p$ is the probability of an accident and $a$ is the loading factor that represents administrative costs. Assuming $a = .25$, which is a reasonable approximation of the national average (see Viscusi and Moore, 1987), and given the accident probabilities of .035 (1977 QES), .047 (1977 PSID), and .046 (1982 PSID) in our sample, the optimal WAGE–BENEFIT trade-offs are $-.05$ (1977 QES), $-.06$ (1977 PSID), and $-.06$ (1982 PSID). The actual tradeoffs calculated from the data are always much larger (in absolute value) than those for the 1977 QES. The 1977 PSID results are smallest in absolute magnitude, perhaps in part because of the greater measurement error in the INJURY variable, which is based on two-digit industry matchups of injuries to workers, whereas the 1977 QES and the 1982 PSID results are based on more refined, three-digit matchups. The 1982 results indicate benefit levels fairly close to the optimal insurance amount, excluding the role of moral hazard (higher benefit levels may increase the frequency of injuries if workers become less careful, and also increase their duration, since higher benefits may reduce the incentive to return to work).

If we focus on the PSID data, it appears that there has been an increase in benefit inadequacy over the five-year period, since workers are increasingly willing to trade off wages for workers' compensation benefits. Some rough calculations could be made to explain this finding. First, although the average weekly benefit level in our sample rose from $148 to

$235, the average after-tax weekly wage based on a forty-hour week rose from $195 to $292. Thus, in our sample, the average weekly earnings replacement rate fell over time by nine percentage points. A further calculation shows that, by translating weekly benefits in 1981 into 1976 dollars using the appropriate price deflator for the period, real benefits are largely unchanged. Since these real benefits are the worker's concern, and since we would expect the demand for real benefits to rise with the observed increase in the injury level, the observed trends in the rates of tradeoff are plausible. Nevertheless, in all likelihood the difference reflects primarily the higher quality of the risk data in the 1982 PSID, so one should be cautious in taking the 1977 PSID results at face value.

For purposes of the subsequent calculations, the general implications of the results are the following. Consider a situation in which the actuarial cost of benefits (plus administrative costs) leads to a 5–6-cent expected additional cost to employers for each additional $1 in benefit levels. Since administrative costs are not high, workers receive an expected benefit of 4–5 cents. In return for these higher expected benefits, they are willing to take a considerably higher wage cut, on the order of 12 cents for the 1977 QES. For this sample, clearly, higher workers' compensation benefits produce wage reductions several times greater than their dollar cost.

In the case of the 1977 PSID results, the higher benefits do not pay their own way. These estimates, which are subject to much more substantial measurement error than the 1977 QES estimates because of the more aggregative industry risk–worker matchups, do not appear to be a reliable reflection of worker preferences, particularly given the much different and more precise results using three-digit matchups.

Finally, for the 1982 PSID, higher workers' compensation benefits lead to wage reductions that are comparable to the levels that one would expect if insurance for injuries were set at an optimal level. If one uses the 1977 QES results as the reference point for the tradeoff four years earlier, then there appears to have been a substantial drop in the rate at which workers will sacrifice wages for higher workers' compensation benefits. Thus, the level of workers' compensation benefits that would be observed with fully efficient insurance markets is similar to that provided in 1981 and above the amount provided in 1976.

## Estimates of the Total Wage Offset

Table 1–5 explores the net cost of workers' compensation after taking into account the wage offset effects. Column 2 in each panel of the table is identical, as it summarizes the after-tax levels of total workers' compensation payments.[7] Before-tax premium levels rose from $10.9 billion in 1976 to $22.9 billion in 1983. Assuming that the marginal tax rate faced by firms is 0.30, the after-tax payments for workers' compensation reported in column 2 of each panel rose from $7.6 billion to $16.0 billion over the same period.[8] Most of this increase occurred from 1976–1980, as after-tax payments almost doubled in this period, rising from $7.6 billion to $13.6 billion.

Panels A to F in Table 5 present calculations of the wage reduction and the net cost of workers' compensation benefits, based on the data in column 2. The key assumptions made, which are summarized in the panel headings, pertain to the rate of tradeoff between wages and workers' compensation and the manner in which benefits relate to workers' compensation payments.

In addition, since the 1977 QES results had a tradeoff of greater absolute magnitude than the 1982 PSID tradeoff, we explored the possible influence of a diminishing magnitude of the rate of tradeoff over time. In Panel C and Panel F the $-.12$ tradeoff is assumed to decrease linearly by .008 annually. As a result, the assumed rate of tradeoff in 1983 is $-.064$, and the rate of tradeoff in 1981 is $-.08$, the result obtained using the 1982 PSID sample A diminishing of the rate of tradeoff is expected on theoretical grounds as benefit levels increase, since the marginal value of insurance declines. This result abstracts from possible moral hazard problems.

Calculation of the wage reductions requires assumptions concerning the relationship between payments, which are made ex post, and benefits, which generate ex ante wage changes. The basic relationship utilized is that total premiums (TP) will equal benefits (b) times the probability of an accident (p), plus the associated administrative costs:

Total Premiums = Benefits × Probability of an Accident
+ Administrative Costs.

If administrative costs equal a cents per dollar of expected benefits, then

$$TP = pb(1 + a).$$

Thus, using information on total premiums and accident probabilities, and the loading factor $a = 0.25$, we can compute the benefit level

$$b = TP/(1.25)p. \qquad (4.2)$$

Once we know b, we can determine the wage reduction due to b by multiplying b by the estimated wage reduction rate. Panels A–F are based on this formula. In Panels A, B, and C, and 1976 risk level of .035 is taken as the measure of p, while in Panels D, E, and F the 1981 risk level of .045 is used. The column 3–5 results are all reported in post-tax dollars, assuming a corporate tax rate of .30.

Based on these assumptions, column 3 in each panel presents the wage reduction effects. For simplicity, let us focus on Panels A-C. With the −.12 wage reduction rate in Panel A, the wage savings range from $20.3 billion to $42.7 billion, each of which is far in excess of the level of insurance payments. With a tradeoff of −.08 in Panel B, the wage effects are one-third lower than in Panel A, as they reach a peak of $28.5 billion in 1983. Finally, in Panel C, in which the rate goes linearly from −.12 in 1976 to

Table 1–5.   Wage Effects and the Net Cost of Worker's Compensation

PANEL A: *Wage reduction = .12 (1977 QES); Benefits = payments/.045*

| Year | Total Payments[a] | Wage Reduction | Total Premiums[a] | Net Cost |
|------|------|------|------|------|
| (in $ billions) | | | | |
| 1976 | 7.6 | 20.3 | 10.9 | −12.7 |
| 1977 | 8.6 | 26.1 | 14.0 | −16.3 |
| 1978 | 9.7 | 30.9 | 16.6 | −19.3 |
| 1979 | 11.9 | 37.6 | 20.0 | −23.5 |
| 1980 | 13.6 | 41.1 | 22.0 | −25.7 |
| 1981 | 15.0 | 42.7 | 22.9 | −26.7 |
| 1982 | 16.3 | 42.1 | 22.5 | −26.3 |
| 1983 | 16.0 | 42.7 | 22.9 | −26.7 |

PANEL B: *Wage reduction = .08 (1981 PSID-lnWAGE eq.);*
*Benefits = payments/.045*

| Year | Total Payments[a] | Wage Reduction | Total Premiums[a] | Net Cost |
|------|------|------|------|------|
| (in $ billions) | | | | |
| 1976 | 7.6 | 13.5 | 10.9 | − 5.9 |
| 1977 | 8.6 | 17.4 | 14.0 | − 7.6 |
| 1978 | 9.7 | 20.6 | 16.6 | − 9.0 |
| 1979 | 11.9 | 25.1 | 20.0 | −11.0 |
| 1980 | 13.6 | 27.4 | 22.0 | −12.0 |
| 1981 | 15.0 | 28.5 | 22.9 | −12.5 |
| 1982 | 16.3 | 28.0 | 22.5 | −12.2 |
| 1983 | 16.0 | 28.5 | 22.9 | −12.5 |

Table 1-5.   (continued).

PANEL C: *Wage reduction = .12 in 1976 (1977 QES), increases linearly by .008 annually; Benefits = payments/.045*

| Year | Total Payments[a] | Wage Reduction | Total Premiums[a] | Net Cost |
|------|------------------|----------------|-------------------|----------|
| (in $ billions) | | | | |
| 1976 | 7.6 | 20.3 | 10.9 | −12.7 |
| 1977 | 8.6 | 24.4 | 14.0 | −14.6 |
| 1978 | 9.7 | 26.8 | 16.6 | −15.2 |
| 1979 | 11.9 | 30.1 | 20.0 | −16.0 |
| 1980 | 13.6 | 30.1 | 22.0 | −14.7 |
| 1981 | 15.0 | 28.4 | 22.9 | −12.4 |
| 1982 | 16.3 | 25.3 | 22.5 | − 9.5 |
| 1983 | 16.0 | 22.8 | 22.9 | − 6.8 |

PANEL D: *Wage reduction = .12 (1977 QES), Benefits = payments/.056*

| Year | Total Payments[a] | Wage Reduction | Total Premiums[a] | Net Cost |
|------|------------------|----------------|-------------------|----------|
| (in $ billions) | | | | |
| 1976 | 7.6 | 16.3 | 10.9 | − 8.7 |
| 1977 | 8.6 | 21.0 | 14.0 | −11.2 |
| 1978 | 9.7 | 24.9 | 16.6 | −13.3 |
| 1979 | 11.9 | 30.2 | 20.0 | −16.1 |
| 1980 | 13.6 | 33.0 | 22.0 | −17.6 |
| 1981 | 15.0 | 34.3 | 22.9 | −18.3 |
| 1982 | 16.3 | 33.9 | 22.5 | −18.1 |
| 1983 | 16.0 | 34.3 | 22.9 | −18.3 |

PANEL E: *Wage reduction = .08 (1981 PSID-InWAGE); Benefits = payments/.056*

| Year | Total Payments[a] | Wage Reduction | Total Premiums[a] | Net Cost |
|------|------------------|----------------|-------------------|----------|
| (in $ billions) | | | | |
| 1976 | 7.6 | 10.9 | 10.9 | − 3.3 |
| 1977 | 8.6 | 14.0 | 14.0 | − 4.2 |
| 1978 | 9.7 | 16.6 | 16.6 | − 5.0 |
| 1979 | 11.9 | 20.1 | 20.0 | − 6.0 |
| 1980 | 13.6 | 22.0 | 22.0 | − 6.6 |

Table 1-5. (continued).

| Year | Total Payments[a] | Wage Reduction | Total Premiums[a] | Net Cost |
|------|------|------|------|------|
| (in $ billions) | | | | |
| 1981 | 15.0 | 22.9 | 22.9 | − 6.9 |
| 1982 | 16.3 | 22.6 | 22.5 | − 6.8 |
| 1983 | 16.0 | 22.9 | 22.9 | − 6.9 |

PANEL F: *Wage reduction = .12 in 1976 (1977 QES), increases linearly by .008 annually; Benefits = payments/.056*

| Year | Total Payments[a] | Wage Reduction | Total Premiums[a] | Net Cost |
|------|------|------|------|------|
| (in $ billions) | | | | |
| 1976 | 7.6 | 16.3 | 10.9 | − 8.7 |
| 1977 | 8.6 | 19.6 | 14.0 | − 9.8 |
| 1978 | 9.7 | 21.5 | 16.6 | − 9.9 |
| 1979 | 11.9 | 24.2 | 20.0 | −10.1 |
| 1980 | 13.6 | 24.2 | 22.0 | − 8.8 |
| 1981 | 15.0 | 22.9 | 22.9 | − 6.9 |
| 1982 | 16.3 | 20.3 | 22.5 | − 4.5 |
| 1983 | 16.0 | 18.3 | 22.9 | − 2.3 |

[a] Data are taken from "Workers' Compensation: Coverage, Benefits, and Costs," *Social Security Bulletin*, for each year included in the table.

−.08 in 1981 and −.064 in 1983, the wage reduction goes from $20.3 billion in 1976 (as in Panel A) to $22.8 billion in 1983.

The final column of each panel is the net cost of workers' compensation, which is simply the difference between total after-tax premiums paid (column 2) and the wage reduction (column 3). In every case considered, workers' compensation benefits have more than paid for themselves in all years through the wage offset.

The most favorable evidence of workers' compensation's desirability is in Panel A. Increasing workers' compensation premiums from $10.9 billion in 1976 to $22.9 billion in 1983 did not cost firms an extra $12 billion before taxes. Rather, it saved them an extra $14.0 billion through the influence of the wage offsets. For the results in Panel B, the additional net cost went from −$5.9 billion in 1976 to −$12.5 billion in 1983, and in Panel C it went from −$12.7 billion in 1976 to −$6.8 billion in 1983. More modest savings result if we use the injury rate of .045, as shown in Panels D-F.

The results in Panel C are a bit deceptive since they seem to suggest that workes' compensation increases are cost-reducing. Overall, the net cost is negative, as is true in every other case considered. However, if it is the higher level of workers' compensation benefits that has led to the dampening of the rate of tradeoff between wages and workers' compensation, as one expects theoretically, then the higher level of benefits is not cost-reducing. In particular, the net cost went from −$12.7 billion in 1976 to −$6.8 billion in 1983, which represents a cost increase of $5.9 billion. Overall costs remain negative, but the costs of benefit increases are positive.

This pattern is not unique to Panel C. Panel F also has a larger cost reduction in 1976 than in 1983. These are both cases in which the rate of tradeoff declines over time, and the dampening of the tradeoff is attributed to the more generous levels of workers' compensation benefits. In these cases, benefit increases do not pay for themselves through wage reductions since the net cost of the benefit increases is positive.

The results in Table 1–5 are strengthened when the net cost of benefits is computed in real terms. In particular, in Columns C and F, where nominal net costs are falling over time, real net costs are falling at an even faster rate, due to the effects of the chronic inflation experienced during the period. In Panel C, for instance, the net cost of workers' compensation decreased by 46 percent in nominal terms from 1976–83. Given the increase in the price level during that period, real benefits fell by $8.6 billion, or over 67 percent.

Three general sets of conclusions emerge from Table 1–5. First, recognition of the wage reductions generated by workers' compensation leads to a lower net cost than the total premiums suggest. The highest annual real net cost estimated was −$2.3 billion (Panel E, 1983), and the least costly was −$26.7 billion (Panel A, 1981). Second, in every instance the annual net cost of workers' compensation is negative. Finally, even though the annual net costs may be negative, the incremental net costs of higher benefits are typically positive if one assumes that the observed changes in the wage-workers' compensation tradeoff from 1976 to 1983 are due to the higher benefit levels.

## Moral Hazard and Related Factors

One potential drawback of the higher workers' compensation benefits from the standpoint of the firm is that they may increase the number of injuries, or at least claims of injuries, and their duration. As the degree of coverage of the income loss from job injuries is increased, workers have less of a financial incentive to avoid the injury, since the size of the loss has been reduced. Similarly, the duration of injuries may increase, since workers have less of an incentive to return to work if they receive close to full earnings replacement without working.

Each of these effects follows directly from standard economic models, but the magnitude of these effects has long been controversial. Recent research by Butler (1983) and Butler and Worrall (1983, 1985) suggests that these influences may be substantial—with an elasticity of injury claims with respect to benefits of 0.4 and a duration elasticity of 0.23.[9] The calculations in table 1–5 take into account the effects of moral hazard on benefits since total net costs, including the costs due to more frequent or prolonged injuries, are reflected in the total payments.

Two additional classes of costs have not been considered. First, if there are more frequent injuries, costs to the firm in terms of interruptions of production and the replacement of injured workers will rise. Empirical evidence on the effect of benefit levels on injury rates is not conclusive. Of the two existing studies, Chelius (1982) finds no relationship, while Ruser (1985b) estimates that the injury rate–benefit elasticity is .5. Kniesner and Leeth (1986), in a numerical simulation, find the injury–benefit elasticity to be extremely low—about .05%.

Second, higher injury rates may boost the level of wages workers require to work on the job. In general, there are substantial compensating differentials for job risks that increase as the injury level rises, as reflected in the positive INJURY coefficients in table 1–4. If, however, the underlying level of workplace safety has not changed but workers, in effect, choose to have a higher accident rate because more generous benefit levels diminish their optimal level of safety precautions, the standard relationship between wages and injury rates will not hold. At the very minimum, there will be some offset of the compensating differential effect because of the diminished safety precautions that are taken.

The only plausible case for a substantial wage increase for greater job risks stemming from diminished precautions must be based either on the ability of unions to use a bad safety record for negotiating purposes or on a failure of other workers to perceive the true source of the greater apparent riskiness. Because of the speculative nature of such adjustments, we did not modify the results in table 1–5 to take such factors into account.

## Conclusions

The most fundamental purpose of this chapter has been to show that one cannot take workers' compensation premium levels at face value as an estimate of the costs to firms of the system. Under a wide range of assumptions, a substantial wage offset is generated by the provision of benefits. This offset is to be expected on economic grounds, since boosting one attractive feature of the compensation mix (workers' compensation) will reduce the wages needed to make a hazardous job acceptable to the worker.

One can take two perspectives on the wage offsets. In terms of the level of net costs (i.e., premiums less wage reductions), workers' compensation more than pays for itself. When viewed incrementally, however, the change in net cost is *positive* due to a substantial diminishing of the rate of tradeoff between wages and workers' compensation as the benefit levels increase. Although workers' compensation increases do not provide an economic "free lunch" to firms, they are cheaper fare than in generally believed.

## Notes

1. See Viscusi (1983, 1986), Smith (1976), and Bartel and Thomas (1985) for reviews of the performance of OSHA.

2. Viscusi (1984) discusses these and related issues.

3. Notable exceptions include Worrall (1983), Worrall and Appel (1985), Worrall and Butler (1985), Viscusi (1980), Darling-Hammond and Kniesner (1980), and the references cited in note 6.

4. In 1970, employed costs of workers' compensation were $4.9 billion, or about $1.13 per $100 of payroll.

5. See U.S. Bureau of Labor Statistics (1974).

6. Estimates of this substitution are found in Viscusi and Moore (1987), Arnould and Nichols (1983), Dorsey and Walzer (1983), Butler (1983), and Ruser (1985a). This prediction is an implication of the equalizing difference model (Smith, 1979; Rosen, 1985; Viscusi, 1978). Ehrenberg (1985) provides a survey of evidence on this and related issues.

7. Data on payments and premiums are taken from Price (1986) and from related issues in prior years.

8. The average tax rate faced by workers in the data sets is about 30%. Thus, the wage savings to firms before taxes are 30% higher than are those calculated using our estimated wage reduction rates, which are estimated on an after-tax basis. Since wage savings to firms must be calculated on an after-tax basis also, we assume for simplicity that firms face the same marginal tax rate, on average, as workers.

9. Similar findings are discussed in Bartel and Thomas (1985), Chelius (1974, 1982) and Worrall and Appel (1985).

## References

Arnould, Richard J., and Len M. Nichols. "Wage-Risk Premiums and Workers' Compensation: A Refinement of Estimates of Compensating Wage Differential." *Journal of Political Economy* 91, (1983): 332–340.

Bartel, Ann P., and Lacy Glenn Thomas. "Direct and Indirect Effects of Regulation: A New Look at OSHA's Impact." *The Journal of Law and Economics* 28, (1985): 1–26.

Butler, Richard J. "Wage and Injury Rate Response to Shifting Levels of Workers' Compensation." In John D. Worrall (ed.), *Safety and the Work Force: Incentives and Disincentives in Workers' Compensation*. Ithaca, NY: ILR Press, 1983, pp. 61–86.

Butler, Richard J., and John D. Worrall. "Workers' Compensation: Benefit and Injury Claims Rates in the Seventies." *Review of Economics and Statistics* 65, (1983): 580–599.

Butler, Richard J., and John D. Worrall. "Work Injury Compensation and the Duration of Nonwork Spells." *The Economic Journal* 95 (1985): 714–724.

Chelius, James R. "The Control of Industrial Accidents: Economic Theory and Empirical Evidence." *Law and Contemporary Problems* 38 (1974): 700–729.

Chelius, James R. *Workplace Safety and Health: The Role of Workers' Compensation*. Washington: American Enterprise Institute, 1977).

Chelius, James R. "The Influence of Workers' Compensation On Safety Incentives." *Industrial and Labor Relations Review* 35, 2 (1982): 235–242.

Darling-Hammond, Linda, and Thomas J. Kniesner. *The Law and Economics of Workers' Compensation*. Rand Institute for Civil Justice Report R-2716-ICJ (1980).

Dorsey, Stuart, and Norman Walzer. "Workers' Compensation, Job Hazards, and Wages." *Industrial and Labor Relations Review* 36, 4 (1983): 642–654.

Ehrenberg, Ronald G. "Workers' Compensation, Wages, and the Risk of Injury." In John F. Burton, Jr. (ed), *New Perspectives in Workers' Compensation*, Ithaca, NY: ILR Press, 1987, pp. 71–96.

Hamermesh, Daniel S., and John R. Wolfe. "Compensating Wage Differentials and the Duration of Wage Loss." National Bureau of Economic Research Working Paper No. 1887 (1986).

Kniesner, Thomas J., and John D. Leeth. "Workers' Compensation with Imperfect State Verification: The Long-run Impact on Injuries and Claims." Paper presented at the Summer Meetings of the Econometric Society, Duke University, June 1986.

Price, Daniel N. "Workers' Compensation: 1976–80 Benchmark Revisions." *Social Security Bulletin*, July 1984.

Price, Daniel N. "Workers Compensation: Coverage, Benefits, and Costs, 1983." *Social Security Bulletin*, February 1986.

*The Report of the National Commission on State Workmen's Compensation Laws.* Washington: U.S. Government Printing Office, 1972.

Rosen, Sherwin. "The Theory of Equalizing Differences." In Orley Ashenfelter and Richard Layard (ed.), *Handbook of Labor Economics*, vol. 2, Amsterdam: North-Holland, 1986, pp. 641–692.

Rosenblum, Marcus (ed.). *Compendium on Workmen's Compensation*. Washington: U.S. Government Printing Office, 1973.

Ruser, John. "Workers' Compensation Benefits and Compensating Wage Differentials." Washington: U.S. Bureau of Labor Statistics, 1985a.

Ruser, John. "Workers' Compensation Insurance, Experience Rating and Occupational Injuries." *Rand Journal of Economics* 16, 4 (1985b): 487–503.

Smith, Robert S. *The Occupational Safety and Health Act: Its Goals and Achievements.* Washington: American Enterprise Institute, 1976.

Smith, Robert S. "Compensating Differentials and Public Policy: A Review." *Industrial and Labor Relations Reivew* 32 (1979): 339–352.

Topel, Robert H. "Equilibrium Earnings, Turnover, and Unemployment: New Evidence." *Journal of Labor Economics* 2, 4 (1984): 500–522.

U.S. Bureau of Labor Statistics, *Employment Compensation in the Private Nonfarm Economy*, 1974 Summary 76-12. Washington D.C.: U.S. Government Printing Office, 1977, pp. 3–4.

Viscusi, W. Kip. "Wealth Effects and Earnings Premiums for Job Hazards." *Review of Economics and Statistics* 60, 3 (1978): 408–416.

Viscusi, W. Kip. *Employment Hazards: An Investigation of Market Performance.* Cambridge: Harvard University Press, 1979.

Viscusi, W. Kip. "Imperfect Job Risk Information and Optimal Workmen's Compensation Benefits." *Journal of Public Economics* 14 (1980): 319–337.

Viscusi, W. Kip. "Structuring an Effective Occupational Disease Policy: Victim Compensation and Risk Regulation." *Yale Journal on Regulation* 2, 1 (1984): 53–81.

Viscusi, W. Kip. "The Impact of Occupational Safety and Health Regulation, 1973–1983." *Rand Journal of Economics* 17, 4 (1986): 567–580.

Viscusi, W. Kip, and Michael J. Moore. "Rates of Time Preference and Valuations of the Duration of life." *Journal of Public Economics*, 38 (1989), pp. 297–317.

Viscusi, W. Kip, and Michael J. Moore. "Workers' Compensation: Wage Effects, Benefit Inadequacies, and the Value of Health Losses." *The Review of Economics and Statistics* 69, 2 (1987): 249–261.

Worrall, John D. *Safety and the Work Force: Incentives and Disincentives in Workers' Compensation.* Ithaca, NY: Industrial and Labor Relations Press, 1983).

Worrall, John D., and David Appel. *Workers' Compensation Benefits: Adequacy, Equity, and Efficiency.* Ithaca, NY: Industrial and Labor Relations Press, 1985).

Worrall, John D. and Richard J. Butler "Some Lessons From the Workers' Compensation Program," in Monroe Berkowitz and M. Anne Hill (eds.), *Disability and the Labor Market.* Ithaca, NY: ILR Press, 1986, pp. 95–123.

# 2 HETEROGENEITY BIAS IN THE ESTIMATION OF THE DETERMINANTS OF WORKERS' COMPENSATION LOSS DISTRIBUTIONS

John D. Worrall
Richard J. Butler

## The Hazards of Estimating Moral Hazard

The potential for someone covered by insurance either to have too many accidents, or to have too large a loss, is termed *moral hazard* in the insurance literature. In a world of perfect information and competitive markets for insurance, there should be no moral hazard with respect to workers' compensation, since both job risk and risk severity would be observed exactly by the insurer, the employer buying insurance, and the workers receiving the benefits. Moral hazard arises because workers, insureds, and insurers do not have perfect knowledge of what the other parties are always doing. In the absence of moral hazard, an increase in benefits should probably have very little impact on either the frequency or the severity of a claim.

Moral hazard may be reflected in an increase in the *frequency of claims*

The authors wish to thank participants at the 1983 NCCI Conference on Workers' Compensation for their comments on this chapter, and the College of Family, Home, and Social Sciences at Brigham Young University for financial support. Comments from Philip S. Borba greatly improved an earlier version of the chapter.

23

when benefits rise, since increased benefits can change workers' incentives regarding self-protection against injuries. In other words, there will be a change in the level of resources devoted a loss reduction either by the insured firm or by its workers. This in turn leads to a change in the probability of filing a claim. For example, a large increase in benefits (such as was experienced in the 1970s) might sufficiently reduce the fear of minor industrial accidents to the point that workers become more willing to undertake risk at the job (not wearing safety equipment, undertaking more risky tasks, etc.). But as risk exposure increases, so does the number of claims. Or suppose that a new, large firm becomes fully experience-rated after being manually rated for a time. It now finds that claim-reduction efforts—such as safety campaigns, classes on the safe use of tools, or a more careful screening of claims—more directly influence its insurance costs. Therefore, greater profit can be realized by devoting resources to claim prevention, and the firm will do so.

Whereas the moral hazard problem discussed above principally would be reflected in claims frequency, another class of moral hazard problems concerns the *reporting of claim severity* when claim severity is not fully observed by the insurer. An increase in benefits means a decrease in the opportunity cost of missing work (since wages are partially replaced by compensation benefits); it costs less to take more leisure time, and some workers may take more time to recuperate than they would if their true severity could be observed exactly by the insurers (and employers).

An important problem for applied researchers in workers' compensation is to estimate these types of responses accurately in order to forecast future costs for any given change in the benefit structure. Estimates of moral hazard effects are complicated when workers differ from each other. In the presence of worker heterogeneity, there are hazards to estimating the moral hazard.

Throughout this chapter, we focus on the moral hazard problem associated with employee behavior; that is, we will be concerned with how one estimates employees' incentives to change their behavior in the face of benefit increases. We ignore some of the issues associated with differences between firms, including experience rating. We do this for pedagogical convenience only, since the heterogeneity problems are even more complicated in models of joint employee/employer behavior, and the *statistical corrections* to be discussed below have even more relevance.

Three types of such biases are especially relevant to the prediction of loss distributions given any change in the level of benefits, wages, retroactive periods, etc. The first type of bias is the generic *omitted variable bias* common to much of the empirical research. In the workers' compensation case, a good example would be the linear regression of wages on some index of job risk (say the likelihood of a fatal injury for that class of worker), where the level of potential compensation benefits is omitted. Indeed, exactly this error of omission is rather common in studies that look for compensating wages for degree of risk of job injury/illness (notable exceptions to this failure are the studies by Arnould and Nichols, 1983; Butler, 1983; Butler and Worrall, 1983; and Dorsey and Walzer, 1983. The problem is that compensation benefits are correlated with both wages and risk. Omitting this important determinant can lead to a negative bias in the estimated risk premium (that is, the coefficient of the risk variable will tend to be understated) if wage–risk premiums fall as compensation benefits rise, and higher benefits lead to more job risks. However, problems associated with omitted variable bias are as well understood as are the techniques available to correct them, and so we will not discuss this type of bias further.

The other two types of heterogeneity problems that are addressed in this chapter arise when estimating the impact on benefits on claim frequency (we discuss this in the next section) and when estimating the impact of benefits on claim severity (we discuss this in the third section).

The claim frequency bias arises because workers and firms sort themselves in the market place according to their preferences for wages and risk. In the presence of differential tastes, rather than a single wage–risk package, the market will generate a variety of wage–risk packages that meets the needs of both buyers and sellers, subject to competitive pressures. This market combination of wages and risks is referred to as a *hedonic equilibrium*. It depends on a number of firm–worker factors, including the level of workers' compensation benefits. We discuss this model more explicitly in the next section, and refer to the frequency bias problem as a *sample selection* problem.

The second bias with which we will concern ourselves in this chapter arises in the estimation of a dynamic process, such those that generate models of workers' compensation disability spells. These models, developed in the third section of the chapter, are especially relevant to the problem of estimating the impact of benefits on the duration of a compensation claim. The problem is one of sorting out the general (moral hazard) effect that an increase in benefits may have on all claims (how quickly would workers return to work when benefits increase if all workers were alike) from the differential effect that it may have on particular claims (unobserved worker differences, e.g., differences in attitudes, cause some workers to return to work more quickly than others). We refer to this as the *claim heterogeneity* problem.

## Estimating Frequency: The Sample Selection Problem

*Market Competition and Hedonic Selectivity*

In a competitive, informed market, competition among buyers and sellers of labor services will generate compensating premiums for risk of injury.[1] Consider such a market, with many informed firms and workers that freely compete with one another. Since a given risk cannot be untied from a given task (with a given potential wage), firms and workers sort themselves— subject to the competitive pressures of others—into a hedonic equilibrium. Such an equilibrium is shown in figure 2–1, and has been discussed by Smith (1979) in the same context of a compensating wage.

Our discussion focuses on the interaction between wages and risk; we are assuming that the levels of benefits are exogenously determined. However, since changes in the benefits are likely to induce changes in the wages as well as changes in the observed level of risk (where *risk* may be interpreted here as the probability of filing a claim), we again have to take the sorting process into account or we will likely get biased estimates of the impact of benefits on risk, resulting in poorly forecasted distributions.

To understand both the nature of this hedonic selection effect and its

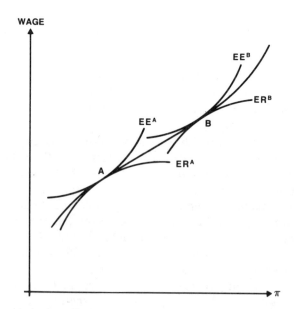

Figure 2–1.  Hedonic selection.

solution, consider figure 2–1. The employee indifference curves ($EE^A$, $EE^B$) are assumed to be increasing in slope due to diminishing marginal utility of income. This is the reason for the bowl-shaped indifference curves; these workers would like to avoid job risk and will, as individuals, only accept more if the compensating wage increases (so the slope of each individual's wage–risk tradeoff gets increasingly large). As seen in the figure, A exhibits greater risk-aversion than B, since for any given increase in risk, A requires a larger wage increase in order to maintain a given level of untility. In the equilibrium as drawn, B is marketing his relative tastes for risk by working at a more risky task but being compensated by a higher wage.

The isocost curves of the firms ($ER^A$, $ER^B$) in figure 2–1 are bowed in the opposite direction because of diminishing marginal productivity of expenditure in safety. At a given firm, the least costly safety technology is employed initially so that the cost of reducing risk (moving left on the isocost curve) is small and only a slight reduction in wage is required to keep costs constant. As more expensive technology is used to gain further reductions in job risk, wage decreases have to be increasingly large in order to maintain constant costs. If firms and individuals were matched in points A and B along the locus, then competition with potential buyers and sellers choosing to locate between A and B forces a monotonic relationship between risk and wages. Workers would like to move to the northwest of the locus to increase their utility, but cannot, since competition assures firms on the locus of lower-cost individuals in the market. On the other side, firms would like to move to the southeast of the locus to lower their costs of production, but cannot, since workers would find higher wages for any level of risk on the wage–risk locus relative to any point southeast from it.

It is important to note that the equilibrium market locus seen in figure 2–1 is determined ultimately by the distribution of the characteristics of demanders and suppliers. The market distributes individuals along the locus, and hence the slope of the locus (as given by the total change in wage per additional unit of risk exposure) is conditioned upon the characteristics of buyers and sellers. As we will see below, this result implies that these characteristics will enter the analysis in a nonlinear way. The omission of these nonlinearities leads to our *sample selection bias*, where the effect of benefits on risk exposure may be poorly estimated.

To develop this argument somewhat more formally, we will let the marginal cost to the worker (and benefit to the firm) of risk exposure and the amount of risk be determined *along with the market locus* (for the *i*th match, which we assume consists of one buyer and one seller) as

$$W_i' = X_i^D \alpha_1 + \alpha_2 \pi_i \qquad \text{Demand (Marginal Return Function),} \qquad (2.1)$$

$$\pi_i = X_i^S \beta_1 + \beta_2 W_i' + \varepsilon_i \qquad \text{Supply (Marginal Cost Function).} \qquad (2.2)$$

Equation (2.1) describes the marginal return ($W_D' = \partial W/\partial \pi$) the firm offers to a worker with given observed risk level, $\pi_i$, when demand conditions are given by $X_i^D$ (which includes those things that characterize a given job type).[2] Equation (2.2) makes the amount of risk exposure, $\pi$, a function of the marginal cost ($\partial W/\partial \pi = W_S'$), observable personal and job-related characteristics, $X^S$ (which includes the level of compensation benefits), and unobserved taste effects, $\varepsilon_i$. A relatively greater taste for risk leads the individual to a higher level of risk exposure for any given values of ($X^S$, $W_S'$), i.e., when $\varepsilon_i > 0$.

The market sorts individuals in a competitive equilibrium where the marginal cost of risk exposure equals the marginal gain ($W_D' = W_S' = W'$), at which prices the amount of risk embodied in a given job is appropriate from both the employer's and employee's perspectives, given the market tradeoff between levels of risk and wage. But note that it is the market wage–risk function ($W$) that we observe directly, rather than the compensating wage ($W'$). The compensating wage $W'$ has to be inferred from the market wage function $W$. Only by appropriately modeling the nonlinear relationships in the model can we retrieve the $\pi$ and estimate the structural relationships in equations (2.1) and (2.2).

That *appropriate nonlinear relationship* for wages and risk is generated by the underlying (marginal cost and return) equations. Since a linear specification for these marginal relationships (linear in the $X$'s and $\varepsilon$) is the simplest possible, it will be useful to derive the resulting market envelope function between wages and risk to see if that is linear as well, and to provide some guidelines in interpreting the extant compensating premium estimates.

The structural marginal cost (MC) and marginal return (MR) equations generate the market envelope, and in doing so imply restrictions between the envelope function and MR, MC functions. Indeed, solving equations (2.1) and (2.2) for the reduced form filing rate function yields

$$\pi_i = X_i^S \tilde{\beta}_1 + X^D \tilde{\beta}_2 \alpha_1 + \tilde{\varepsilon}_i, \qquad (2.3)$$

where

$$\tilde{\beta}_1 = \frac{\beta_1}{1 - \alpha_2 \beta_2}, \quad \tilde{\beta}_2 = \frac{\beta_2}{1 - \alpha_2 \beta_2}, \quad \text{and } \tilde{\varepsilon} = \frac{\varepsilon_i}{1 - \alpha_2 \beta_2}.$$

This reduced form claim rates function is easy to estimate using OLS regression techniques. But many researchers in workers' compensation have augmented their specification by including wages on the right-hand side, and then estimating the model by two-stage least squares regression (see, for example, Chelius, 1983; Butler, 1983; and Butler and Worrall, 1983). The inclusion of a wages variable, even if it is treated as endogenous, is inappropriate[3] if there is a hedonic market for risk as described in equations (2.1) and (2.2). This is explained at greater length in a different context in Butler (1984). Briefly, the problem is this: observed wages are the integrated value of the wage premium ($\partial W/\partial \pi$), i.e., the sum of all the compensating differentials with the sum being taken over levels of risk ($\pi$). Since the wage premium and risk functions are determined by the shift variables $X^D$ and $X^S$, it follows that wages, risk, and these shift variables will be related to one another in a nonlinear fashion. To account for both nonlinearity of the wage/risk relationship and the wage/risk, endogeneity, Butler (1984) suggests simply interacting instrumented values of the wage variable with all the other regressors.

We note that this procedure differs from the simple OLS and two-stage least squares procedures commonly used for hedonic markets. The conceptual experiment is to take the market locus as given, and then note that a particular risk level on the market locus will be associated with specific values of $X^D$ and $X^S$. But since every match is conditioned by the characteristics of the participants, leaving out the nonlinear relationship between wages and the shift variables ($X^D$, $X^S$, and $\varepsilon$) means that the measured impact of wages on risks ($\pi$) includes *both* a marginal return component and a component due to market sorting.

Simple OLS estimation may recover more than just the effect of marginal costs on risk ($\beta_2$ in equation (2.2)). If the market for risks is truly hedonic and we ignore the implications of sorting, then the estimated impact of wages on risk will not equal the true impact. Rather, the relationship will be as follows:

$$\hat{\beta} = \frac{d\pi}{dW} = \frac{\partial \pi}{\partial W} \text{ (true ``}\beta\text{'')} + \frac{\partial \pi}{\partial X^S}\frac{dX^S}{dW} + \frac{\partial \pi}{\partial X^D}\frac{dX^D}{dW} + \frac{\partial \pi}{\partial \varepsilon_i}\frac{d\varepsilon_i}{dW} . \quad (2.4)$$

Only the first term on the right-hand side represents the effect of the wage on the amount of risk exposure in a given job, and other terms arise when we omit the nonlinearities between wages and $X^S$, $X^D$, and $\varepsilon$, and represent and *selectivity bias* effects or the job shifting induced by, say, the level of compensation benefits (one of the $X^S$ terms). This can be seen readily in figure 2–1: the change in risks for an additional dollar to wages at point B reflects the marginal wage increase required by worker B (the first right-hand-side term) and the set of exogeneous variables that leads individual B to locate on this proportion of the hedonic locus (since worker A would have a much smaller decrease in risks than worker B does for an additional dollar of wages, when these changes are evaluated at any given level of risks). The $X^S$, $X^D$, and $\varepsilon$ effectively sweep out a market equilibrium so that a term like $\partial W/\partial X^S \, dX^S/d\pi$ in equation (2.4) combines the variation between $\pi$ and $X^S$ along the equilibrium locus (where the $dX^S/d\pi$ is computed with the effect of that variation on the observed samples of wages ($\partial W/\partial X$) at any given point. This is called selectivity bias in the economics literature.

### Hedonic Selection: Am Empirical Example

In the last section we have discussed how heterogeneity, operating through sample selection, can bias estimates of the impact of benefits on risk (i.e., can distort the estimated impact of benefits on the frequency of compensation claims). We present estimates of the magnitude of the hedonic bias using a worker's compensation data set from South Carolina on 15 industries over a 32-year period (1940 to 1971). The data set, and the rationale for the economic variables included in the analysis, is discussed at greater length in Butler (1983). Estimates from the claims (injury) rate models are given for each class of compensable injury (except death and medical only) in tables 2–1 and 2–2.

The reduced form claim rate model (corresponding to equation (2.3)) is given in table 2–1 separately for each class of compensable injury. The theoretical expectation of the variables DAY (number of days per year the average plant was in operation as a measure of the pace of industrial activity) and SIZE (the number of employees per firm, to capture economies of scale in the provision of safety equipment) are fairly well worked out (see Chelius, 1974). As the pace of employee activity increases or the size of the firm decreases, accidents tend to increase as expected. As the proportion of black males increases relative to white males, the injury rate rises. One would expect this result if the RACE variable is interpreted as a composition variable—that is, that blacks have the less skilled and more accident-prone jobs. The resulting positive sign on the human capital variable HKM is somewhat puzzling, but may simply be capturing a younger work force with both more years of education and a more expensive education.

Since we are chiefly concerned with the potential bias on the compensation benefit variable resulting from a misspecified hedonic function, we focus our discussion on the benefit variable. The use of actual benefits paid as the workers' compensation variable in tables 2–1 and 2–2 may be inappropriate, since it is an ex post measure that reflects workers of other than average characteristics (i.e., wages). As such, measured benefits will actually reflect the impact of sorting along the equilibrium locus. Hence bias from hedonic sorting may be difficult to detect.

The problem with using actual benefits paid is that their estimated impact potentially mixes the true benefit effect with outcomes induced by the existence of the benefits. For example, raising the minimum benefit

Table 2–1. Reduced Form (OLS) Estimates of Claim Rates by Type (absolute *t*-statistics)

| Independent Variable | IRPD | IRPP | IRTT |
|---|---|---|---|
| Intercept | −9.747 | −10.491 | −8.004 |
| | (5.89) | (6.69) | (5.83) |
| WC | .858 | 1.146 | .313 |
| | (2.19) | (3.08) | (.96) |
| DAY | .394 | .031 | .876 |
| | (1.02) | (.08) | (2.73) |
| RACE | .649 | .737 | .598 |
| | (5.84) | (6.99) | (6.49) |
| HKM | .280 | .545 | .190 |
| | (.96) | (1.98) | (.79) |
| TIME | −.053 | −.063 | −.083 |
| | (3.49) | (4.40) | (6.62) |
| SIZE | −.291 | −.329 | −.272 |
| | (6.88) | (8.21) | (7.78) |
| N | 468 | 468 | 468 |
| $R^2$ | .322 | .365 | .522 |

[1] Variables used in the claim rates equations are as follows:
*Dependent Variables (all measured in logs)*
IRPD: Annual injuries per employee resulting in permanent dismemberment or disfigurement; IRPP: Annual injuries per employee resulting in permanent partial injuries; IRTT: Annual injuries per employee resulting in temporary total injuries.
*Independent Variables (all measured in logs except time)*
WAGE: After-tax weekly male wage of production employees; RACE: Ratio of black to white male production employees; DAY: Average number of days the industry was operating; HK: Quality-adjusted measure of human capital (real accumulated expenditures for the average worker in South Carolina, adjusted for migration and age distributions); SIZE: Number of employees per establishment; TIME: Time-trend variable; WC: Expected workers' compensation (for the average worker; see text).
See Butler (1983) for more discussion of the data set.

Table 2–2. Two-Stage Least Squares Estimates of South Carolina Claim Rates by Type (absolute *t*-statistics)

| Independent Variables | IRPD | | IRPP | | IRTT | |
|---|---|---|---|---|---|---|
| | *No Correction* | *Hedonic Correction* | *No Correction* | *Hedonic Correction* | *No Correction* | *Hedonic Correction* |
| Intercept | -8.448 | -39.944 | -9.713 | -8.777 | -7.488 | -34.874 |
| | (5.07) | (1.95) | (6.09) | (.35) | (5.35) | (2.52) |
| WAGE | 1.898 | -9.801 | 1.136 | -15.493 | .754 | 3.473 |
| | (3.98) | (1.02) | (2.49) | (1.32) | (1.88) | (.53) |
| WC | -1.157 | 15.887 | -.060 | 9.542 | -.487 | 5.523 |
| | (1.81) | (2.15) | (.10) | (1.06) | (.91) | (1.11) |
| DAY | -.120 | 10.427 | -.277 | 6.168 | .672 | 8.778 |
| | (.30) | (2.24) | (.72) | (1.09) | (21.98) | (2.80) |
| RACE | .808 | -1.259 | .832 | -2.062 | .661 | -5.493 |
| | (6.91) | (.68) | (7.44) | (.91) | (6.73) | (4.39) |
| HK | .476 | 2.088 | .662 | 2.407 | .268 | -.854 |
| | (1.63) | (.52) | (2.38) | (.50) | (1.10) | (.32) |
| TIME | -.080 | -.042 | -.080 | .082 | -.093 | -.591 |
| | (4.86) | (.15) | (5.04) | (.24) | (6.79) | (3.11) |

| | | | | | | |
|---|---|---|---|---|---|---|
| SIZE | -.294 | -4.607 | -.331 | -4.909 | -.274 | -3.518 |
| | (7.05) | (7.89) | (8.29) | (6.92) | (7.81) | (8.94) |
| WAGE² | — | 4.360 | — | 3.587 | — | .991 |
| | | (2.71) | | (1.83) | | (.91) |
| WC-Wg | — | -3.443 | — | -1.642 | — | -1.079 |
| | | (1.96) | | (.77) | | (.91) |
| DAY-Wg | — | -2.432 | — | -1.378 | — | -1.801 |
| | | (2.10) | | (.98) | | (2.31) |
| RACE-Wg | — | .368 | — | .560 | — | 1.347 |
| | | (.84) | | (1.05) | | (4.58) |
| HK-Wg | — | -.718 | — | -.768 | — | -.162 |
| | | (.69) | | (.61) | | (.23) |
| TIME-Wg | — | .009 | — | -.020 | — | .136 |
| | | (.12) | | (.23) | | (2.94) |
| SIZE-Wg | — | 1.019 | — | 1.083 | — | .762 |
| | | (7.36) | | (6.44) | | (8.17) |
| R² | .342 | .381 | .372 | .295 | .523 | .636 |
| Claims Rate Elasticity | -1.16 | 1.74 | -.06 | 2.79 | .49 | 1.09 |

*Note:* See notes to table 2–1 for explanations of variables.

payment will disproportionately affect those with the lowest wages. If these low-wage workers are the only ones that respond to the change in the minimum, we will observe the frequency increasing while the average level of benefits paid actually falls. (Note that expected benefits, average ex ante payments, actually increase.) So there may be a dampening effect that causes *acutal* benefits to understate changes in *expected* benefits. A change in the maximum can similarly lead to an overstatement.

Since workers' behavioral response reflects changes in expected benefits, where expected benefits have changed as much as or more than actual benefits, the estimated benefit effects may be as large as they are with the hedonic sorting mechanism correctly specified. However, the magnitude of the bias is impossible to determine a priori. An alternative measure would be the expected benefits that the average worker receives if injured. This variable, WC, was constructed by taking the average observed wages and then computing the expected benefits. Its construction is discussed in detail in Butler (1983). Note that it has large, statistically positive impact on both the IRPD claim rates and IRTT claim rates, as one would expect, given employee incentives in an imperfectly experience-rated world.

The interesting result, however, is the standard claim rate model (without nonlinearities), given for each class of claim rates as the *No Correction* model. We first note that the pattern of coefficients in table 2-2 for the nonbenefit measures is similar to that in the first table. However, in the selectivity-adjusted results that include the nonlinear wage terms, the effect of expected benefits is to significantly increase the claims rate, whereas in the No Correction (or standard) model, benefits appear to decrease the claims rate.

The filing claims rate elasticities are given in the last row of table 2-2. The elasticity measures the percentage change in the claims rate given a 1% change in benefits. Note that in all cases, not only is there a significant quantitative effect when the hedonic correction is applied, but also the sign of the effect changes. The negative elasticity in the standard model for temporary total claims, for example, suggests that claims rates would fall by 5% given a 10% rise in benefits (that is, the claim rate elasticity is about $-1\frac{1}{2}$). However, in the appropriately specified hedonic model, the claim rate elasticity is actually positive, implying about a 10% rise in claim rates for each 10% increase in benefits.

### Estimating Severity: The Claim Heterogeneity Problem

Claim heterogeneity arises when there are unobservable differences in claimants that result in observed severity differences for the same type of claim. There is a simple sorting problem associated with uncompleted spells that is in a rough sense analogous to the omitted variable bias problem. Here the omission is the unobserved (as of the date that sample was drawn) proportion of the spell—that is, some claims may still be in progress at the that the sample was taken, so they are *right censored*. These uncompleted spells are *selective* (they are often uncompleted simply because they tend to be the longest), and our estimation of the impact of benefits on claim duration must necessarily account for this or we will probably get biased estimates of the effects we want to measure. Butler and Worrall (1983) present a further discussion of this problem and its solution, using some robust regression techniques. While the sorting discussed above arises from the way in which we draw our observations (if we observed the completed duration for everyone, then there would be no bias in the estimate of the benefit elasticity), there may still be a self-sorting problem if there was some variance across individuals in the sample regarding their propensity to stay on a claim due to unobserved differences in tastes or unobserved socioeconomic factors. It is the second type of heterogeneity that we call *claim heterogeneity*, and we discuss it in the remainder of this section.

Since we want to estimate the impact of an increase in benefits on the expected duration of a claim in the presence of claim heterogeneity, we need to model how the unobservables will affect the *empirical* (or *observed*) distribution of time on a claim. Let $g(t)$ be this observed probability density function for $t$ (so $t$ is a random variable for the duration of a compensation claim). To get this function, we will have some parameter of the true function of time vary according to some mixing distribution function $\phi(\theta)$, so that

$$g(t) = \int f(t|\theta)d\phi(\theta), \qquad (2.5)$$

where the true conditional probability density function for duration, given $\theta$, is $f(t|\theta)$. Claim heterogeneity arises because $\theta$ distorts the observed distribution (in equation (2.5)) relative to the true distribution (given by the $f(t|\theta)$ function). A very rough analogy would be coming upon a four-year-old who has mixed himself a drink. In the refrigerator there are the "conditional probability, $f(t|\theta)$" fluids consisting of milk, apple juice, orange juice, and pineapple juice. There are also the "mixing distribution, $\phi(\theta)$" dry mixes in the cupboard: instant coffee, instant hot chocolate mix, and instant strawberry mix. The mess has been cleaned up (analogies can be fanciful), and all there is left to observe (or taste in this case) is the glass containing just one of the four liquids and one of the dry mixes. The statistical problem is to discover which of the four liquids were used from the resulting mixed drink that one has in the glass.

We could generalize $\theta$ so that it is a function of both the observable characteristics of the claim and an unobservable part. Then we have

$$\theta = \beta \cdot B + \varepsilon, \tag{2.6}$$

where $\beta$ is the parametric constant, $B$ the level of workers' compensation payments, and $\varepsilon$ an unobservable taste variable distributed randomly among the population. In particular, if higher values of $\theta$ tended to *lower* the expectation duration, then we may expect that $\beta < 0$ in equation (2.6), since benefits might be expected to increase the duration of a claim, as discussed in the first section of this chapter. In this context, positive values of the unobservable component $\varepsilon$ also decrease duration—$\varepsilon$ could be interpreted as a factor indicating relative perference for work.

In our discussion, we have interpreted $f(t|\theta)$ as the true population (conditional) probability density function that we want to estimate, and let $\phi(\theta)$ be the distribution of unobservables for *those in our sample*. The problem is that our sample probability density function, $g(t)$, may have characteristics that are significantly different from our population distribution. Since in equation (2.6), $B$ is assumed to be observable, we can control for its impact on $\theta$ relatively easily. So in the remainder of our discussion, we suppress discussion of the $\beta \cdot B$ term and let $\phi(\theta) \equiv \phi(\varepsilon)$ be the distribution function for our unobservable.

An equivalent formulation of the estimation problem, the one usually presented in the empirical literature, is based upon a transformation of the density function. Instead of talking about the estimation of $f(t|\theta)$ directly, often the *hazard rate* of the process is computed:

$$\lambda = \frac{f(t|\theta)}{1 - F(t|\theta)} \qquad \text{Population hazard rate.} \tag{2.7}$$

The hazard rate is the instantaneous rate, or probability, of leaving a compensation claim now, given that one has not yet left it (see Butler and Worrall, 1983, and references cited there). In the case dealt with here, when adjustment is not made for claim heterogeneity, the *sample* hazard rate will be

$$h = \frac{g(t)}{1 - G(t)}, \tag{2.8}$$

and may vary in important aspects from the population hazard rate. A biased estimate of the duration distribution again biases our ability to forecast the impact that demographic changes (including the level of workers' compensation benefits) have on compensation loss distributions.

We illustrate these problems with the simplest case, in which time is exponentially distributed so that

$$F(t|\theta) = 1 - \exp(-\theta t),$$
$$f(t|\theta) = \theta \exp\{-\theta t\}. \tag{2.9}$$

Since for the exponential distribution, we know that

$$\text{Prob}(t > a + b | t > a) = \text{Prob}(t > b), \tag{2.10}$$

we might suspect that the hazard rate, namely the conditional probability of leaving a claim, must also be independent of time when time is distributed as an exponential random variable. Indeed, this is confirmed as

$$\lambda = \frac{\theta \exp(-\theta t)}{1 - (1 - \exp(-\theta t))} = \theta. \tag{2.11}$$

Hence $\partial \lambda / \partial t = 0$, i.e., the length of stay on a compensation claim has no effect on the rate at which one leaves recipient status. Hazard rates (and their corresponding distribution functions) for which $\partial \lambda / \partial t \neq 0$ are said to exhibit *duration dependence*. This means that the length of stay on a claim acutally affects the rate at which a recipient returns to work.

The duration dependence could go in either direction in workers' compensation. It will tend to be positive if the workers' assets begin to depreciate rapidly during claimant status—the longer a worker is out, the more incentive there is to return, so the hazard rate increases. On the other hand, it may be negative if there are *welfare dependency* effects or declining firm-specific human capital. In these cases, the longer a worker is on a claim, the less incentive there is to leave it.

Although by assumption our *population hazard rate*, $\lambda$, exhibits no duration dependence, the *empirical hazard rate population function in which the exponential is mixed with another distribution* will exhibit negative duration dependence *regardless of the form of the mixing distribution function $\phi(\theta)$* so long as it is nondegenerate. To see why this is the case, consider the following distribution for $\phi(\theta)$:

$$\phi(\theta) = \frac{\bar{\lambda} + \delta \text{ with } \alpha \text{ probability,}}{\bar{\lambda} - \delta \text{ with } 1 - \alpha \text{ probability,}} \qquad \bar{\lambda} > \delta > 0. \tag{2.12}$$

The case where $\theta = \bar{\lambda}$ corresponds to the case of no duration dependence. Taking the natural logarithm of $(f(t|\theta))$, the probability density function, we have in the case of no heterogeneity

$$\ln(f(t|\theta)) = \log\bar{\lambda} - \bar{\lambda}t, \tag{2.13}$$

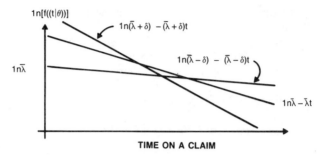

Figure 2–2.   The case of no heterogeneity: a simple linear function in time.

a simple linear function in time that you will recall, shows no duration dependence of the hazard rate function. This is illustrated in figure 2–2. Relative to this linear benchmark, any $\ln(f(t|\theta))$ that was convex for all values of time and was strictly convex for at least some values of time would exhibit negative duration dependence. If it were strictly concave for at least some values of $t$, the implied hazard would exhibit some positive duration dependence. In the exponential case, the integration of any distribution for the unobservables induces convexity into the observed distribution of claim spells and so always leads to empirical hazard rates with negative duration.

In our example above, heterogeneity divides the sample population into two groups. The first group has a relatively positive value of the unobservable—implying that its members are prone to return to work earlier—with a (log)probability density function

$$\ln(f(t|\theta = \bar{\lambda} + \delta)) = \ln(\bar{\lambda} + \delta) - (\lambda + \delta)t. \qquad (2.14)$$

This function intersects the no-duration-dependence line from above, implying shorter expected durations. The group that is less prone to return to work, which has a (log)probability density function

$$\ln(f(t|Y = \bar{\lambda} - \delta)) = \ln(\bar{\lambda} - \delta) - (\bar{\lambda} - \delta)t,$$

has a lower intercept than the no-duration-dependence curve, cutting it from below, and exhibiting a longer expected duration than those functions with no duration dependence.

Intuitively, groups with $\theta = \bar{\lambda} + \delta$ (with shorter expected duration) will leave the sample earlier than those for which $\theta = \bar{\lambda} - \delta$ is more typical of the latter stages of the spell. This is why the observed distribution appears convex and yields a function exhibiting negative duration dependence.[4]

There are both parametric and nonparametric controls possible for the distribution of unobservables. The nonparametric approach is to estimate the heterogeneity function $\phi(\theta)$ nonparametrically using *points of increase* while retrieving the parameters of the conditional duration distribution $F(t|\theta)$. This is attractive in the sense that we need not impose any additional structure of interest, $F(t|\theta)$, although the computational costs of making these adjustments appears to be large. (See Heckman and Singer, 1982, for further discussion on this issue). The second and most common control for unobservables has been to explicitly assume a one- or two-parameter distribution function for $\phi(\theta)$, and then simultaneously to estimate the parameters of both $f(t|\theta)$ and $\phi(\theta)$. However, as the empirical examples in Heckman (1982) show, the estimation of the parameters in $f(t|\theta)$ are very sensitive to the assumed form for the $\phi(\theta)$. Here we draw upon the recent results of McDonald and Butler (1984) to show how more general parametric models can be developed.

The usual assumption is that the distribution of duration times on a claim is either exponential (which implicitly assumes no duration dependence) or Weibull (which allows for duration dependence). As McDonald (1984) shows, both distributions are specialized cases of the generalized gamma (GG) distribution. McDonald and Butler (1984) show that when the scale parameter for the GG distribution is mixed with the inverse generalized gamma (IGG) function, the resulting distribution is the GB2 distribution derived in McDonald (1984). Special cases of this GB2 distribution include the Fisk, Lomax, F, Beta-2, Burr 12, and K3 distributions (among others). This suggests that if one assumes that the duration on claimant status follows a GB2 distribution, then one can parametrically test for the "best" for both the conditional distribution ($f(t|\phi)$) in equation (2.5)) and the mixing function (the ( ) in equation (2.5)). Details and proofs are provided in McDonald and Butler (1984). We illustrate the importance of heterogeneity effects on estimated duration elasticities using some results from Butler and Worrall (1985).

There were no individual claim severity cases from South Carolina from which we could estimate the models outlined above. However, the National Council on Compensation Insurance has kindly provided us with a sample of claim durations from Illinois, using their Detailed Claim Call data set. (Again, the reader is referred to Butler and Worrall (1985) for a detailed discussion of the variables and results.) In table 2–3, we present maximum likelihood estimates of hazard rate estimates for low back claims from that Illinois sample, using both the Weibull and Burr-12 distributions. In both cases, the scale parameter has been made a linear function of the indicated exogenous variables. The parameters from the Weibull distribu-

Table 2–3.  Full Information Maximum Likelihood Estimates of Duration Using the Weibull and the Singh–Maddala Distributions

|  | Weibull | Singh–Maddala |
|---|---|---|
| A | 0.890 | 1.8486 |
|  | (39.68) | (15.47)* |
| Q |  | 0.6140 |
|  |  | (7.30)* |
| Intercept |  | −1.0263 |
|  |  | (1.23) |
| Benefit | −0.352 | 0.1830 |
|  | (4.43) | (1.23) |
| Wage | 0.173 | −0.0346 |
|  | (1.90) | (0.22) |
| Age | −0.158 | 0.1179 |
|  | (1.55) | (0.72) |
| Married | −0.212 | 0.1527 |
|  | (2.61) | (1.28) |
| Hospital | −0.150 | 0.1461 |
| Days | (11.62) | (9.46)* |
| Employment | 0.419 | 0.0983 |
| Status | (2.10) | (0.38) |
| Lawyer | −2.259 | 2.3275 |
|  | (7.73) | (6.69)* |
| ln-likelihood | −1937.03 | −1839.59 |

* Absolute value of the asymptotic $t$-statistic in parentheses.

tion are given in the left-hand column of the table. In this example we assume that the true conditional distribution, $f(t|\theta)$, follows a Weibull distribution. Hence, in the absence of claim heterogeneity, the Weibull estimates in the left-hand column of table 2–3 represent the "true" impact of the indicated variables on the duration of a claim. In particular, the effect of the benefits on compensation loss distributions is such that a 10% increase in benefits increases average duration by 4%—i.e., elasticity of duration with respect to benefits is .4.

To control for potential unobservable heterogeneity in the scale parameter of the Weibull distribution, we have assumed that the mixing distribution for the scale parameter is an inverse gamma distribution. The resulting mixture is a Burr-12 (also known as Singh-Maddala distribution).

The right-hand column of table 2–3 contains the MLE estimates for the Burr-12 model, and while the signs and relative magnitudes of the other variables remain the same, the estimated benefit effect is lower. Expected signs are reversed in the Burr-12 model from the Weibull model due to the form of the specification. The elasticity of duration with respect to benefits is about .2, or about half the size it was when there was no control for claim heterogeneity.

## Conclusions

As we begin to accumulate information on the important elasticities necessary to forecast compensation loss distributions, care needs to be taken that we do not ignore the sample selection implications of the same economic models that are used to formulate our statistical procedures. Hopefully more thinking about the nature of the solution to the heterogeneity problem will take place, with careful applications made to the models we use to forecast compensation losses. We have provided some empirical examples where control for such heterogeneity has proven important.

In this chapter, we have suggested how heterogeneous workers can generate sample selection biases in the estimation of the population functions. In all of these cases, the estimation of the impact of rising benefits on the *observed outcome* (the probability of filing a claim, or its average duration) includes both the *population effect* and a *sample selection effect*, the latter being generated by population heterogeneity. Throughout, the presumption has been that the unbiased estimation of the parameters of the population function is important, our models clearly illustrating how heterogeneity induces bias into the parameters of the empirical function. Our preference for the unbiased estimation of the population function is undoubtedly correct when one is interested in behavioral tests suggested from economic theory. However, it may be argued that when the selection rule is invariant across different sample populations, then for the purposes of *forecasting* costs, the sample function would be sufficient, even though it provides biased estimates of the population. Hence, for forecasting the impact of small, marginal changes in workers' compensation, the sample (as opposed to population) function may be sufficient for many purposes. Clearly, it would be most useful to have information on both the selection rule and the population functions. Hopefully, the brief discussion here will help stimulate further research into how heterogeneity affects our ability to forecast workers' compensation costs.

## Notes

1. Simpler models of sorting were discussed at length in an earlier version of this chapter. Those simpler models, as well as the hedonic model discussed in this section, draw heavily on Butler (1984).

2. Recall that our model assumes that the firm is not experience-rated. Hence, benefits may not directly affect the offered wage premium (although they will indirectly through the supply side).

3. While the data for the Butler and Worrall (1983) study examine interstate variations in claim rates and hence would not be modeled appropriately as a hedonic models, the Chelius (1974) and Butler (1983) data samples would satisfy the hedonic model. Indeed, the Butler data set to be discussed (looking at manufacturers within a given state) is the most likely hedonic candidate.

4. The following proof for any nondegenerate distribution function of the unobservable when $F(t|\theta)$ is an exponential distribution is due to Heckman:

$$h(t) = \frac{g(t)}{1 - G(t)} = \frac{\int \theta \exp(-\theta t) d\phi(\theta)}{\int \exp(-\theta t) d\phi(\theta)}.$$

The ratio on the right hand side is negative, since the Cauchy–Schwartz inequality for integrals implies that the numerator is negative.

## References

Apostol, Tom. *Mathematical Analysis*, 2nd edition. Reading, M. A., Addison-Wesley, 1974.

Arnould, Richard J., and Lem Nichols. "Wage-Risk Premiums and Workers Compensation: A Refinement of Estimates of Compensating Wage Differentials." *Journal of Political Economy* 91 (1983): 332–340.

Butler, Richard, J. "The Effect of Education on Wages—Hedonics Makes Selectivity Bias (Sort of) Simpler," *Economic Inquiry* 22 (January 1984): 714–724.

Butler, Richard, J. "Wage and Injury Rate Response to Shifting Levels of Workers' Compensation." In John D. Worrall (ed.), *Safety and the Workforce: Incentives and Disincentives in Workers' Compensation*. Ithaca, NY: ILR Press, 1983.

Butler, Richard J., and John D. Worrall. "Work Injury Compensation and the Duration of Nonwork Spells." *Economic Journal* 95 (1985):714–724.

Butler, Richard J., and John D. Worrall. "Workers' Compensation: Benefit and Injury Claims Rates in the Seventies." *Review of Economics and Statistics*, 65 (1983):580–589.

Chelius, James. "The Control of Industrial Accidents: Economic Theory and Empirical Evidence." *Law and Contemporary Problems* (Summer/Autumn 1974):700–729.

Chelius, James. "The Influence of Workers' Compensation on Safety Incentive." *Industrial and Labor Relations Review* 35 (1982):235–242.

Chelius, James. "Workers' Compensation and the Incentive to Prevent Injuries."

In John D. Worrall (ed.), *Safety and the Workforce: Incentives and Disincentives in Workers' Compensation*. Ithaca: ILR Press, 1983.

Cox, D. R. "Regression Models and Life Tables." *Journal of the Royal Statistical Society* 34 (1972):187–220.

Dorsey, Stuart, and Normal Walzer. "Compensating Differentials and Liability Rules." *Industrial and Labor Relations Review* (1983):36 (4):642–642.

Heckman, James J., "Sample Selection Bias as a Specification Error." *Econometrics* 47 (1979):153–162.

Heckman, James J., and Burton Singer. "The Identification Problem in Econometric Models for Duration Data." In W. Hildenbrand (ed.), *Advances in Econometrics*. Cambridge: Cambridge University Press, 1982.

Johnson, William G. "The Disincentive Effects of Workers' Compensation Payments." In John D. Worrall (ed.), *Safety and the Workforce: Incentives and Disincentives in Workers' Compensation*. Ithaca, NY: ILR Press, 1983.

McDonald, James B. "Some Generalized Functions for the Size Distributions of Income." *Econometrica* (1984):52 (4) 647–663.

McDonald, James B., and Richard J. Butler. "Generalized Mixing Distributions." Unpublished manuscript, August 1984.

Rosen, Sherwin. "Hedonic Prices and Implicit Markets: Product Differentiation in Pure Competition." *Journal of Political Economy* 82 (1974):34–55.

Roy, Andrew D. "Some Thoughts on the Distribution of Earnings." *Oxford Economic Papers* 11 (June 1951):135–146.

Smith, Robert S. "Compensating Wage Differentials and Public Policy: A Review." *Industrial and Labor Relations Review* 32 (1979):339–352.

Worrall, John D., and David Appel. "The Wage Replacement Rate and Benefit Utilization in Workers' Compensation Insurance." *The Journal of Risk and Insurance* 49 (1982): 361–371.

Worrall, John D., and Richard J. Butler. "Benefits in the Workers' Compensation System and the Duration of Claims." Revised 1984. Forthcoming in NCCI volume on Workers' Compensation.

# 3 WORKERS' COMPENSATION DISABILITY BENEFITS DURING RETIREMENT YEARS: PROPER AND PRESENT ROLE

C. Arthur Williams, Jr.
Peter C. Young

About 70% of the $17.5-billion workers' compensation benefits paid to workers with job-related injuries or diseases in 1983 were cash benefits (Price, 1986). The remaining payments went to providers of medical care to these workers. Of the cash payments, about 87% went to disabled workers either as income replacement benefits or as compensation for physical impairments. The other 13% were death benefits payable to survivors of deceased workers. An unknown, but not negligible, proportion of the disability benefits were paid to workers who, if they had not been disabled by job-related injuries or diseases, would have retired prior to 1983.[1] This chapter deals with a seldom-discussed aspect of workers' compensation—whether workers' compensation disability benefits should be continued past the age at which the worker, if not disabled, presumably would have retired. This chapter will 1) present a case for discontinuing these benefits at the presumed retirement age, 2) summarize similar proposals made by others, 3) indicate whether United States jurisdictions currently make any adjustments during postretirement years, 4) explore the political and administrative reasons that explain the disparity between the proposed discontinuance and present practice, and 5) present a modified proposal that may be more acceptable.

## Proper Role

The *proper* role of workers' compensation disability benefits after the worker, if not disabled, presumably would have retired depends upon the stated or implied objective of the workers' compensation program. State laws vary as to these objectives.

### Wage-Loss Replacement

All states pay temporary total disability, temporary partial disability, and permanent total disability benefits that presumably are based on the actual wages lost. A few states pay permanent partial disability benefits based on actual wages lost; most of the others relate the benefit to the presumed loss of wages or the loss of earning capacity.

If the objective of the workers' compensation program is to replace actual or presumed wages lost, should the worker continue to receive benefits past the presumed retirement age? Since wages would stop at that age, the consistent procedure would be to terminate disability benefit at the presumed retirement age.[2]

Because employer-financed employee benefits may be an important part of the workers' total compensation package, however, workers' compensation should also replace part of these benefits. If these benefits include a pension, the worker should, following the presumed retirement age, receive a pension based on service prior to the date of disability plus part of the employer-financed pension that would have been earned from that date to the retirement age. The worker should also be eligible for part of any employer-financed life insurance and medical care insurance benefits he or she would have received during the disability, including any postretirement life insurance and medical care insurance benefits.

Logically, also, the disability benefit should be indexed to reflect the wage increases the worker would have received because of career progressions and general average-wage increases. Because it is extremely difficult to adjust the benefit for expected career progressions, only general average-wage adjustments are included in this proposal.

To illustrate this proper role, assume that a worker, aged 45, is totally and permanently disabled. The worker's salary at the time of disability was $360 per week. The worker had been covered for 20 years under an employer-financed pension plan that at age 65 would provide 1% per year of service of the worker's average salary over the last five years for each year of service. The worker was also covered under an employer-financed plan that provided medical care insurance benefits and life insurance equal to one year's salary.

If the workers' compensation benefit is designed to replace two thirds of the lost wages, the disability benefit to the date of retirement should be two thirds of the indexed wages plus two thirds of the life insurance and medical expense insurance benefits.[3] At retirement age, the worker should receive a pension equal to the amount earned because of service prior to the disability (20% of the average indexed wages during the previous five years) plus two thirds of the amount that the worker would have earned during the disability years (two thirds of 20%, or 13%). Two thirds of any postretirement life insurance or medical expense insurance benefits should also be included in the disability benefits.

The employer-financed employee benefits, of course, are commonly much less generous than those assumed in this example. Indeed, the employer might not at the date of the injury (or later) finance any private employee-benefit plans. In this case, if the worker had remained with this employer until reaching retirement age, and the employer never had financed any employee benefits, a total disability would result "only" in the loss of cash wages. The disability benefit should be two thirds of the indexed wage loss ending on the day the worker would have retired. To pay this worker any income after retirement would result in a pension the worker would not have received if the disability had never occurred.

The theory of compensating wage differentials provides some justification for terminating disability payments at the retirement age.[4] According to this theory, if two workers have jobs that are identical in every respect except than one job provides a pension plan and the other does not, the worker without the pension plan should receive the higher wage. Because workers' compensation benefits are expressed as a percent of the worker's wage, if the worker without the pension is disabled, he or she will usually receive a higher weekly workers' compensation cash benefit than would the worker with a pension plan. (The cash benefits would be the same, however, if both workers were paid enough to receive the maximum weekly benefit.) Because the worker without a pension plan has been compensated for the absence of a pension by higher wage payments to the disability date and higher workers' compensation payments thereafter, he or she should receive no disability benefits after retirement. Because the worker with the pension plan received lower wages and lower workers' compensation benefits prior to retirement, he or she should receive a pension benefit after retirement based upon service up to the date of disability and workers' compensation status thereafter.

Let us now consider three different scenarios, each of which depict two

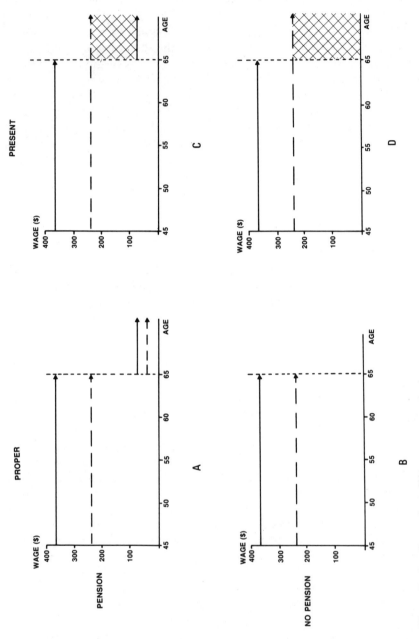

Figure 3–1.   Scenario 1:  Wages are constant.

possible variations. The first scenario, figure 3–1, depicts our worker, aged 45, in two situations: first, the worker's pension (described earlier) exists; second, no pension exists for the worker. Further assumptions include

1. The worker's weekly salary at the time of total disability is $360;
2. If total disability had not occurred, the worker would have retired at age 65 with no spells of unemployment;
3. Wage would have remained constant;
4. The pension benefit, if it exists, is not indexed after retirement; and
5. The employer provides no other employee benefits.

Figures 3–1A and 3–1B illustrate these two situations. In figure 3–1A, the worker receives two thirds of the presumed level salary until age 65. At that point the worker receives 100% of the pension earned prior to the disability plus two thirds of the pension that would have been earned had no disability occurred.

Figure 3–1B indicates that, if no pension is otherwise available, all benefits cease at the presumed retirement age.

The second scenario, Figure 3–2, represents a situation similar to figure 3–1 except that wages are no longer assumed to remain constant.

In figure 3–2A, the proper workers' compensation benefit rises with the presumed rise in the worker's wage. Whether this benefit remains two thirds of the presumed wage loss at any given times depends on how the benefit is indexed. Thus, if the benefit is indexed by increases in the state average weekly wage, it is possible that

1. A worker in a high-wage-growth occupation might be under-compensated in later years, and
2. A worker in a low-wage-growth occupation might eventually receive more in workers' compensation benefits than would ever be received through wages.

These outcomes, of course, may be largely offset through a more flexible indexing approach.

It should be noted that the relationship between the workers' compensation retirement benefit and the presumed pension benefit should remain roughly constant. However, since the pension is based on the final five years' wages, both the presumed pension and the workers' compensation retirement benefits will be higher in figure 3–2A than in figure 3–1A.

The third scenario, figure 3–3, is identical to figure 3–2 except that the worker's pension is now indexed. Figure 3–3B is identical to figure 3–2B,

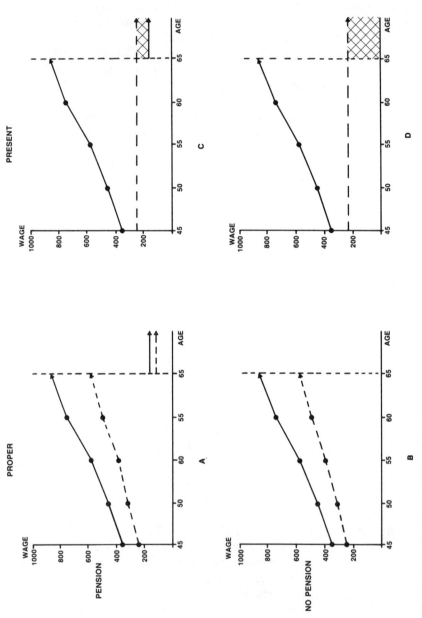

Figure 3–2. Scenario 2: Wages are not constant.

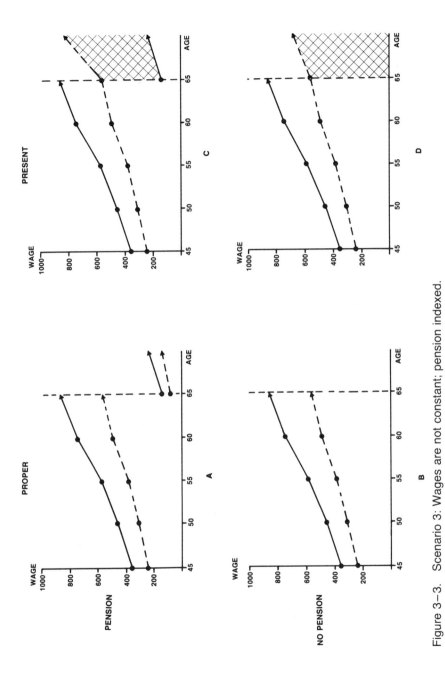

Figure 3–3.    Scenario 3: Wages are not constant; pension indexed.

but figure 3–3A illustrates that the worker's presumed pension is indexed, and the workers' compensation retirement benefit is indexed as well. Obviously, if the worker's compensation is to represent a constant proportion of the presumed pension, the method of indexation must be identical.

Figures 3–1, 3–2, and 3–3 also show what the actual workers' compensation benefit would be in a typical state for a permanent and total disability (see figures 3–1C, 3–1D, 3–2C, 3–2D, 3–3C, and 3–3D). The typical benefit is a nonindexed lifetime income equal to two thirds of the wage loss subject to a weekly maximum and a weekly minimum. Present practices will be discussed in much more detail later in this chapter. Figure 3–3 also shows what the workers' compensation benefit might be in the states that index these benefits for changes in the state average weekly wage. To simplify the discussion, Old Age, Survivors, and Disability Insurance benefits have been ignored in these illustrations. The discussion also ignores the fact that workers' compensation benefits are tax-free whereas private pension benefits are not. Foregone career progressions are assumed to be zero.

In figure 3–1C, the present benefit exceeds the proper benefit after retirement (the excess is represented by the cross-hatching). The proper benefit would be two thirds of the 20% pension that the worker would have received for the last 20 years of service if he or she had not been disabled. In figure 3–1D, the disabled worker receives a pension that would not otherwise be received (cross-hatched area).

Figure 3–2C shows a present benefit that, because it is not indexed, is less than the proper benefit prior to the retirement. Like the figure 3–1C situation, however, the present benefit is more than the proper benefit after retirement. In figure 3–2D, as in figure 3–2C, the present benefit is less than the proper benefit prior to retirement age but much greater thereafter.

As Figures 3–3C and 3–3D show, in states that index the workers' compensation disability benefit, prior to retirement age the current benefit is the proper benefit proposed in this chapter. However, after the worker would have presumably retired, the present benefit would be much higher than the proper benefit, especially in figure 3–3D, which assumes no pension plan.

Numerous scenarios could be described. The basic concept, however, is clear. Continuing the disability retirement income past retirement age will in many, if not most, cases produce a better retirement income for the worker than the worker would have earned by working during the pre-retirement disability period. The smaller the pension that would have been earned during that period and the older the worker, the more important this workers' compensation pension would become. An indexed workers' compensation benefit would greatly increase its importance. As the percentage of active workers in the older age brackets increases, these pension costs will become an increasingly important part of workers' compensation costs.

### Benefits Based on Loss of Earning Capacity or Presumed Loss of Earnings

Most states base permanent partial disability benefits on either the loss of earning capacity or the presumed loss of earnings, not the actual wage loss. The benefit is typically a lump sum equal to the weekly benefit times a specified number of weeks that varies with the perceived degree of disability. The benefit is the same whether or not the disabled person returns to work, which depends largely upon the occupations to which that person can return. The benefit, therefore, may be more or less than the actual wage loss. This feature of permanent partial disability benefits has been debated frequently and extensively. Supporters argue that the described person is more likely to return to work under this procedure because it removes an important disincentive against returning to work.[5]

The proposal suggested in this chapter would accept the present practice subject to these modifications:

1. Instead of paying the cash benefit in a lump sum, the weekly benefit would be paid each week for the specified number of weeks.
2. On each anniversary date, the cash benefit would be adjusted for increases in the state average weekly wage.
3. The worker would continue to receive the same fraction of employee benefits as the percentage used to determine the weekly cash benefits for the specified number of weeks. If the worker became eligible for some or all of these employee benefits upon returning to work, the workers' compensation employee benefit would be reduced accordingly.

### Benefits Based on Impairments

In addition to acutal or presumed wage-loss benefits, some states provide a permanent disability benefit that is related to the physical or mental impairment only. The worker's prior earnings are not considered. Although it might be argued that, for example, the loss of an arm, aside from its economic impact, is more important to a younger worker than to an older worker, this chapter is concerned only with comparative income replacement benefits.

## Earlier Proposals

For the most part, workers' compensation literature has not dealt with continuation of disability benefits past the actual or presumed retirement age. Four major exceptions are 1) the 1977 Report of the Interdepartmental Workers' Compensation Task Force, 2) Paul C. Weiler in his 1980 monograph entitled *Reshaping Workers' Compensation for Ontario*, 3) the 1983 Crum and Forster Occupational Disease Task Force, and 4) a 1985 National Association of Insurance Committee Occupational Disease Advisory Committee.

### Interdepartmental Workers' Compensation Task Force

Although *The Report of the National Commission on State Workmen's Compensation Laws* (1972) contained numerous recommendations for changing state workers' compensation laws, none dealt specifically with the subject of this paper. However, the report did state that

> ...it is appropriate to integrate workmen's compensation benefits with other benefits provided by an employer. As in the past...employers and other interested parties should be free to develop provisions which either supplement workmen's compensation benefits or reduce retirement or disability benefits paid for by the employer in the presence of workmen's compensation benefits.
> (p. 66)

The Commission also recommended that the Disability Insurance (DI) component of Old Age, Survivors and Disability Insurance (OASDI) continue to reduce DI payments if the combined DI and workers' compensation benefits exceed 80% of the worker's prior wage.

Another Commission recommendation led to the establishment in 1974 of an Interdepartmental Workers' Compensation Task Force that included a Policy Group consisting of the Secretaries of Labor, Commerce, and Health, Education, and Welfare, plus the Federal Insurance Administrator. The Task Force's assignment was to encourage and assist the states in administering worker's compensation and to examine certain aspects more closely. In 1977 the Policy Group encouraged states to go beyond the

National Commission's 19 "essential" recommendations (*Workers' Compensation: Is There a Better Way?*, 1977). One of the Group's additional recommendations would stop workers' compensation disability benefits at the worker's retirement age. Specifically, the Policy Group recommended that, in the long run,

> ...workers' compensation wage replacement benefits be superceded by Social Security and other retirement benefits at the age of 65. In preparation for this, we have recommended that employers continue to pay Social Security taxes on workers' compensation wage replacement benefits. The question of who should pay the employee's share must have further study. For the present, we recommend that Social Security retirement benefits be supplemented by workers' compensation up to the level of the workers' compensation benefits alone, if those benefits are higher. The full change-over should take place when those who have had Social Security and other retirement contributions paid on their workers' compensation benefits reach the age of 65. Retired persons who return to work should be covered by workers' compensation, but should not be able to receive both benefits based on the same work experience.                (p. 15)

This recommendation is consistent with the proposal in this chapter, in that 1) conceptually, at age 65, disability benefits would be replaced by retirement benefits, and 2) employers would treat the workers' compensation disability benefits as wages in determining their OASDI taxes and employee benefit obligations.[6] The short-term recommendation differs, however, in that the retirement benefit may include some workers' compensation disability benefit if the workers' compensation benefit alone exceeds the OASDI retirement benefit. If the employer had no private pension plan, the retirement benefit for most workers would be the workers' compensation benefit less the OASDI benefit (presumably including the portion of the OASDI benefit financed by employee contributions).

### The Weiler and Ontario Proposals

In *Reshaping Workers' Compensation for Ontario*, Professor Paul Weiler (1980) argued that

> The regular workers' compensation pension should be specifically designed to compensate fore the loss of earnings during the normal working life. But after the anticipated retirement age (which can either be set of a flat 65 or vary for different industries and workers depending upon relevant and predictable factors), the function of workers' compensation should be to compensate for loss of expected *retirement* income; i.e., for the loss of accumulated pension plan benefits under either public or private plans.'                (p. 45)

Weiler also recommended that the workers' compensation system

> ...be designed to maintain the private benefit package previously provided by the employer, or at least to compensate the injured worker for loss of these benefits...(s) such significant benefits as...contributions to a private pension scheme have become too important to be left out of consideration by workers' compensation.                                           (p. 44)

In addition to continuing coverage under the private pension plan, Weiler proposed that workers' compensation continue coverage under the Canada Pension Plan. Weiler also recommended that workers' compensation benefits be adjusted for inflation. Weiler's proposal, therefore, was essentially the same as the one proposed in this chapter.

The Weiler proposal was more fully developed in the 1981 *White Paper on the Workers' Compensation Act* prepared by the Ministry of Labor in response to Professor Weiler's review of the Ontario system. The Ministry made 21 recommendations for change, one of which would replace permanent disability awards at age 65 with retirement income loss benefits. The report acknowledges that

> Implementing this principle will require that the Board develop formulas which measure the impact of an occupational injury on the amount of retirement income that would have been received had the injury not occurred....
>
> Certain of the several government-sponsored benefits will be unaffected by the injury; e.g., the non-earnings related Old Age Security scheme. Benefits which are lost under the Canada Pension scheme, which is based on contributions for years of employment, will have to be made up by the Workers' Compensation Board, since...federal legislation...now restricts the accumulation of benefits during periods of unemployment due to an occupational injury.
>
> As regards private pension plans, a disabled worker who must leave his current employer and/or take a lower-paying job will suffer a loss in some of his ultimate retirement income as a result. Thus the Board must be directed to set aside funds which will provide a standard retirement benefit—at the maximum level permitted by the Income Tax Act for private pensions—to accrue while wage loss compensation is being paid because of an occupational injury.
>                                                                       (pp. 18–19)

The Weiler recommendation, as developed in this *White Paper*, differs from the proposal described in this chapter in only one way. The replacement retirement benefit is not the actual retirement income lost because of the disability, but what that loss would be if the worker had been covered under a private pension plan providing the maximum level permitted by the Income Tax Act. That maximum level would be 2% per year of the full net disposable earnings lost because of the worker's disability. The workers' compensation retirement benefit, therefore, would exceed the retirement benefits lost if the worker's employer had no pension plan or paid less than the maximum amount.

The *White Paper* acknowledges that one may question whether workers whose employers do not provide a pension plan would receive a retirement income considerably in excess of what they would have received had they not been injured at all.


### Crum and Forster Occupational Disease Task Force

In their report on the role of state workers' compensation laws in compensating occupational disease victims, Crum and Forster's Occupational Disease Task Force (1983) recommended that for those states using a wage-loss system, wage-loss benefits should terminate at the time an employee begins to receive retirement benefits under OASDI. The worker, however, would receive a workers' compensation retirement supplement equal to any diminution of OASDI retirement benefits because of the job-related benefit.[7] Similarly, for those states not adopting a wage-loss system, employees receiving partial or total disability benefits at the time they begin to receive retirement benefits should receive as a workers' compensation benefit only the diminution of their OASDI retirement benefit.

This proposal is consistent with the proper role recommended in this chapter, except that it ignores any private pension benefits that may have been lost and does not propose indexed benefits.


### NAIC Occupational Disease Advisory Committee

In 1985, the NAIC Occupational Disease Advisory Committee made a similar proposal as follows:

> The financial resources of the workers' compensation system should be focused on injured workers in their pre-retirement years... This principle requires that income benefits paid to workers or their spouses should be reduced or eliminated entirely after retirement. Two approaches are possible. The first provides that workers' compensation income benefits would continue to be paid but would be reduced by benefits paid by social security and private retirement programs. The second approach provides that workers' compensation income benefits would be paid after retirement only if social security retirement benefits are less than they would have been if the workers had not been injured. If social security retirement benefits are reduced, workers' compensation would provide supplementary benefits to make up for the lost social security benefits.     (p. 2)

The Advisory Committee's proposal differs from the one presented in this chapter in that 1) under the first approach, the postretirement benefit is not related to the loss in OASDI and private pension benefits, 2) under the second approach, the postretirement benefit is the loss in the OASDI benefit, but the loss of any pension income is ignored, and 3) the Advisory Committee did not propose any indexing or replacement of any private employee benefits.[8]

## Present Role

What is the present role of workers' compensation disability benefits in the United States after the age at which the disabled worker presumably would have retired? If the role just described is the proper one, the present role is incorrect. With rare exceptions, disability benefits do not stop at the worker's presumed retirement age. Instead the system often provides a lifetime pension, even if the employee would not otherwise have received such a pension had the injury not occurred. On the other hand, the disability benefit is not indexed and employee benefits lost are not replaced.[9]

The ways in which the actual or presumed retirement age is reflected in current United States workers' compensation laws can be summarized under the following categories: 1) termination of benefits, 2) reduction of benefits, and 3) offset provisions. Table 3–1 lists 1) the three states that terminate some benefits after retirement, 2) the one state that may reduce benefits, and 3) the ten states with offset provisions.

### Termination of Benefits

Only three states terminate disability benefits at the actual or presumed retirement age, and then only under certain conditions.

**Montana.**    Montana is the only state that, according to its law, terminates permanent total disability benefits upon presumed retirement. Because Montana's approach is so important for the purpose of this chapter, the relevant statutory provision is reproduced below:

> If a claimant is receiving total disability compensation benefits and the claimant receives retirement social security benefits or disability social security benefits paid to the claimant are converted by law to retirement benefits, the claimant is considered to the retired and no longer in the open market. When the claimant is considered retired, the liability of the insurer is ended for payment of

Table 3–1. States with Laws that Terminate, Reduce, or Offset Workers' Compensation Disability Benefits after Presumed Retirement Age

| Terminate | | Reduce | Offset |
|---|---|---|---|
| Permanent Total Disability | Permanent Partial Disability | Permanent or Temporary Disability | Permanent Total Disability Only |
| Montana | Louisiana Minnesota* | Michigan** | Alaska District of Columbia Colorado Florida Louisiana Michigan Minnesota North Dakota Oregon Wyoming |

* Minnesota also terminates temporary total disability benefits after maximum medical improvement.
** Worker receives better of 1) reduced amount or 2) the benefit less an offset.

such compensation benefits. This section does not apply to permanent partial disability benefits. Medical benefits are expressly reserved to the claimant.

In Montana, therefore, totally disabled workers are treated "properly" according to this chapter, assuming that the presumed retirement age is properly measured by receipt of an OASDI retirement benefit. Montana law, however, provides no automatic adjustments for increases in average statewide earnings or for increases in consumer prices prior to the worker's presumed retirement. It also does not compensate the worker for any diminution in OASDI or private employee benefits.

Workers with permanent partial disabilities in Montana receive weekly benefits equal to two thirds of "the actual diminution of the worker's earning capacity measured in dollars," but no more than half the state average weekly wage, for the duration of the disability but no more than 500 weeks. The duration, however, is limited to 300 weeks for the loss of one leg at or near the hip joint, 280 weeks for the loss of one arm at or near the shoulder, 200 weeks for the loss of one hand, 165 weeks for the loss of an eye, 15 weeks for the loss of one first finger at the distal joint, and other periods for the losses of other members included in the list. This benefit is the same regardless of the worker's age except that "the actual diminution of the worker's earning capacity" may be judged for a specified condition to be greater the older the worker. For many older workers, therefore, the income replacement benefit will be continued past the presumed retirement age.

Although the Montana statute states that the permanent total disability benefit stops when the disabled worker retires, both the Montana State Fund and the private insurers in that state convert this benefit to a 500-week permanent partial disability benefit.[10]

**Louisiana.** Unlike Montana, Louisiana does not stop permanent total disability benefits when the worker retires or would have retired. However, it *may* terminate that part of the permanent partial disability benefit based on the worker's actual wage loss, called a "supplemental earnings benefit." Again, the exact wording of Louisiana Revised Statutes, Vol 16A, R.S. 23:1221, is important enough to reproduce below:

> The right to supplemental earnings benefits pursuant to this paragraph shall in no way exceed a maximum of five hundred twenty weeks, but shall terminate: (iii) When the employee retires or begins to receive old age insurance benefits under Title II of the Social Security Act, whichever comes first; however, the period during which supplemental earnings benefits may be payable shall not be less than one hundred four weeks.                                   (pp. 362–364)

**Minnesota.** Minnesota has two provisions relating to termination of post-retirement disability benefits. First, temporary total disability compensation ends 90 days after an employee has reached maximum medical improvement or 90 days after the end of an approved retraining program, whichever is later. However, it ends earlier if the employer provides suitable employment during that 90-day period or if the worker actually retires. Receipt of OASDI creates a rebuttable presumption that the worker has retired from the labor force.

Second, workers with permanent partial disabilities receive either impairment compensation or economic recovery compensation depending upon whether, within 90 days following maximum medical improvement, the employer furnishes available work to the employee. The impairment compensation, which is triggered by a job offer, is a lump-sum payment related only to the percent of disability determined by a schedule that specifies a percentage of disability for each entry on a long list of impairments. The economic recovery compensation, triggered by absence of a job offer, is two thirds of the worker's prior earnings, but no more than the state average weekly wage, for a number of weeks that depends upon the percent of disability. If during the 90-day period the worker retired, only the impairment compensation is paid. Again, receipt of OASDI retirement benefits creates a rebuttable presumption that the worker has retired. Retirement or presumed retirement after the 90-day period, however, does not reduce the economic recovery compensation.

Permanent total disability benefits are not terminated if the worker retires.

### Reduction of Benefits

Only one state, Michigan, reduces disability benefits after the worker reaches the age at which he or she would presumably have retired, in this instance age 65. Michigan reduces the benefit that could otherwise be payable by 5% per year, subject to a maximum reduction of 50%. In no case, however, is this reduction permitted to reduce the benefit below the minimum weekly benefit. More importantly, this reduction does not apply to persons 1) who are not eligible for OASDI retirement benefits, or 2) whose benefits are reduced under the offset provision described in the next section. In practice, a worker whose benefit would be reduced more by the offset provision than by the 5% per year reduction can elect to be subject to the reduction provision. About three quarters of the disabled workers have chosen the offset.

### Offset Provisions

Instead of, or in addition to, terminating or reducing workers' compensation disability benefits at the workers' actual or presumed retirement age, nine states offset part or all of the workers' compensation benefit by retirement benefits received under OASDI. Wyoming may offset the benefit by state or federal pension plan benefits, but not by OASDI. Table 3–2 shows the various offsets that are used. Five states relate the OASDI offset to the entire OASDI benefit; the other four consider only half the OASDI benefit. Six states reduce the workers' compensation benefit by either the entire OASDI benefit or half that benefit; the other three limit the OASDI offset to either half the workers' compensation benefit or to the amount that would push the combined total of workers' compensation and other benefits above 80% of the worker's prior earnings. Three of the nine states add employer-paid pension benefits to the OASDI offset.

Offset provisions serve two major purposes. First, they recognize that workers' compensation disability benefits continued past retirement age are essentially a retirement benefit that should be offset by retirement

Table 3–2.   Offset Amounts at the Actual or Presumed Retirement Age

| Method | State |
|---|---|
| The amount that would reduce the combined workers' compensation and OASDI benefits to less than 80% of the worker's prior earnings | Louisiana |
| The entire OASDI benefit, but no more than half the workers' compensation benefit | Florida |
| One half the OASDI benefit | Alaska, North Dakota |
| The entire OASDI benefit after the worker has received $25,000 of disability benefits | Minnesota* |
| The entire OASDI benefit | Oregon |
| The amount necessary to qualify the worker for maximum benefits from any other state or federal pension plan after the worker has received 275 weeks of benefits | Wyoming |
| One half the OASDI benefit plus employer-paid pension benefits | Colorado, Michigan |
| The amount that would reduce the combined workers' compensation, employer-paid pension, aand OASDI benefits to less than 80% of the worker's prior earnings | District of Columbia |

* In Minnesota, the offset provision does not apply until the worker has received $25,000 in weekly total disability benefits. From that point on, the workers' compensation benefit is reduced by the full amount of the OASDI benefit subject to special treatment of a supplementary minimum benefit. Except for the offset provision, for a worker who has been totally disabled either for 208 weeks or as a result of an occupational disease, the minimum weekly benefit (called a supplementary minimum benefit) becomes and remains 65% of the current state average weekly wage. Under the offset provision, the reduced workers' compensation benefit cannot be less than the supplementary minimum benefit minus 5% of the difference between this supplementary minimum benefit and the reduced workers' compensation benefit that would otherwise be payable. For more than half the totally disabled workers, the combined income will exceed the worker's prior earnings.

benefits received from some other source. Second, they stop a worker from receiving a combined workers' compensation, OASDI, and sometimes private pension that is too high a percentage of the worker's earnings prior to his or her disability. Offset provisions, however, are not consistent with the proper role proposed in this chapter. First, they do not reduce workers' compensation benefits at retirement for persons not eligible for OASDI. Because most disabled workers are covered under OASDI, however, relatively few workers would not have benefits reduced by this offset. When, however, the offset also includes employer-paid private pensions, the workers without such pensions are treated much more favorably. Second, if the entire OASDI benefit is included in the offset, part of the offset is financed by the worker, not the employer. Third, this offset does not, except by chance, produce a retirement income that is equal to the retirement income based on predisability service plus some percentage of the retirement income that would have been earned during the disability period if the worker had not been disabled.

## States with Automatic Escalation Adjustments

An important factor affecting the cost of continuing disability benefits past the presumed retirement age is whether the benefits are indexed to reflect increases in either the state average weekly wage or the Consumer Price Index. Table 3–3 summarizes the current escalation provisions in the 13 states that index the benefits in some fashion.

The most common approach, used by nine states, is to adjust the benefits annually to match increases in the state average weekly wage, thus preserving the worker's standard of living. The second approach, used by three states, differs only in that the annual increases are limited to either

Table 3–3. States with Escalation Provisions

| Provision | States |
|---|---|
| Benefits adjusted annually to match increases in the state average weekly wage | Connecticut |
| | District of Columbia |
| | Illinois |
| | Maine |
| | Massachusetts |
| | New Hampshire |
| | New Jersey |
| | Vermont |
| | Washington |
| Benefit adjusted annually to match increases in the state average weekly wage but limited to stated percentage increase | 5% — Florida |
| | Michigan |
| | 6% — Minnesota |
| Benefits adjusted annually to match increases in the Consumer Price Index (but combined workers' compensation and OASDI benefit cannot exceed 80% of the worker's prior earnings) | Virginia |

5% or 6%. Virginia is the only state that relates the adjustments to increases in the Consumer Price Index. Virginia matches these increases, but limits the combined workers' compensation and OASDI benefit to 80% of the worker's prior earnings.

Except in Connecticut, Maine, Minnesota, New Hampshire, and Vermont, these adjustments are limited to permanent total disability benefits. In all of the excepted states, both temporary and permanent total disability benefits are adjusted automatically. Maine and Vermont also adjust permanent partial disability benefits.

As noted earlier, indexing the workers' compensation benefit increases greatly the disparity between the present and proper workers' compensation benefits. Yet nine of the 13 states with escalation provisions do not terminate, reduce, or offset workers' retirement benefits during the retirement years. Only the District of Columbia, Florida, Michigan, and Minnesota appear in both table 3–3 and table 3–1.

Other things being equal, one would expect workers to find permanent total workers' compensation benefits more attractive when they are indexed and not terminated, reduced, or offset during the retirement period. Consequently, other things being equal, one might expect workers aged 50 or over to be a larger proportion of the permanent total disability cases in states with indexed benefits and no termination, reduction, or offset provisions. Table 3–4 shows this proportion for each of the 12 states included in the Detailed Claim Information Survey conducted by the National Counsil on Compensation Insurance, classified into three categories according to 1) whether they index the benefit, and 2) whether they terminate, reduce, or offset the benefit during retirement years.

The sample is too small and the other factors affecting the disability rates are too numerous to draw any firm conclusions from the data. The unweighted averages, however, run counter to the hypothesis. The Information Survey data averages are higher for the three index states with reductions or offset provisions than for the four index states with no reduction or offset provisions. Even with Pennsylvania omitted, among the nine states with no termination, reduction, or offset provisions, these averages are higher for the no-index states than for the index states. The same relationship, however, exists for all disability cases, not just permanent total disability cases, starting at age 50.

A second hypothesis is that among older workers, permanent total disability cases are a larger percentage of total disability cases in states that index, especially if they have no reduction or offset provisions. Table 3–5 shows these percentages for each of the states and the three categories used in table 3–4. As mentioned earlier, these data should be interpreted

Table 3–4.   Percent of All Disability Cases and All Permanent Disability (PTD) Cases that Started at Ages 50–59 or Ages 60–69, for Selected States, 1979–1980

| | Ages 50–59 | | Ages 60–69 | | Ages 50–69 | |
|---|---|---|---|---|---|---|
| *States* | *All* | *PTD* | *All* | *PTD* | *All* | *PTD* |
| *Indexing but no termination, reduction, or offset provisions* | | | | | | |
| Connecticut | 14.41 | 10.00 | 5.45 | 3.33 | 19.87 | 13.33 |
| Illinois | 13.09 | 22.73 | 4.86 | 15.91 | 17.95 | 38.64 |
| Maine | 13.45 | 22.22 | 3.87 | — | 17.32 | 22.22 |
| Virginia | 13.21 | 36.65 | 7.81 | 17.61 | 21.02 | 54.26 |
| Weighted average | 13.67 | 30.84 | 5.02 | 15.32 | 18.69 | 46.17 |
| Unweighted average | 13.54 | 22.90 | 5.50 | 9.21 | 19.04 | 32.11 |
| *No indexing, termination, reduction, or offset provisions* | | | | | | |
| Georgia | 10.94 | 21.74 | 4.71 | 10.14 | 15.65 | 31.88 |
| Kentucky | 14.77 | 34.32 | 7.31 | 31.11 | 22.08 | 65.43 |
| Massachusetts | 14.70 | 12.31 | 5.78 | 15.38 | 20.49 | 27.69 |
| New York | 16.61 | 12.90 | 6.54 | 12.90 | 22.71 | 25.81 |
| Pennsylvania | 15.82 | 38.00 | 6.69 | 43.67 | 22.51 | 81.67 |
| Weighted average | 13.55 | 21.79 | 5.64 | 29.76 | 19.19 | 61.55 |
| Unweighted average | 13.96 | 24.04 | 5.88 | 20.53 | 19.84 | 44.58 |
| Unweighted average minus Pennsylvania | 13.59 | 21.25 | 5.71 | 15.91 | 19.31 | 37.16 |
| *Indexing and reduction or offset provisions* | | | | | | |
| Florida | 13.28 | 28.95 | 5.82 | 15.79 | 19.09 | 44.74 |
| Michigan | 16.45 | 26.67 | 8.39 | 14.67 | 24.84 | 41.33 |
| Minnesota | 12.53 | 28.81 | 5.77 | 13.56 | 18.30 | 42.37 |
| Weighted average | 14.10 | 27.91 | 6.74 | 14.53 | 20.84 | 42.44 |
| Unweighted average | 14.09 | 28.14 | 6.66 | 14.67 | 20.74 | 42.81 |

*Source:* Derived from National Council on Compensation Insurance Detailed Claim Information Survey Data.

with care because of the small small sample and the many factors affecting the percentages. However, in this case, if Kentucky, which has an unusually high percentage, is omitted, the raw data support the hypothesis. The unweighted average percentage is highest in the states with indexing but no termination, reduction, or offset provisions. It is lowest in the three states (all of which are index states) that have reduction or offset provisions.

Table 3–5.   Total Permanent Disability Cases as a Percent of All Disability Cases for Ages 50–59 and 60–69, for Selected States, 1979–1980

| State | 50–59 | 60–69 | 50–69 |
|---|---|---|---|
| *Indexing but no termination, reduction or offset provisions* | | | |
| Connecticut | .33 | .29 | .32 |
| Illinois | 2.62 | 4.95 | 3.25 |
| Maine | .98 | 0 | .76 |
| Virginia | 7.65 | 10.13 | 8.31 |
| Weighted average | 3.50 | 4.73 | 3.83 |
| Unweighted average | 2.90 | 3.84 | 3.16 |
| *No indexing, termination, reduction, or offset provisions* | | | |
| Georgia | 1.37 | 1.49 | 1.41 |
| Kentucky | 24.70 | 45.28 | 31.51 |
| Massachusetts | .52 | 1.64 | .84 |
| New York | .55 | 1.37 | .79 |
| Pennsylvania | 4.65 | 12.62 | 7.02 |
| Wisconsin | .62 | .65 | .62 |
| Weighted average | 5.66 | 12.73 | 7.74 |
| Unweighted average | 5.40 | 10.51 | 7.03 |
| Unweighted average minus Kentucky | 1.54 | 3.55 | 2.14 |
| *Indexing and reduction or offset provisions* | | | |
| Florida | 1.23 | 1.53 | 1.32 |
| Michigan | .96 | 1.04 | .99 |
| Minnesota | .89 | .91 | .90 |
| Weighted average | .98 | 1.07 | 1.01 |
| Unweighted average | 1.03 | 1.16 | 1.07 |

## Reduction of Private Employer Benefits

Instead of reducing the workers' compensation benefit, OASDI may, as already explained, reduce the OASDI benefit. Private employee benefits, particularly disability benefits and pension disability benefits, might logically also be reduced if the worker's disability is job-related. Current practices in this regard are summarized briefly below.

**Short-Term Disability Plans.** Short-term disability plans may cover only nonoccupational disabilities, in which case they have no effect on workers' compensation benefits. If the plan also covers occupational disabilities, however, the benefits are reduced by workers' compensation benefits. If a worker continues to receive these benefits beyond his or her presumed retirement age, the benefit violates the wage-loss concept. Because short-term disability benefits seldom are paid for more than 26 weeks, however, the payments beyond the presumed retirement age are probably small in number and amount. Reducing the temporary disability benefit by the workers' compensation benefit has no effect on the workers' compensation benefit itself.

**Long-Term Disability Plans.** Long-term disability plans almost always cover both occupational and nonoccupational disabilities. Almost always they also subtract from the long-term disability benefit any workers' compensation benefits received. Although some long-term disability plans pay benefits for the remainder of the disabled workers' life, most stop the benefits at age 65 or 70 on the assumption that the responsibility for retirement benefits rests with the employer's pension plan and OASDI. These plans, therefore, are consistent with the proper role proposed in this chapter for workers' compensation.

**Disability Benefits under Pension Plans.** Pension plans may provide disability benefits in the following ways:

1. Early retirement may be limited to workers who are permanently and totally disabled. Alternatively, disabled persons may become eligible for early retirement at an earlier age or with less service. If the pension benefit is actuarially reduced to reflect the early retirement, this option does not increase the present value of the benefit paid. If the pension benefit is not reduced this much, the benefit may include a disability component payable past the presumed retirement age.
2. The worker's pension benefit may continue to accrue, assuming constant earnings, from the date of the disability until the normal retirement age. This accrual is consistent with the proposal advanced in this chapter except that the proposed pension accrual would be based on indexed workers' compensation benefits, not constant salaries.
3. The plan may provide a separate disability income benefit that the worker will receive for the rest of his or her life. After the worker reaches his or her presumed retirement age, the disability benefit in effect replaces the retirement benefit. Alternatively, the plan may replace the disability benefit at the presumed retirement age; the worker then becomes entitled to the retirement benefit preserved under point 2.

No data are available on how often workers' compensation benefits are deducted from the disability benefits paid under any of these methods. In his discussion of pension disability benefits, however, McGill (1984) states that "the disability benefit formula must take into account, by offset or otherwise, the disability benefits provided under social security, workers' compensation, and possibly veterans' legislation."

## Why the Disparity between the Proper Role and Present Practice?

Current practices in the United States are clearly not consistent with the proper role of postretirement workers' compensation benefits proposed in this chapter or with similar proposals made by several other persons during the past 10 or 15 years. The reasons appear to be 1) political and 2) administrative.

### Political Reasons

Replacing workers' compensation disability benefits at retirement age with a retirement income that might be zero would not be a popular political move. Benefits would be terminated or reduced for aged workers whose physical or mental condition understandably would cause others to sympathize with their plight.

Despite the fact that under the proposal only those who were not eligible for a pension would receive no insurance income during retirement, most workers with permanent total disabilities would be worse off after retirement than under the present system.[11]

A second reason why legislators would hesitate to support this proposal is that it would represent a dramatic change in the system, which would generate considerable attention and lengthy debates.

Third, one of the essential recommendations of the National Commission on State Workmen's Compensation Laws was that permanent total disability benefits be continued for life.

Fourth, the employee's status with respect to employee benefits is determined by what benefits the employer provided at the date the disability commenced. With the passage of time, the employer might have increased or decreased the benefit package without compensating decreases or increases in cash wages. Of course the employer might also have increased or decreased the general level of cash wages with or without changing the employee benefits.

Fifth, except possibly in states that already index benefits, discontinuing total disability benefits at the retirement age would probably not reduce workers' compensation costs significantly.[12] Furthermore, replacing part of the employee benefits lost because of the disability and indexing the disability income benefits would increase costs substantially. These benefit improvements, however, would affect many workers and might on balance be considered more valuable than the benefit lost by the discontinuance of disability income benefits at retirement.

The cost impact of this proposal is so important that it merits more discussion. Table 3–6 quantifies the effect of the proposed changes on the cost to the employer (value to the employee) of permanent total disability benefits provided to workers who become disabled at ages 25, 45, and 60. For each age, the table first shows for nonindexed states the effect of 1) stopping the income payments at age 65. The table next shows the effects of stopping the income payments at age 65 but 2) increasing the benefits prior to that time by 20% (a percentage that would actually vary among employers and possibly employees) to continue part of the employee benefits, including any pension, 3) indexing the benefits 4% a year

Table 3–6. Percentage Changes in Present Value of Permanent Total Disability Benefits Under Four Sets of Modifications of the Present Law

| | Age | | |
|---|---|---|---|
| *Modifications* | *25* | *45* | *60* |
| *Nonindexed States* | | | |
| Benefit stops at age 65 | −5.06% | −19.46% | −61.62% |
| Benefit stops at age 65, benefit increased 20% for employee benefits | +14.92% | +3.35% | −53.94% |
| Benefit stops at age 65, benefit indexed until then | +48.38% | +11.12% | −58.64% |
| Benefit stops at age 65, benefit increased 20% for employee benefits, benefit also indexed until then | +78.06% | +33.40% | −50.37% |
| *Indexed States* | | | |
| Benefit stops at age 65 | −18.09% | −34.08% | −70.95% |
| Benefit stops at age 65, benefit increased 20% for employee benefits | −1.70% | 20.89% | −65.14% |

up to age 65, and 4) doing both (2) and (3). The present values were calculated assuming the Commissioners' 1980 Standard Ordinary mortality rates, a 5% annual interest rate, and salaries earned at the end of each year.

For workers disabled at age 25, the percent value of the benefit is reduced about 5.1% if the benefit stops at age 65. However, when some employee benefits are added, when the benefits are indexed, or when both of these occur, the present value increased over 78% under the complete proposal. For the worker disabled at age 45, the effect of stopping the benefit at age 65 is greater, but the present value still increases over 33% under the complete proposal. For the worker disabled at age 60, the present value is reduced substantially under all of the options, including a 50% drop under the complete proposal.

For indexed states, only two versions of the proposal would represent changes because the benefits are already indexed. For both these versions are for all ages, the result is a reduction in the present value of the benefit. For the complete version, however, the reduction is only about 2% for the worker disabled at age 25. For the two older workers, the reductions are substantial.

To determine the effect of these changes on aggregate permanent total disability benefits, one would need to 1) perform similar calculations for each of the other possible ages and 2) know the age composition of persons who are permanently and totally disabled at each of those ages. Such a calculation is beyond the scope of this chapter. However, if the only possible ages were 25, 45, and 60, with 20% of the disabled workers being age 25, 60% age 45, and 20% age 60, the percentage changes in the aggregate benefits would be as shown in table 3–7.

The termination of the weekly cash benefits at the presumed retirement age should have little or no effect on the other types of workers'

Table 3–7.  Percentage Change in Aggregate Benefits

|  | Nonindexed States | Indexed States |
| --- | --- | --- |
| Benefit stops at 65 | −25.0% | −38.3% |
| Benefit stops at 65, employee benefit increase | −5.8% | −25.9% |
| Benefit stops at 65, indexed benefit | 4.6% | Not applicable |
| Benefit stops at 65, employee benefits increase, indexed benefits | 25.6% | Not applicable |

compensation benefits, but the indexing and especially the addition of employee benefits may. Specifically, medical expense benefits for the job-related injury or disease should not be affected. Because temporary total disability benefits seldom exceed 52 weeks, indexing the benefits on the anniversary date should not be a costly addition. Continuing some fraction of the employee benefits, however, could increase their cost by some substantial percentage, say, 20%. This cost increase would be reduced to the extent that the employer would normally continue part or all of the employee benefits during periods of temporary disability. Paying permanent partial disability benefits in weekly installments would offset to a large extent the cost of indexing these benefits. Continuing the employee benefits, however, would increase the cost by, say, 20%. Death benefits would not be affected by the proposal.

How much workers' compensation rates would be increased in nonindexed states by the complete proposal would depend upon 1) the increase in the cost of the aggregate benefits of each type and 2) the percent of the total benefits consisting of each type. Based on the discussion thus far and one possible distribution of types of benefits, the average increase in workers' compensation rates would be 13%, as calculated in table 3–8.

In states already indexing permanent total disability benefits, the major difference would be a 26% decrease in the cost of the permanent total disability benefits, causing the increase in cost for all types of benefits combined to drop to 11%.

More detailed data and a more careful analysis may suggest a larger or smaller cost increase. For example, not considered in this analysis was the effect of these benefit changes on workers' propensity to file disability claims and the duration of their disabilities.

Finally, under the proposed change, other things being equal, employers

Table 3–8. Average Increase in Workers' Compensation Rates in Nonindexed States

| Type of Benefit | Increase in Cost | Present Percent of Total Benefits |
|---|---|---|
| Medical expenses | 0% | 34% |
| Temporary total disability | 20% | 20% |
| Permanent total disability | 26% | 4% |
| Permanent partial disability | 20% | 40% |
| Death | 0% | 2% |
| All types combined | 13% | 100% |

with generous employee benefits would incur higher workers' compensation costs than employers with less generous or no private employee benefits. (Of course, their employees lose more by becoming disabled.) The proposal, therefore, might provide a strong disincentive to establishing and expanding such benefits. On the other hand, as noted earlier, the theroy of compensating wage differentials suggests that an employer who does not provide employee benefits must pay higher wages to get the same type of work done.

## Administrative Reasons

If adopted, the proposed change would create more work and some problems for state workers' compensation administrators. Anticipation of these administrative problems, of course, would cause some additional political problems. Key administrative problems are associated with 1) the age at which the workers' compensation disability benefits should stop, 2) the retirement income amount, and 3) whether the workers' compensation insurer (or self-insurer) should pay the retirement income (and other employee benefits) lost.

**Age at Which Disability Benefits Should Stop.** At what age should the workers' compensation disability income benefit be replaced by a retirement benefit? Should the retirement age be the same for all disabled workers? One possibility is the normal retirement age in the employer's private pension plan. According to *Employee Benefits in Medium and Large Firms, 1986*, published by the U.S. Department of Labor Bureau of Labor Statistics (1987), the normal retirement ages in defined benefit pension plans vary greatly. The ages reported were 65 (36%) any age with sufficient service (24%) 62 (19%), 60 (14%), 55 (3%), and other ages (4%). Employees, however, cannot be forced to retire at any age merely because of their age. Retirement prior to the normal retirement age is also possible. At what age should a totally disabled worker be presumed to have retired? If, in the interests of simplifying workers' compensation administration, the disability benefits always stopped at age 65, should the worker receive pension credits for the workers' compensation benefits received from the normal retirement age, if earlier, to age 65? Would setting the presumed age equal to the actual normal retirement age create too much administrative expense? If the normal retirement age were earlier than age 65, a common situation, the workers' compensation disability benefit would be less than it would be if the normal retirement age was

65. Would this be fair? If so, because the "normal" retirement age is earlier than age 65, would it be perceived to be fair?

Because many workers are still not covered under any private pension plans, their presumed retirement age cannot be determined by these plans. Most workers, however, are covered under Old Age, Survivors, and Disability Insurance. The normal retirement under OASDI is age 65, but about two thirds of the beneficiaries elect to retire prior to age 65 and many delay claiming benefits until as many as five years later. Thus the same questions arise as under the private plans. If the worker is covered under both OASDI and a private pension plan, which of these two systems determines when a worker retires?

**Retirement Income Benefit Amount.** If the retirement income benefit is some fraction of the retirement income lost because of the disability, this loss must first be determined. In most cases, the retirement income loss will include some loss of 1) OASDI and 2) private pension plan benefits. If the worker had been receiving Disability Income benefits, the worker would not have suffered any reduction in OASDI retirement benefits because of the disability freeze explained earlier.[13] However, if the worker was not eligible for Disability Insurance payments, the worker's OASDI retirement benefit would be reduced if excluding the last earnings during the disability years prior to retirement would reduce the average indexed monthly earnings upon which the OASDI is based. Congress would have to amend the Social Security Act to count workers' compensation benefits as covered income subject to OASDI taxes.

As for private plans, workers' compensation disability benefits paid prior to the retirement age should be treated the same as if they were salaries. The major problem is that each worker's retirement income loss would require a separate calculation. For each employer the calculations should be relatively easy, but for workers' compensation system administrators, checking each calculation would be time-consuming. The number of benefit formulas they would encounter would be extremely large.

**Should the Workers' Compensation Insurer Pay the Retirement Income Benefit?** If the workers' compensation insurer (or self-insurer) is obligated to pay the retirement income benefit (and other employee benefits), like the workers' compensation system administrator, it should probably rely, after checking, on the employer's calculations. The advantage of assigning this responsibility to the workings' compensation insurer (or self-insurer) is that the security arrangement would be the same for all workers' compensation benefits. A complicating factor is that in pricing workers' compensation, the insurer should consider the types of employee benefits provided by the employer. For example, one would expect the workers' compensation rates to be higher for an employer with a private pension plan than for one with on plan. A distinction might be made between plans that are modest and those that are generous. Pricing the annual cost of a pension benefit would be easy for a defined contribution money purchase plan but not for a defined benefit plan. If workers' compensation insurers recognized these and similar considerations in their pricing, the workers' compensation pricing structure would be much more complicated than at present.

An alternative approach would make the employer directly responsible for the employee benefits contained under the proposal. Administrative costs would be less and workers' compensation insurance pricing would not be complicated. On the other hand, the benefits might be less secure and the true cost of all workers' compensation benefits would be more difficult to determine.

## Conclusions

Under the wage-loss approach, workers' compensation should replace some fraction of a disabled worker's income including employer-financed employee benefits until the time when the worker would have retired. From that point on, the workers' compensation system would replace some fraction of the retirement income and other postretirement employee benefits the worker lost because he or she was disabled. Otherwise workers, especially older workers with no private pensions in states with indexed benefits, may have a strong financial incentive to be declared disabled. They certainly have an incentive to remain disabled once a disability has occurred. As older workers become a larger share of the workforce, the cost of continuing the disability benefit past the normal retirement age may increase dramatically. The effect may be to reduce other benefits, either in effect or proposed, that it is more important to preserve.

The replacement of workers' compensation disability benefits at retirement age with a lesser or no retirement benefit is not a new idea. Nevertheless, only one state legislature has embraced this concept, and even in that state the law has been interpreted as requiring replacement of the permanent total disability benefit with a permanent partial disability benefit. Two other states also terminate some disability benefits upon retirement, but not permanent total disability benefits. Several states do reduce benefits after retirement, but they do not pay zero benefits to those with no private pension plan. Several subtract part or all of any OASDI retirement benefit; two also subtract employer-paid pension benefits. In most states, the disability benefit continues without any reduction or offset.

Why has such a logical idea failed to attract any legislative support? The legislator proposing the termination of disability benefits at retirement age would almost certainly incur more political debits. The people whose benefits would be reduced would be the most seriously disabled. The change would be so dramatic that it would attract significant attention; because of its complexity it would not be easy to explain. Initially at least, the savings that would be generated by discontinuing the cash benefits past the retirement age probably would be more than offset by the cost of indexing the disability benefits and replacing part of the employee benefits. On the other hand, the indexed disability benefit and replacement of part of the employee benefits lost would be significant benefit improvements, especially in no-index states.

Administratively, the replacement of the workers' compensation benefit with an OASDI benefit may require some negotiations with Congress. Replacing part of a private pension poses several complex questions. These questions center around 1) the age at which the disability benefits should stop, 2) the retirement income benefit amount, and 3) whether the workers' compensation insurer should pay the replacement retirement benefit.

For these and other reasons, the pure form of the proposal presented in this chapter is unlikely to be adopted. Some modifications that might increase the probability of its being accepted are as follows:

1. To reduce costs, the indexing and replacement of part of the employee benefits lost, other than retirement income, could be omitted from the proposal. The authors very reluctantly suggest this modification because logic dictates that these benefits should be included. Furthermore, including these benefits would make the proposal much more acceptable to the average worker.
2. Instead of terminating completely workers' compensation disability benefits at the presumed retirement age, the program could continue a small impairment pension that is not related to the worker's prior earnings. This pension should be paid in addition to any private pension or OASDI benefits. The rationale for this pension is not to replace lost income; instead it should compensate the worker for some nonwage losses that would continue during retirement.
3. The presumed retirement age could be set equal to the OASDI normal retirement age unless the employer provides a private pension plan with an earlier normal retirement age, in which case that age would

be the termination age. Currently this retirement age is 65, but it is scheduled to increase during the early part of the next century to age 66 first and then to age 67.

4. The employer could be made directly responsible for providing the pension and other preretirement and postretirement employee benefits that the proposal would include. This modification would greatly simplify the administration and pricing of workers' compensation. These benefits might be less secure than if the workers' compensation insurer were responsible, but no less than for similarly situatied nondisabled workers.

If the workers' OASDI pension, survivorship, and health insurance benefits are not protected by the DI freeze, the employer should be required by state law and permitted by Congress to pay OASDI taxes on the workers' compensation disability benefits until retirement.

## Notes

1. According to the National Council on Compensation Insurance's Twelve-State Detailed Claim Information Survey, the proportion of disability cases that started at age 60 or later ranged during 1979–1980 from 3.87 in one state to 8.30 in another. The proportion of per- manent total disability cases ranged from 0 to 43.67. See table 3–4 in this chapter.

2. For the same reasons that disability benefits should stop at the workers' presumed retirement age, workers' compensation survivorship benefits should cease at that age. This chapter, however, deals only with disability benefits.

3. Instead of reducing the medical expense benefits by one third, administratively it would be easier to require the worker to pay one third of what the employer would otherwise pay.

4. For a discussion of the joint determination of wages and employee benefits and how these two forms of compensation are reflected in explict and implicit contracts, see Ehrenberg and Smith (1985), chapter 11.

5. For a discussion of the issues involved in these debates, see Burton (1983).

6. If the worker is also eligible for Disability Insurance benefits, the disability freeze benefit under that program will protect the worker from losing OASDI retirement or survivorship benefits. Consequently, in this instance the employer would not have to pay OASDI taxes.

7. A worker would suffer such a diminution of OASDI benefits if his or her disability qualifies him or her for workers' compensation benefits but not for the DI disability freeze described in footnote 5.

8. The Committee (1985) explained that private pension benefits were not included under the second approach because many employees are not covered under a pension plan. Furthermore, they argued, because of pension plan provisions such as vesting conditions, it would be virtually impossible to determine the private pension benefit a worker would have earned if the injury had not occurred.

9. The concept, however, has been accepted in some form by several Canadian provinces, including Newfoundland.

10. The Montana state fund pays the benefit in a lump sum, the private insurers in installments. The Montana Division of Workers' Compensation is currently reviewing their interpretation of the statute.

11. Supplemental Security Income guarantees a specified minimum income to all aged persons, but the monthly benefit is low and the program imposes some rigid property requirements on its beneficiaries.

12. The cost impact would be more favorable in states that already index benefits because 1) employers in these states are already providing indexed benefits and 2) under the proposal, in most cases, employers would not provide an indexed retirement income. In many cases, they would provide no retirement income.

13. The worker would lose any additional benefit he or she would have received because of salary increases received as a result of career progressions; however, these are not considered in the proposed change.

## References

Burton, John F., Jr. "Compensation for Permanent Partial Disabilities." In John D. Worrall (ed.), *Safety and the Work Force* Ithaca, NY: ILR Press, 1983, chapter 2.

Ehrenberg, Ronald G., and Robert S. Smith. *Modern Labor Economics*, 2nd edition. Glenview, IL: Scott, Foresman and Company, 1985.

*Employee Benefits in Medium and Large Firms, 1986*, Bulletin 2281. Washington, D.C.: U.S. Department of Labor Bureau of Labor Statistics, June 1987.

McGill, Dan M. *Fundamentals of Private Pensions*, 5th edition. Homewood, IL: Richard D. Irwin, Inc., 1984.

*Occupational Disease Issues*. Report of the NAIC Occupational Disease Advisory Committee, June, 1985.

Price, Daniel N. "Workers' Compensation: Coverage, Benefits, and Costs." *Social Security Bulletin* 49, (1986): 5–11.

*The Report of the National Commission on State Workmen's Compensation Laws*. Washington, D.C.: U.S. Government Printing Office, July 31, 1972.

*Role of the State Workers' Compensation System in Compensating Occupational Disease Victims*. Report of Crum and Forster's Occupational Disease Task Force, June, 1983.

Weiler, Paul C. *Reshaping Workers' Compensation for Ontario*. A Report Submitted to Robert G. Elgie, M. D., Minister of Labor, November, 1980.

*White Paper on the Workers' Compensation Act*. Government of Ontario, 1981.

*Workers' Compensation: Is There a Better Way?*. A Report on the Need for Reform of State Workers' Compensation by the Policy Group of the Interdepartmental Workers' Compensation Task Force, January, 1977.

# 4 REHABILITATION AND WORKERS' COMPENSATION: INCOMPATIBLE OR INSEPARABLE?

Monroe Berkowitz

It is intuitively reasonable and eminently logical to give injured workers the opportunity to receive rehabilitation services designed to speed their return to work. Rehabilitation would seem to be an inseparable part of workers' compensation, and yet recent events demonstrate anew how incompatible the two programs may be. The states of Washington and Colorado have amended their laws to cut back on their commitment to mandatory rehabilitation, and the rehabilitation provisions of the workers' compensation laws in California, Minnesota, and Florida are under attack. Our purpose is to explore the uses of rehabilitation in workers' compensation, and to examine whether the programs are inseparable, as has been the traditional claim, or incompatible, as recent experience would suggest.

We begin by briefly examining the nature of compensation and rehabilitation. Next, we turn to a historical overview of the relations between them. Until quite recently, the vocational rehabilitation of compensation clients was the province of the public rehabilitation programs. Today, especially in those states that have made aspects of rehabilitation mandatory, the private sector providers have largely displaced the public program. Such a change has vast implications for the role of the compensation agency in the monitoring and oversight of the rehabilitation process. For one thing, it means that rehabilitation services must now be paid for by the insurance carrier. We look at the admittedly sparse data on rehabilitation expenditures of insurance carriers and then move on to a theoretical examination of the problems posed in attempting to arrive at the optimal amount of rehabilitation services to be offered injured workers. In the absence of good aggregate data, we examine the experiences of several states to illustrate the variety of approaches to the problem of combining the two systems. We conclude with observations about the future relationships and the problems that remain to be solved.

## The Nature of Workers' Compensation

By its very nature, workers' compensation is an interference with the free choice of both the employer and the employee in the labor market. Employees who are risk-preferers might well opt for higher wages and less protection in the event of an injury. Some employers might prefer to invest heavily in safety programs and take their chances of large losses should they be proven negligent. The state, in its wisdom, does not allow either alternative. Instead, it prescribes a program whereby all persons injured in work accidents are guaranteed a modest recovery regardless of fault. In addition, the worker is to receive the medical care necessary to cure and relieve the effects of his injury. To an extent that varies from state to state, the worker is also entitled to medical rehabilitation services if indicated. All workers' compensation programs go further and prescribe the terms and conditions under which medical and income replacement benefits are to be paid. Particularly relevant are those provisions that govern payment of indemnity benefits in the case of permanent disability.[1] Jurisdictions that compensate permanent partial disabilities on the basis of actual wage loss provide different incentives for employees to participate in rehabilitation than do those jurisidictions which compensate on the basis of impairments. Whether an employer saves money by rehabilitating an employee is at least partially dependent upon the type of workers' compensation law under which he is operating. More important, the workers' compensation scheme is now an independent variable that can be changed to encourage or discourage the provision of rehabilitation services.

## The Nature of Rehabilitation

There is no single, universally agreed-upon definition of rehabilitation. For purposes of this discussion, it is useful to think of rehabilitation as a set of services, ranging from medical management to formal education, designed either to restore a worker to his former job, or to his former level of efficiency, or to the highest level of functioning of which he is capable, given his residual functioning capacities. There is probably less controversy about what rehabilitation is and does than there is about what its objectives should be.

Operationally, rehabilitation consists of a range of services bracketed by the two mentioned above—medical management and formal education. Among these services are counseling, guidance, evaluation, retraining, and job placement. Rehabilitation may involve job redesign and modifications to the work place or even to the home environment, although, most commonly, rehabilitation services are directed toward improving the individual and his job chances, rather than the environment in which he functions.

Rehabilitation is said to be a team effort involving the physician, allied health professionals, and persons from a host of assorted disciplines— vocational education, social work, work evaluation, etc.The coordinator of the team may be a professional rehabilitation counselor.[2] It is a continuous integrated progress, with one service melding into and flowing from the other. The focus is on the client and the accomplishment of the stated objectives, be they return to the worker's old job, or possibly some more ambitious objective such as restoration of the maximum capabilities of the person given his residual functioning capacities. If the process is truly a continuous one, then there is no real dividing line between medical and vocational rehabilitation. Yet one of the difficulties of bringing rehabilitation into workers' compensation is that the laws of some jurisdictions require such a distinction, since they provide for different payers for the different types of services.

The objectives of rehabilitation are most controversial and will vary depending on who is paying for and who is providing the services. If the objective is return to work, this might be accomplished with minimal services. If the objective is the improvement of the worker so that he might attain his maximum potential, an objective which the traditional professional counselor is most sympathetic with, additional and more expensive services may be indicated. Once rehabilitation services are mandated, it becomes vitally necessary to spell out these objectives since the employer may now be obligated to pay for rehabilitation, and this may turn out to be a blank check unless the objectives are specified.

## The Historically Close Relationship between Workers' Compensation and Rehabilitation

At the inception of workers' compensation, rehabilitation was looked upon as one of its principal objectives.[3] As early as 1916, the annual meetings of the workers' compensation administrators, the International Association of Industrial Accident Boards and Commissions (IAIABC), were being advised that rehabilitation of injured persons should be the first concern of workers' compensation, followed by financial relief and then accident prevention, in that order.[4] From 1916 onwards, almost each year's committee of the IAIABC raised the flag of rehabilitation and exhorted the troops to rally around. From time to time, new initiatives are begun, but one does not sense very much lasting forward progress. It should not be surprising to discover that it is difficult to integrate rehabilitation into workers' compensation. Workers' compensation has tended to become increasingly litigious over the years, and rehabilitation seems to call for a clinical case-by-case approach. Yet, there have been many attempts over the years to have the two systems operate together.

The state of New Jersey, for example, had a perfect example of close coordination and cooperation between the state workers' compensation agency and the state program of vocational rehabilitation as far back as 1919. The relationship between workers' compensation and rehabilitation was so close that it was difficult to separate the two. As workers came into the Newark compensation office to review the financial adequacy of a pro- posed settlement, they would be examined at a state-run clinic. The same physician would determine the correctness of the cash indemnity payment and would be available to provide any necessary physical restoration services. At the same time, the worker would be seen by a vocational rehabilitation counselor for possible training and placement services.[5]

The close coordination lasted only a relatively few years until it foundered because of difficulties that have hardly been resolved even today. The state-run clinics found themselves in head-to-head competition with private medical providers, and their physicians became involved in conflicts of interest as they sought both to fix the degree of disability and to recommend rehabilitation programs. Although several rehabilitation models have been tried over the years, today New Jersey's workers' com- pensation program has no rehabilitation program save for the statutorily mandated referral of permanent total cases long after such referral can do anyone any good.

### The Federal–State Vocational Rehabilitation Program

The two agencies that closely cooperated in New Jersey were the state workers' compensation agency and the New Jersey vocational rehabilitation agency. Beginning in 1920, the federal government authorized grants-in-aid to the states for the purpose of establishing these vocational rehabilitation programs. That federal legislation was the result of successful lobbying by IAIABC, which came into being in 1913.[6] The primary clients of the newly established vocational rehabilitation agencies were the industrially injured, and close relationships existed between these agencies.

Now all of that is gone. We will note below some special cases. We recognize that each state workers' compensation agency has a formal written agreement of cooperation with the state's vocational rehabilitation agency, but the record indicates that workers' compensation cases have become an insignificant proportion of the total number of rehabilitation clients. Table 4–1 shows, for 13 states (states for which we have some additional data as to rehabilitation expenditures), the number of closed rehabilitation-agency cases that were referred by workers' compensation. Only New York has more than 2% of its cases referred from the workers' compensation agency. If we consider all jurisdictions, not only the 13 listed, the proportion of workers' compensation referrals is 1.6% of the total number of cases closed in 1984. Table 4–2 lists all rehabilitation jurisdictions where 4% or more of the closed cases in 1984 were referred from workers' compensation agencies.

Among these jurisdictions, Puerto Rico and West Virginia have exclusive state funds that have a record of cooperation with the state agency. At one time, several of these states (West Virginia and Montana, for example) referred all their cases to the state agency. Today West Virginia refers approximately 50% of its cases to the state vocational rehabilitation agency and the other half to private providers. Montana has recently changed its practices and now refers to private vendors as well as to the state agency. Kansas, Nebraska, and Mississippi are states without mandatory provisions. Screening units in these state workers' compensation agencies have no authority to compel carriers to pay for vocational rehabilitation, and where referrals are indicated, they are made exclusively to the state agency where services can be provided without cost to the parties. Up until quite recently, the New Hampshire agency had an employee of the state rehabilitation agency outstationed in its office. That employee screened cases and took referrals. In accordance with the ever-changing pattern of relationships between these agencies, that practice has recently been discontinued. The agency now notifies the carrier of any cases where it believes some rehabilitation inquiries are warranted, and it is up to the carrier to follow through.[7]

Granted that there are exceptions in a few states, overall the picture shows that the formerly close cooperation between the workers' compensation agencies and the state vocational rehabilitation programs is a thing

Table 4–1. Number of Workers' Compensation Cases Referred to 13 State Vocational Rehabilitation Agencies in 1984

| State | Number of Workers' Compensation Referrals | Percent of Total | Number of Other Referrals | Percent of Total | Number not Reporting Referral Source | Percent of Total | Total Number of Referrals |
|---|---|---|---|---|---|---|---|
| Connecticut | 42 | 0.6% | 7,433 | 99.4% | 1 | 0.0% | 7,476 |
| Florida | 368 | 1.1% | 32,249 | 93.8% | 1,763 | 5.1% | 34,380 |
| Georgia | 133 | 0.8% | 16,462 | 99.2% | 0 | 0.0% | 16,595 |
| Illinois | 15 | 0.1% | 21,363 | 99.9% | 0 | 0.0% | 21,378 |
| Kentucky | 34 | 0.3% | 13,432 | 99.7% | 0 | 0.0% | 13,466 |
| Maine | 15 | 0.5% | 3,171 | 99.5% | 0 | 0.0% | 3,186 |
| Massachusetts | 242 | 1.3% | 18,610 | 98.3% | 75 | 0.4% | 18,927 |
| Michigan | 168 | 0.9% | 18,130 | 99.0% | 14 | 0.1% | 18,312 |
| Minnesota | 117 | 0.8% | 13,659 | 99.0% | 27 | 0.2% | 13,803 |
| New York | 872 | 2.7% | 30,695 | 95.1% | 724 | 2.2% | 32,291 |
| Pennsylvania | 346 | 1.0% | 32,632 | 99.0% | 0 | 0.0% | 32,978 |
| Virginia | 291 | 2.0% | 14,475 | 98.0% | 0 | 0.0% | 14,766 |
| Wisconsin | 266 | 1.5% | 17,692 | 98.5% | 9 | 0.1% | 17,967 |
| Total—13 States | 2,909 | 1.2% | 240,003 | 97.8% | 2,613 | 1.1% | 245,525 |
| All Jurisdictions | 10,548 | 1.6% | 638,789 | 96.8% | 10.479 | 1.6% | 659,726 |

Table 4–2.  Percent of Total Closed State Vocational Rehabilitation Agency Cases Referred by Workers' Compensation

| State | Percent of Total Cases |
|---|---|
| New Hampshire | 4.9% |
| Puerto Rico | 7.5% |
| West Virginia | 11.2% |
| Mississippi | 7.2% |
| Kansas | 4.7% |
| Nebraska | 4.7% |
| Montana | 19.1% |
| Oregon | 13.3% |

of the past. The fault, if fault there be, cannot be ascribed to one agency or the other. The vocational rehabilitation program found other clients, such as the mentally ill, the mentally retarded, and the severely handicapped, who posed possibly fewer disincentive problem.[8] The workers' compensation agencies did not necessarily give up on rehabilitation. Employers and insurance carriers, especially when rehabilitation services were being offered voluntarily and not in response to any mandate of law, turned to alternative suppliers in the private sector.

## Rehabilitation Activity in 13 States

Table 4–3 shows the costs of workers' compensation insurance carrier's rehabilitation activities. Although these are largely costs incurred in the purchase of rehabilitation services from private providers, some of the costs may be due to purchases of services from the public program.[9] We look first at the averages for the 13 states that report to NCCI in their detail claim survey. Costs are broken down into three categories—evaluation, indemnity, and education. As is usual in such instances, the data leave a good deal to be desired. Medical rehabilitation costs are merged with all medical costs and are not reported separately. Indemnity costs attributable to rehabilitation should capture that portion of benefits paid to a worker undergoing rehabilitation that would not be paid if the worker were not receiving such services. Although this is clear conceptually, it is difficult to isolate such payments. One way to do so is to count only those payments made to workers after they have reached maximum medical improvement. But even such a rule is not easy to follow, and it should be modified in cases of permanent disability. At any rate, we take the indemnity data

Table 4–3. Average Rehabilitation Costs in 13 States

| | Average Total Cost | Average Evaluation Cost | Percent of Total | Average Indemnity Cost | Percent of Total | Average Education Cost | Percent of Total |
|---|---|---|---|---|---|---|---|
| Open 1 | $16,963.03 | $1,785.82 | 10.53% | $14,976.50 | 88.29% | $200.71 | 1.18% |
| Open 2 | $31,521.05 | $1,933.97 | 6.14% | $29,383.90 | 93.22% | $203.18 | 0.64% |
| Open 3 | $58,889.07 | $2,627.89 | 4.46% | $55,971.70 | 95.05% | $289.48 | 0.49% |
| Open 4 | $73,642.61 | $3,394.97 | 4.61% | $69,543.40 | 94.43% | $704.24 | 0.96% |
| Closed 1 | $4,004.99 | $266.16 | 6.65% | $3,710.90 | 92.66% | $27.93 | 0.70% |
| Closed 2 | $12,759.59 | $672.36 | 5.27% | $12,002.80 | 94.07% | $84.43 | 0.66% |
| Closed 3 | $26,669.38 | $1,557.29 | 5.84% | $24,662.70 | 92.48% | $449.39 | 1.69% |
| Closed 4 | $30,616.31 | $1,257.42 | 4.11% | $29,257.20 | 95.56% | $101.69 | 0.33% |

*Source:* NCCI Detailed Claim Information.

as reported and suspect that some carriers may have reported all of the indemnity payments in a particular case.

The evaluation costs may be more credible. These are the costs incurred in evaluating a worker to determine what, if any, services should be offered to him. Education costs are also suspect in that they may include all of the vendor costs for training programs but may fail to include costs incurred for counseling, guidance, and perhaps placement services. Such services precede and follow education and training programs and must be included somewhere.

Taking the data at face value, we see that regardless of whether a case is open or closed, and no matter which report, it is the indemnity costs which predominate. Evaluation costs also tend to be considerable, although typically these are only 5% or 6% of the costs. Under the laws of some jurisdictions, and under the carriers' practice in others, the first step in the rehabilitation process is to have the employee evaluated to determine if any rehabilitation services would be appropriate. Obviously many more cases are evaluated than will receive services. Evaluation costs are highest for those cases still open at the fourth report, some 42 months after the date of accident. For cases closed at the first and second report, costs are modest, but for those closed at later reports, evaluation costs on the average are about $1500.

What emerges in striking form is how little, on the average, is spent for education programs. Presumably this category also contains training expenses as well. Expenditures here vary in the low hundreds of dollars, and it is obvious that few extensive educational programs are being financed. This would accord with the conventional wisdom that education and retraining is a last resort, to be used only when all else fails. The controversy over the role that retraining should play in the rehabilitation of an individual is intimately tied up with the quarrel over the objectives of rehabilitation discussed above. If the objective is return to work, then providing some counseling and guidance and perhaps some discussion with the employer may be all that is necessary. Or perhaps the job may have to be modified so that it can be done by the worker even with his reduced capacities. If the objective is to develop the client to his full potential, then education and retraining may be prescribed. Quite naturally, when the rehabilitation is being provided voluntarily, the objective is to get the worker back on the job with the minimum of services.

Something of the comparative picture among 12 of the 13 states can be seen from table 4–4. In order to make the information comprehensible, we have concentrated on cases that are closed at the third report. For all 12 states, 10% of these cases receive some rehabilitation services. Florida,

Table 4-4.   Percent of Cases With Rehabilitation Permanent Partial Cases—
Closed at Third Report

| Jurisdiction | No. of Cases | Percent No Rehab | Percent Rehab |
|---|---|---|---|
| Connecticut | 233 | 86% | 14% |
| Florida | 100 | 50% | 50% |
| Georgia | 167 | 78% | 22% |
| Illinois | 1500 | 96% | 4% |
| Kentucky | 140 | 93% | 7% |
| Maine | | | |
| Michigan | 40 | 88% | 13% |
| Minnesota | 213 | 86% | 14% |
| New York | 1500 | 97% | 3% |
| Pennsylvania | 120 | 94% | 6% |
| Virginia | 98 | 87% | 13% |
| Wisconsin | 390 | 97% | 3% |
| All 12 States | 4652 | 90% | 10% |

with its rehabilitation nurse program, which preceded its current mandatory rehabilitation system, has relatively few cases, but 50% of them received rehabilitation. Georgia, which had a mandatory referral program in effect, is next with 22%. At the bottom of the list are Wisconsin and New York, a fact that is surprising since New York has its so-called R program under which carriers are supposed to report all cases out of work more than a specified number of days. If no return to work is expected, the carriers are supposed to indicate the type and nature of the rehabilitation plan designed to get the worker back into the labor force.[10] In Wisconsin, there has long been a tradition of close cooperation between the state agency and the vocational rehabilitation agency.

These percentage comparisons may be deceiving, given the disparities in the size of the workers' compensation case loads in the several states. Nonethelss, Illinois and New York, which show exactly the same number of workers' compensation cases closed at the third report, show about the same percentage of cases referred to rehabilitation. When it comes to rehabilitation activity and monitoring on the part of the workers' compensation agencies, these are certainly two different states. Illinois is not distinguished for its activity in this area, whereas New York, in addition to its R program, has a rehabilitation section in the compensation agency that monitors its referral program.[11] This similarity in the two states whose workers' compensation rehabilitation provisions differ so much again raises the issue of whether carrier activity is not motivated more by its analysis of the costs and benefits of rehabilitation than it is by the differences in the state statutes.

It is likely that the data sources are too crude to determine whether statutory provisions mandating rehabilitation make any difference. It is unfortunate that evaluative information is not at hand, especially since there now seems to be some reaction to the mandatory provisions in several states. Even as some states seek to extend their rehabilitation provisions, others are pulling back.

In the traditional public program and in workers' compensation, rehabilitation has been looked upon both as a humanitarian program and as a cost-reducing device. The allegation that the costs of rehabilitation are less than its benefits becomes especially appealing when premiums rise and the parties scurry to find ways to cut costs. Workers' compensation premiums increased dramatically after benefit levels were increased following the report of the National Commission. Total workers' compensation costs paid by employers rose from $4.9 billion in 1970 to $22.3 billion in 1980, after which they declined.[12] The provision of rehabilitation services was seen as one method of reducing costs.

This piece of reasoning was familiar, although this time around it was reinforced by what was happening in other cost areas. The increase in workers' compensation costs came about at the same time as the rise in health care costs in general. Management began to realise that health care vendor costs had to be controlled in much the same way as the cost of other goods and services it purchased. As *disability management* programs became the order of the day,[13] it was recognized that long-term disability was a potentially expensive item, perhaps even more so than acute care.[14] Having the rehabilitation counselor on board as the manager of the rehabilitation team might be one way to control these costs.

For management to react rationally in order to control increased costs is one thing; to compel management to provide a service on the theory that it is good for them and will save them money is quite another. At the very least it requires some examination. We turn now to a look at the theoretical, or at least more abstract, considerations underlying the market for rehabilitation services. At issue is whether the intervention of the state is necessary to induce employers to provide the right amount of rehabilitation services. Will they arrive at this point in the absence of compulsion?

## The Demand and the Supply of Rehabilitation in the Absence of Compulsion

We follow Worrall and Butler[15] in recognizing that the process of rehabilitation can be thought of as a profit-maximizing activity from the point of

view of the employer. In the absence of any mandate to provide rehabilitation services, but with all other constraints of the compensation system
operating, the employer[16] will purchase that amount of rehabilitation
services such that the marginal dollar expended will yield a dollar's benefit.

Operating in the absence of compulsion, the employer will be concerned
about the quality of the services purchased and the efficiency of their use.
The employer would presumably volunteer to offer rehabilitation services
only where there was a expectation of benefit commensurate with the costs
of the proffered service. Problems of selection of workers for services,
selection of the providers, and decisions about the amount of the services
offered would all be left to the employer. He might make mistakes, he
might miscalculate benefits or costs, but presumably he would bear the
burden of these mistakes and would learn from them. It is possible to think
of an intensive and an extensive margin. In the first case, the problem is
to determine how much in the way of services should be offered to an
individual worker. In the second case, the problem is to figure out how
many workers ought to be offered services. Both margins are relevant, but
for sake of simplifying the discussion, let us discuss the extensive margin.

Assume that the employer has 100 cases in the pool and can estimate the
costs of providing a bundle of rehabilitation services and the benefits that
would be derived from making these services available. Let us assume that
each of these workers is willing to accept the services. (In this example,
there are no relevant disincentives to the employee accepting whatever
services are offered.) Armed with this knowledge and motivated by a
desire to maximize profits, the employer will select first the employee
for whom the differences between the costs and the benefits will be the
greatest. Assuming that there are no constraints on the funds available for
rehabilitation services, the employer will continue to select employees and
offer services until the last employee selected yields benefits just equal to
the costs involved. At this extensive margin, the marginal benefits are
equal to the marginal costs involved. Under these conditions, let us say
that only 60 of the 100 clients will be offered the services and the other 40
will not. Under our assumptions, offering services to the 61st person,
assuming that the persons are arrayed in order of the diminishing marginal
returns, would be irrational. The costs involved are greater than the
benefits expected.

Should a workers' compensation jurisdiction seek to change this state of
affairs, it could either change the law so as to increase the benefits to the
employer from providing rehabilitation service to the 61st employee, or
mandate the provision of the service to that employee, forcing the extra
cost on the employer, and, in effect, distributing it over all companies in

the insurance pool, or perhaps over all employees in the organization in the form of lower wages or benefits.

There would be no need to mandate rehabilitation for the first 60 employees in the pool. Of course, in a mandated program, there would be reporting, monitoring, and supervisory costs involved for all the employees, including the first 60. The state agency will supervise these services and the employer will be called upon to make the necessary reports.

There is also the issue of the intensive margin. How many services ought to be offered to any individual employee? If the system were purely voluntary on the part of the employer, there would be no need for sophisticated discussions about the objectives of rehabilitation. The employer would offer services up to the point where the marginal savings would equal the marginal costs.

Implementation of such rules, whether at the intensive or the extensive margin, requires some knowledge on the part of the provider as to the technology of rehabilitation and the probabilities that the provision of a particular service will have the expected effects. Obviously such knowledge will never be complete, but there is every reason to believe that the employer with real costs at stake will invest the optimal amount of time and funds in seeking the requisite amount of knowledge. If, in some instances, a particular procedure is a crapshoot with no one having the ability to forecast its efficacy, then that is the state of the world and we would hazard the guess that the profit-seeking employer can do as well as anyone in playing the game.

There is another side to the market, namely the employee—the person who is on the receiving end of the services. If we now allow him to have something to say about all this, the picture changes somewhat. Assume that the employee is a utility maximizer and that the rehabilitation services cannot be forced on him. Just as there is no mandated proffer of rehabilitation services on the part of the employer, there is no obligation on the part of the employee to accept the services offered. Neither does the employee have the right to demand services that are not offered. In such circumstances, the employee will accept services up to the point where the marginal gains in satisfaction are equivalent to the cost to the employee. The amount of the services may be conceptualized in terms of the time spent in the program, or in terms of the discrete types of services offered.

Each individual can be thought of as having a demand schedule for rehabilitation services. The employee may place a value on the expected state of improved health should the program be completed. He might also anticipate a higher wage if the program is a success, or perhaps an earlier return to his old job with the proffered services than he could expect without them. If the rehabilitation program carries with it a continuation of benefits or some maintenance allowance, that would be an added incentive to participate.

On the other hand, there are costs to the employee. One real cost might be the decline in the workers' compensation award that might be forthcoming should rehabilitation be accepted and should it be successful. The perception that lower cash awards may be the reward for cooperation may have a chilling effect on the employee's willingness to participate. There may also be some disutility to the effort and exertion involved in participating in a physical therapy or even a retraining program. The employee must weigh these various factors and decide whether to part-icipate and if so, how much of what type of services to accept. We think of the employee as conceptualizing the process so that units of rehabilitation services offered have a net cost to him, which is the sum of the positive gains and negative costs. We see the employee as having a demand schedule for these services, with more and more services being demanded as the price (net cost) to the individual employee declines.[17]

The rising supply curve of services offered and the declining demand curve intersect at the equilibrium point. At this point, for the particular market under consideration, the amount of rehabilitation services that will be offered is equivalent to the amount that will be taken, and in light of the cost structure and the anticipated gains of the employee and the employer, this point can be said to be optimal in this partial equilibrium example. This equilibrium is based upon the parameters that are set by the particular workers' compensation statute. Given any changes in compensation levels or eligibility rules that affect the incentive structures, we would expect the demand and supply schedules to shift. Should rehabilitation benefits increase, for example, the net costs to the employee would be lower and the amount of rehabilitation demanded would increase. The same ben-efit increase might increase the costs of offering services and affect the amount proffered.

We would expect the amount of rehabilitation activity to vary among the states in accordance with the factors that influence the market for rehabilitation. If we could standardize for such variables, the interesting issue would be whether the mandating or monitoring of the process affects the type or amount of services offered. If such mandating or monitoring is found to have an effect on the quantity of services, the more interesting question would be whether such changes move the system towards or away from the socially optimal amounts where the marginal benefits and costs are equal.[18]

We do not yet have the information necessary to examine these issues. Since a comprehensive data base is absent, we use a case study approach and look at the statutory provisions and some of the experience in selected jurisdictions where rehabilitation has been mandated. We begin with California, where the recent trend towards compulsory rehabilitation began.

## California

To understand rehabilitation in California requires some examination of California's system of paying benefits, especially in permanent partial cases.[19] In California, after the injured worker reaches maximum medical improvement, he may be evaluated by the compensation agency's rating bureau to determine the extent of permanent partial or permanent total disability. The basic impairment rating is adjusted in accordance with the worker's age and occupation by increasing or decreasing the standard rating by predetermined loadings. Theoretically, the amount of the permanent partial impairment award is not affected by whether the worker is or is not working, or even expects to return to the labor market.

Before 1974, medical rehabilitation was the responsibility of the carrier, some vocational services were provided voluntarily, and the more extensive retraining types of programs were carried out by the state vocational rehabilitation agencies. The situation changed when California added a mandatory rehabilitation component to its workers' compensation statute in 1974. The amendments read, in pertinent part,

> When a qualified injured worker chooses to enroll in a rehabilitation program, he or she shall continue to receive temporary disability indemnity payments, plus additional living expenses necessitated by the rehabilitation program, together with all reasonable and necessary vocational training, at the expense of the employer....[20]                                                    (p.9)

The employee has an option to choose to participate or not. Also, entitlement to rehabilitation services cannot be compromised and settled. If an employee entitled to rehabilitation first declines it and then later requests such a benefit, say, after his permanent partial disability case has been settled, or after the proceeds of his award have been exhausted, he is entitled to it if he qualifies.

Under administrative regulations, disabled workers must pass a two-part test to qualify for the vocational rehabilitation benefit. The first criterion is medical, namely, whether the injury prevents the employee from returning to his or her usual occupation—a determination usually made by the treating physician.

If medical eligibility is met, the second step is vocational feasibility— whether rehabilitation services will be beneficial, given the individual employee's injury, interests, and motivation. These standards are comparable to the eligibility criteria for the state vocational programs where the applicant must show a mental or physical impairment and the feasibility of return to the labor market after the receipt of vocational rehabilitation services. According to the data compiled by the California Workers' Compensation Institute, one third of potential candidates fail to meet one or the other tests, medical eligibility being the predominant disqualifier.

The statute vests the authority to monitor and supervise in the rehabilitation bureau of the division of industrial accidents—the state administrative agency. The bureau employs rehabilitation consultants who do not provide services directly. Their function is to foster, review, and coordinate the rehabilitation activities undertaken by insurers and employers.

The actual rehabilitation services are delivered by private rehabilitation vendors who evaluate and develop plans that must be approved by the division's rehabilitation bureau. As mentioned above, up until 1985 the California Department of Vocational Rehabilitation (DVR)—the agency which administers the joint federal–state program of vocational rehabilitation—participated in the program. Counselors from that agency conducted evaluations and provided services in competition, as it were, with carrier-provided and other private vendors. As did the private vendors, the state rehabilitation agency counselors charged the going rate for their services, approximately $55 an hour. After studying the situation, the agency decided to withdraw from the field in 1985.

There were a number of reasons for the agency finally deciding to abandon the field and to leave the actual provision of services to private vendors. For one thing, the agency found it difficult to emulate the private sector and conduct its workers' compensation activities on a self-supporting basis. The state agency had little experience in having its employees bill clients for their services. Some counselors never learned quite how to do this, and the number of billable hours fell below expectations. Some billable hours were never compensated as carriers disputed the eligibility of certain clients.

In addition to these difficulties, there were personnel problems. The productive counselors found the private sector attractive and left for greener pastures. The less efficient were protected by civil service procedures and could not be held to the same productivity standards as the private vendors, who had the added advantage of operating with relatively low overhead costs.

Apparently the agency found it frustrating to have to submit their plans to the rehabilitation bureau of the workers' compensation agency for approval, and when other demands were made on the agency, it decided to give up the work with the compensation agency. Since the compensation agency itself does not employ any service providers, these tasks are in the hands of private consultants.

As the law is written, vocational feasibility must be determine before a claimant is accepted for services. Expenditures in these so-called *nonplan* cases (essentially evaluation expenditures in cases where it was decided that rehabilitation was not appropriate) accounted for about 28% of all rehabilitation expenditures in 1980, down from 34% two years earlier. As with any screening program, the evaluation to determine if services are necessary can be expensive.

The costs of rehabilitation are considerable. Between 1978 and 1980, the average rehabilitation expenditure on claim files that were closed during that period increased by 42% ($2327 versus $3303).

If only cases where specific return to the work plan are included, the increase is greater. The California Workers' Compensation Institute (CWCI), which has completed several studies of rehabilitation in California, estimates the average expense of rehabilitation plans completed in 1982 at the $11,000 level, rising to more than $13,000 in 1983.

When the system of mandatory vocational rehabilitation was introduced in 1975, the California Workers' Compensation Rating Bureau calculated that the new benefit would increase employers' cost an average of 2.7%. This estimate proved accurate for 1975, but costs soon began to increase. In 1976, actual costs turned out to be 3.7% of total incurred losses. In 1982, this Figure rose to possibly 7% — upwards of $130,000,000, with an expected rise according to WCI of 10% in the near future.

Programs that provide for training and formal schooling are more expensive and possibly less effective than those which provide guidance and placement services, although these contentions are difficult to evaluate. According to WCI data, 85% of the workers who complete modified or alternative work programs that capitalize on the employee's transferable skill do in fact return to work. By comparison, only 52% of workers who participate in formal schooling programs find suitable work after completion. These comparisons may be inappropriate because those people for whom modified or alternative work programs can be found may be quite different from those who are deemed suitable only for some formal schooling program. Nonetheless, the message that the Institute derives from this example is worth considering.

WCI puts it this way:

The message in these findings seems apparent: Make as few changes as possible in the disabled employee's life. Modified or alternative work—a substantially similar job in a substantially similar workplace, frequently with substantially similar co-workers—provides the best chance for successful rehabilitation. Other, more complex training cannot match the cost effectiveness of short-term rehabilitation programs that minimize the upheavals in the worker's environment. In contrast, formal schooling programs are the longest, most expensive and least successful. ("A Report to the Industry—Vocational Rehabilitation," California Workers' Compensation Institute, November 1983).

The WCI studies point to other problems, including what they term *benefit duplications*. On the one hand, the California workers' compensation law requires the employer to restore the employability of the disabled worker, but other provisions in the same law require the employer to compensate the employee's reduced ability to compete in the open labor market—the very condition the employer is obliged to correct in the first instance.

Complaints are voiced about delays. These complaints are apart from any problems arising from normal case-processing delays. Unlike the laws in Minnesota or New York, the law in California does not require referral to rehabilitation at a specified time, say 60 days after data of injury if the worker has not returned to work. The time for starting rehabilitation is up to the employee. Many qualified workers apparently elect to postpone rehabilitation until the dollar value of their claim is determined.

There is also a problem in the identification or recognition of need by employers and insurers. Half of the potential rehabilitation cases reported to the state agency for monitoring are submitted late, on average nearly 10 months after the disabling injury. Late reporting can be expensive. Employers and insurers must pay the rehabilitation maintenance allowance retroactive to the date the report should have been submitted.

There are some data on attorney involvement. A recent decision of the Workers' Compensation Appeals Board permits the worker's attorney a separate additional fee for services in connection with the vocational rehabilitation. WCI concludes that attorney involvement and rehabilitation is becoming commonplace.

Apparently the rehabilitation bureau has some of the same legalistic orientation as does the agency. Bureau consultants issue *notices of intent* and *decisions and orders*. Notices are sent advising injured workers of their possible rights to rehabilitation benefits and encouraging them to contact an attorney. Other requirements are complex and convoluted, according to the CWCI.

The incidence of appeals of rehabilitation bureau decisions has increased three-fold from 1980 to 1983. As of the latter year, the body of decisional law in vocational rehabilitation in workers' compensation exceeded 100 cases, up from 58 cases in 1981.

The California Workers' Compensation Institute study concludes that changes are necessary. One of these would be a more explicit enabling statute so as to eliminate confusion, uncertainty, misunderstanding, and controversy that affects both program operation and outcome.

The courts adjudicating the controversies have shown a consistent ignorance of the return-to-work objectives of vocational rehabilitation and workers' compensation and, according to CWCI, "instead, substitute a doctrine of entitlement that encourages additional litigation."

WCI believes that an active, adequately funded state agency is necessary—that these provisions are not going to be self-administering. The state agency must take the initiative to provide meaningful assistance to create an ambience of protection and mediation.

A third need is the introduction of incentives. The employee's participation is self-determined and may be motivated by short-term consequences. The employer's responsibility is dictated by statute, which, when combined with the concurrent and concomitant liability for permanent disability indemnity, produces a grudging response. The solution lies in devising a program that encourages a willing participation of both employee and employer. WCI believes that the mandatory statute is a step forward from the voluntary one in which the amount of the employee's permanent disability indemnity was calculated after rehabilitation, invariably at a lower amount. What was intended to be an employer incentive became a disincentive for the employee, and little happened during the 10-year life of the voluntary vocational rehabilitation provision. The conclusion is that there is a need to integrate the various parts of the system.[21]

Evaluation of any rehabilitation program is notoriously difficult. The basic problem is that in the absence of scientifically valid control group studies, there is no way to measure the effect of the treatment variables. We know what happens to persons who undergo the rehabilitation, but we can never be sure that what happened to them was the result of that rehabilitation experience. Consequently, what follows are impressions gleaned from the California experience in light of the conventional wisdom about rehabilitation.

1. Usually, rehabilitation takes place in a clinical and not in a legal setting. Rehabilitation sevices are not thought of as a right, but a service to be dispensed to those who can benefit from it. Workers' compensation benefits are prescribed by the legislature and are dispensed as a matter of

right, with due-process safeguards and provisions for appeals from administrative decisions. Since these two services are blended in the California system, it is not workers' compensation that has become more clinically oriented, but rehabilitation that has taken on all the legal trappings.

2. While we recognize the difficulties of evaluation, the overall statistics in California appear impressive. From the inception of the new rehabilitation program through 1983, some 22,000 severely injured workers returned to work after vocational rehabilitation, with some 80% working in modified, alternative, or retrained occupations. The system appears to be providing a needed service.

3. The system is expensive. Premium increases have been greater than forecast and are increasing. These are major expenditures, which may signal that California has not found the most efficient system for identifying cases, assuring that the optimal amount of services are provided, and providing a least-cost method of administration.

4. The rehabilitation system was grafted onto the existing system of workers' compensation benefits. Employer groups see it as an add-on benefit duplicating existing benefits. Whether this is a valid criticism or not, there was no restructuring of the benefit system with an eye towards the incentives issue.

We turn next to an examination of Minnesota's rather different system. In Minnesota, the state mandates referrals for rehabilitation evaluation after a specific number of days following the date of injury.

## Minnesota

The rehabilitation provisions of the Minnesota law were changed in 1979 and again in 1983, when fundamental revisions were made in the benefit and administrative provisions of the statute. A so-called two-tier system of benefits was introduced, designed to encourage employers to take back injured workers and to encourage injured workers to return to work. Employers were made responsible for the costs of rehabilitation if services were indicated after the mandatory referral for evaluation.

The 1983 amendments were greeted with a good deal of enthusiasm. The chair of the citizens' committee that had studied the old law and recommended the substantial revisions assumed office as the commissioner of the workers' compensation division. The enthusiasm proved to be short-lived. By 1987, the new commissioner had been replaced, and the legislature had made some major changes in how litigation is to be handled under the law. The same legislation (Minnesota Laws, 1987, Chapter 332) authorized a series of research studies to help account for the rise in workers' compensation premiums, and to inquire into a number of other topics. One such inquiry is being directed towards the rehabilitation experience in Minnesota, signaling some disillusionment with the 1983 amendments. To understand the present situation in Minnesota, it is necessary to trace the background of the system's involvment with rehabilitation.

Prior to the 1979 amendments, rehabilitation was synonymous with retraining. Workers who received permanent disability awards were eligible for retraining 26 weeks after the date of injury if it was determined that retraining would reduce or remove barriers to employability. The Minnesota Division of Vocational Rehabilitation could certify the need for the retraining, and the compensation authorities could authorize up to 156 weeks of benefits at the temporary total rate plus reasonable expenses. The system encouraged a late start and a long program.

The 1979 amendments repealed the retraining provisions and required the employer to provide a rehabilitation consultation within 30 days of receiving medical information that the employee would be unable to return to his previous job. Since that date proved difficult to fix with precision, and since it sometimes came quite late and only after the worker had been off the job for months, the 1983 changes provided for earlier intervention. In addition, these amendments authorized a broad range of services, and, most important, provided for the two-tier system with its changes in methods of benefit payments designed to encourage early return to work.

The Minnesota law now requires employers to refer an injured worker for a rehabilitation evaluation after 60 lost workdays, or 30 days in the case of back injuries. The costs of this evaluation, designed to determine whether the employee requires services to be able to return to his preinjury job, are paid by the employer.

The broadened range of possible services include medical evaluation, physical rehabilitation, work evaluation, job modification, on-the-job training, counseling, and guidance, as well as retraining. Although the options are not set forth in the statute, the regulations of the Department of Labor and Industry, the home agency of the workers' compensation division, present these options in a priority scheme. First preference is given to those plans designed to return the worker to a job with the former employer either by job modification or by utilization of existing skills. If this is not possible, plans calling for placement with a new employer utilizing existing skills come next. Training for work in a new field is to be considered only when the other options are not feasible.

The rehabilitation provisions of the law are significant in that they place Minnesota in the category of a compulsory rehabilitation jurisidiction, at least insofar as the referral for evaluation is concerned. More dramatic perhaps are the 1983 amendment provisions for a two-tier system of benefits for permanent disabilities.

Under this system, the size of the permanent disability award depends on whether the employer, or any employer, makes an offer of a "suitable job" no later than 90 days after the worker has attained "maximum medical improvement." The concept of maximum medical improvement is the traditional one in workers' compensation. It is the point in an injured worker's recovery at which no further significant lasting improvement can be anticipated based on reasonable medical probability.

Whatever the problems involved in the definition of a suitable job, Minnesota has the advantage of having worked with the concept since the 1979 amendments. Controversies surroundisng similar terms plague all benefit programs and played a telling role in the state of Washington's retreat from its comprehensive rehabilitation program. In essence, as Minnesota's employer's manual points out, a suitable job is one within the employee's medical restrictions and one that restores the employee as close as possible to the economic status he enjoyed before the injury.[22] The rules are more specific in their definition of "suitable gainful employment" as

> ...employment which is reasonably attainable and which offers an opportunity to restore the injured employee as soon as possible and as nearly as possible to employment which produced an economic status as close as possible to that which the employee would have enjoyed without disability. Consideration shall be given to the employee's former employment and the employee's qualifications including, but not limited to, the employee's age, education, previous work history, interests and skills.[23]

An injured worker who receives a suitable job offer from any source any time before 90 days after reaching maximum medical improvement (MMI) is entitled to a relatively limited *impairment award* as compensation for his permanent injury. The amount of the award is determined by the extent of his impairments with reference to a detailed schedule patterned after the American Medical Association's *Guides to the Evaluation of Permanent Impairment.*[24]

Impairment awards are based on a flat-rate schedule and are not wage-related. Any worker with a 25% or less disability of the whole body would receive his or her percentage of disability times $75,000. A worker with a 25% disability rating would receive $18,750. A worker with a 50% disability would be entitled to 50% of $100,000 or $50,000. The scale is not linear; dollar amounts increase more than proportionately as the disability ratings increase. The schedule of these awards are shown in table 4–5.

Table 4–5.  Impairment Award Schedule

| Percent of Disability | Amount |
| --- | --- |
| 0–25% | $75,000 |
| 26–30% | $80,000 |
| 31–35% | $85,000 |
| 36–40% | $90,000 |
| 41–45% | $95,000 |
| 46–50% | $100,000 |
| 51–55% | $120,000 |
| 56–60% | $140,000 |
| 61–65% | $160,000 |
| 66–70% | $180,000 |
| 71–75% | $200,000 |
| 76–80% | $240,000 |
| 81–85% | $280,000 |
| 86–90% | $320,000 |
| 91–95% | $360,000 |
| 96–100% | $400,000 |

These are purely impairment ratings, and the reasoning is that since they are compensation for parts of the body, there is no reason to assume that these values should be wage-related. They are not meant to be even proxies for wage loss.

If the employee returns to work for at least 30 days, he receives the impairment award as a lump-sum payment at the end of the 30 days. The return to work incentive for the employee is contained in the lump-sum provision. Should he refuse to accept the suitable job offer, the impairment award is paid out as a weekly benefit.

The interesting aspect of the Minnesota law is that if the employee is not offered a suitable job, he becomes entitled to a larger benefit. He becomes eligible for a so-called *economic recovery* benefit, which is wage-related (see table 4–6). His disability would be rated on the same *impairment* basis, but now he would be paid his percentage of disability times *the number of weeks* specified on the schedule times 66⅔% of his wage rate. The worker who earns $450 per week would have a compensation rate of $300. Should that worker sustain a 25% disability, he would be entitled to 25% of 600 weeks times $300 or $45,000. This contrasts with the award of $18,750 that the worker would receive as an impairment award. Of course, the economic recovery benefit is wage-related, and a lower-wage worker would receive less. The economic recovery benefit is paid

Table 4-6.    Economic Recovery Schedule

| Percent of Disability | Weeks of Compensation |
| --- | --- |
| 0-25% | 600 |
| 26-30% | 640 |
| 31-35% | 680 |
| 36-40% | 720 |
| 41-45% | 760 |
| 46-50% | 800 |
| 51-55% | 880 |
| 56-60% | 960 |
| 61-65% | 1040 |
| 66-70% | 1120 |
| 71-100% | 1200 |

weekly in the same amount and frequency as temporary total, and continues until the employee goes back to work or until the amount of the award is exhausted.

If the employee goes back to work at any job, suitable or not, and works at it for 30 days, he receives the balance of his economic recovery benefits as a lump sum. If he takes a suitable job and is then laid off (except for specified reasons) he is entitled to so-called monitoring benefits. He is eligible for these during the monitoring period, which for the 25% disability would be 25% of 600 weeks or 150 weeks.

The benefit system for permanent disability is obviously quite complicated, and that fact may prove to be its undoing. An evaluation of the system is part of the research agenda authorized by the 1987 amendments. These reports have not yet been issued, but conversations with participants in the system in Minnesota reveal a good deal of confusion about how the two-tier system operates. There is also little understanding about what the two benefit schemes are supposed to accomplish.

Such distrust and confusion may be unfortunate, since the two-tier system is an attempt to deal with the incentives facing both parties. Unlike the California amendments, which grafted a compulsory rehabilitation system onto an existing law (as did Minnesota in 1979), there is an attempt to wed rehabilitation and incentives.

If the employer takes the employee back, his compensation liability is much less. He becomes liable for the lower impairment award rather than the higher economic recovery award. Preliminary indications are that an overwhelming number of the awards, perhaps more than 94%, are made on an impairment basis. This proportion serves as a valuable reminder that most cases in any workers' compensation system do not pose any problem when it comes to return to work. Return to work is the usual, normal, and expected outcome, even for those cases that are serious enough to warrant some permanent partial disability award. It is the minority of cases that pose problems, but these tend to be the expensive cases and the ones in which rehabilitation services are supposed to speed up the process of return to the labor market.

The two-tier system was designed to provide incentives for the worker as well. If he accepts a suitable job offer, he receives the impairment award in a lump sum. If he refuses, it is paid out in weekly installments. There are sticks as well as carrots. The employee is obligated to cooperate in a rehabilitation plan and can be refused benefits if he does not. He must undergo medical examinations and evaluations, and if rehabilitation is found to be appropriate, he must cooperate with the Qualified Rehabilitation Consultant (QRC) in the development of a rehabilitation plan.

The original designation of QRC is made by the insurer, but the employee has the right to object and can change QRCs. The question of who chooses the QRC, and of whether the QRC is supposed to be neutral, has been a matter of controversy in the state. Up until the 1987 amendments, the employee could exercise his right to object to the employer's choice of QRC only once. The rule providing for the right of the employee to object only once came only in 1983. Prior to the 1983 amendments, the employee could be halfway through a program and then decide to change the rehabilitation consultant. Presumably, such a change could take place more than once. The allegations were that such changes led to confusion and lack of progress, and hence the rule changes were made that allowed the employee the right of one refusal only. However, objections were raised that an employee had to have a ongoing sympathetic relationship with the QRC, and to force a person to stay with a QRC that he did not get along with was counterproductive. In the new law, changes were made allowing the employee to choose a different QRC once during the first 60 days following the first inperson contact between the employee and the first QRC, and that the employee might choose a different QRC once again after this 60-day period. "Subsequent requests to change will be determined by the Department or compensation judge according to the best interests of the parties."[25]

Under the 1979 amendments, the Commissioner of Labor and Industry had broad powers to supervise the rehabilitation process. The commissioner interpreted the statutory language to mean that he could determine who was eligible for services whenever a dispute arose. The Workers' Compensation Court of Appeals in *Strandmark v. Century Motor Freight*,

35 WCD 252 (1982) found otherwise and held that the commissioner had no authority to determine eligibility but only to approve or disapprove plans submitted after eligibility was decided. The 1983 amendments seem to have the effect of changing the court decision. They state in explicit terms that the commissioner has the sole authority to determine eligibility and to approve and reject plans. These decisions are not to be made by the compensation judges, but may be appealed to a rehabilitation review panel and from there to the Workers' Compensation Court of Appeals.

The 1983 amendments distinguished between rehabilitation and re-training. Retraining is limited to a maximum of 156 weeks and persons undergoing retraining may petition the commissioner for additional compensation not to exceed 25% of the compensation otherwise payable. Such additional compensation is to be paid in unusual or unique circumstances, in contrast to the 1979 law where the additional compensation was paid on a routine basis.

Under the 1979 amendments, the Department of Labor and Industry was given the power to approve rehabilitation consultants. These powers were broadened in 1983 so that the commissioner now has the authority to determine fees, to assess the fitness of the QRCs and vendors, and to discipline, by fine or otherwise, those consultants and vendors who violate the rules and regulations.[26]

### Assessing the Minnesota Changes

Minnesota has completed several studies of both open and closed claims. By and large, the result are encouraging for the proponents of the changes, but sufficient experience has not yet been accumulated.[27] The Minnesota legislature was obviously concerned about the effects of the changes on small employers. The very preliminary results show no startlingly different effects on small versus larger employers, but no evaluation of these changes can take place until more time has elapsed.

We can note some of the features of the Minnesota system and point out some of the advantages and probable difficulties.

1. The definition of rehabilitation services is a broad one, encompassing medical management, job modifications, work evaluation, and the usual gamut of traditional rehabilitation services. Retraining is included, but is to be considered only when all else fails.

2. The timing of rehabilitation is specified. An assessment or evaluation is to be made after 60 days of time lost or 30 days in the case of back injuries.

3. If a rehabilitation plan is indicated, it is to be worked out by the QRC with the consent and cooperation of the worker. The system has had problems with defining the exact role of the QRC and deciding who the QRC represents and whether the employee should have an unlimited right to change QRCs.

4. Under the 1983 amendments, a separate procedure was used to settle any disputes or differences of opinion between the parties as to any of these rehabilitation decisions. The disputes were handled initially by an informal conference, and then by a rehabilitation board whose decisions were appealable to the Workers' Compensation Court of Appeals. The 1987 amendments changed the procedure and provided that rehabilitation matters would no longer go through the rehabilitation board but would be handled by the usual workers' compensation procedures.

5. Rehabilitation consultants and vendors are regulated by the commissioner; rates are regulated and rules of conduct are specified. The commissioner may fine and otherwise discipline consultants and vendors. The regulations in effect have not solved the problems of QRC selection nor their role in the system. Although QRCs presumably are thought of as being neutral and not favoring the interests of employer or employee conversations with the parties in Minnesota indicate that they perceive some QRCs as plaintiffs' consultants and others as defendants' consultants.

6. The system of permanent disability benefits is constructed with the intention of minimizing litigation and maximizing the return to work of injured employees. Attention has been paid to the incentives of both the employer and the worker. It will take a good deal of time and effort to determine whether the system has had the intended effect. Conversations with the parties and the administrators reveal a good deal of confusion about the purpose of the two tiers, and the current research studies are looking for policy options to change the system once again.

We turn next to an examination of the experience in the state of Washington, where the initial commitment to a mandatory system has been curtailed.

## Washington

Washington is an exclusive-fund state with no private insurance carriers but with self-insurance allowable for eligible employers. Private insurance carriers have been seeking legislative changes to allow them to operate in the state, a move which has been strenuously opposed by the state AFL-CIO.

Washington's latest vocational rehabilitation amendments went into effect on May 16, 1985. Chapter 51.32 of the Laws of 1985 makes "enabling the injured worker to become employable at gainful employment" the primary goal of vocational rehabilitation. This was a major change from the prior statutory goal of return to work at *suitable* gainful employment.

It seems ridiculous that the inclusion or omission of the word *suitable* could make much difference. That word carried a good deal of freight in Washington, although similar language in Minnesota has caused no problems. Apparently, through administrative regulations in Washington as much as anything else, the phrase *suitable gainful employment* was interpreted as a position that paid at least as much as the job the employee held prior to the injury. Dropping the word *suitable* meant eliminating the pre-injury wage requirement. A worker could be rehabilitated to gainful employment even though the job to which he returned paid less than his pre-injury position. In addition, control over private rehabilitation vendors was tightened, and long, expensive retraining programs were discouraged.

The amendments passed the legislature only after widespread concern about the increasing costs of rehabilitation. One would assume that it would be politically infeasible for organized labor to oppose what could be interpreted as a reduction in rehabilitation benefits. However, there was apparently no opposition to such changes from the trade unions. Possibly labor was concerned that the system not appear to be unreasonably expensive, lest that be used as an excuse to bring in private carriers.

As set forth in the amendments, the legislature found that the vocational rehabilitation program created by chapter 63, Laws of 1982, failed to assist injured workers to return to suitable gainful employment without undue loss of time from work, and that the program increased costs of industrial insurance for employers and employees. The legislature also found that the administrative structure established within the Industrial Insurance Division of the Department of Labor and Industries to develop and oversee the provision of vocational rehabilitation services was not providing efficient delivery of vocational rehabilitation services. Thus it was determined that a restructuring of the state's vocational rehabilitation program under the Department of Labor and Industries was necessary.

The law was changed, and the current law reads in part as follows:

> One of the primary purposes of this title is to enable the injured worker to become employable at gainful employment. To this end, the Department shall utilize the services of individuals and organizations, public or private, whose experience, training and interests in vocational rehabilitation and retraining qualify them to lend expert assistance to the Supervisor of Industrial Insurance

on such programs of vocational rehabilitation as may be reasonable to make the worker employable consistent with his or her physical and mental status.[28]

The Office of Rehabilitation Services was created within the Department of Labor and Industries independent of the Industrial Insurance Division. Its functions were to supervise the process and to evaluate the private-sector vendors.

In October 1985, the claims administration units assumed responsibility from the Office of Rehabilitation Services for reviewing and approving all vocational rehabilitation employability assessments, plans, and plan revisions. The Office of Rehabilitation Services remains responsible for vocational-rehabilitation-provider performance evaluations and audits and assistance to the director in the resolution of rehabilitation disputes. In effect, a separation of function took place. The claims units reviewed and approved and rehabilitation-vendor recommendations, and the rehabilitation office audited the overall performance of the vendors and helped resolve rehabilitation disputes.

To determine whether an injured employee is eligible for vocational rehabilitation, an eligibility statement form is to be completed by the vocational rehabilitation counselor. The form contains medical/physical information, employment and education history, transferrable skills analysis, occupational possibilities, labor market information, and a statement of whether or not the injured worker is employable.

The report is reviewed and a decision is made by the claims administration unit as to whether the injured employee is currently employable at gainful employment or whether rehabilitation services are both necessary and likely to enable the injured employee to obtain gainful employment. Gainful employment is defined as any occupation, not to exclude self-employment, that allows a worker to be compensated with wages or other earnings. Those eligible will be referred to a counselor so that a rehabilitation plan may be developed.

When it is determined that vocational rehabilitation is both necessary and likely to make the worker employable at gainful employment, then a series of prioritized options are available. They include (in descending priority)

1. Return to the previous job with the same employer
2. Modification of the previous job with the same employer, including transitional return to work
3. A new job with the same employer in keeping with any (limitations or restrictions)
4. Modification of the previous job with a new employer

5. A new job with a new employer or self-employment based (upon transferable skills)
6. A new job with a new employer, or self-employment (involving on-the-job training
7. Short-term retraining and job placement

Under the new law, there are no special appeals to the Board of Industrial Insurance Appeals. However, a written request may be made for reconsideration of the supervisor's determination.

When it has been determined that an injured employee is eligible for vocational rehabilitation, then the fund or the self-insurer becomes liable for the costs. These include the payment of temporary total compensation while the worker is in the program as well as the other program costs, which may include the costs for books, tuition, fees, supplies, equipment, transportation, and other necessary expenses. However, in light of its experience under the old law where the costs of some retraining and educational courses rose dramatically, a limit of $3000 in any 52-week period was placed on these expenditures. The expenses may include training fees for on-the-job training and the cost of furnishing tools and other equipment necessary for self-employment or reemployment. However, these payments are authorized only for a period of 52 weeks unless extended upon the sole discretion of the supervisor after review.

The law of 1982 (Section 13, chapter 63) provides that the supervisor at his/her discretion may pay job-modification costs in an amount not to exceed $5000. The funds are not chargeable to any employer account but are to be taken from the appropriate account within the second injury fund.

The Washington experience shows, quite dramatically, that consideration must be given not simply to whether rehabilitation should be voluntary or compulsory, but also to the amount and kind of rehabilitation to be mandated. Such issues are important for a number of reasons, not the least of which is that the resolution of such issues can effect costs. And the Washington experience does demonstrate how rehabilitation can cost more than the parties are willing to pay.

## Conclusions

Most injured workers return to their old jobs, and the issue of rehabilitation services never arises. The possible demand for rehabilitation services occurs in those cases where some difficulty is experienced in having the worker return to his old job with his old employer. It is quite understandable that the early administrators of the state workers' compensation laws greeted the rehabilitation movement enthusiastically. The success of rehabilitation in restoring the injured combat veteran of World War I argued that the same techniques would be effective for the injured worker. It seemed a natural marriage between two agencies with complementary purposes.

Although the state vocational rehabilitation and the state workers' compensation programs grew up together in this country, the programs have gone their separate ways. When the typical industrial injury was thought of as an amputee, the tasks of both programs were simpler. The scheduled award for the loss of the limb was paid by workers' compensation, and the worker might be fitted with a prosthesis. The vocational rehabilitation agency might take over the necessary training in the use of the prosthesis and begin the vocational retraining of the worker to fit him for a new job.

Over the years, each of the programs found different clientele. The nature of industrial injuries changed, as did the typical worker, who now had an increasing amount of human capital and a wider-range adaptability. The vocational rehabilitation agencies were increasingly challenged by more difficult cases and were told by Congress to serve new and different groups, such as the mentally ill and the mentally retarded. Equally important were the necessary bureaucratic safeguards that accompanied the spending of the federal monies by the state vocational rehabilitation agencies. Clients had to meet eligibility criterion. They had to show the existence of a physical or mental condition that prevented their entry into the labor market, and the agency had to be reasonably sure that with the provision of services, the worker could reenter the labor market. The amount and type of services were necessarily limited by the yearly budgets that came from both the state and the federal governments. Whether these were real obstacles to the agencies that were taking workers' compensation clients is not the issue. The mere checking of these requirements with the sometimes limited staff of the agency and the filling out of the necessary paperwork often meant that some weeks and perhaps month might elapse from date of application to date of services. When rehabilitation was made compulsory in California in 1975, the state agency became one of many providers of services, and after some years, they abandoned the field to the private-sector vendors and providers.

It is clear, however, that the bulk of the work is in the hands of private-sector rehabilitation providers and will likely remain there. It is not the public–private difference that is significant. That fact is attested to by several public rehabilitation agencies that handle workers' compensation cases. The Michigan rehabilitation agency maintains an active presence in the field, and a largely self-supporting division of the agency, not dependent on federal funding, takes workers' compensation cases on a for-fee basis. What is significant is that rehabilitation has now become an expense that must be controlled. It is no longer a public service available to the worker and his employer without charge.

The experience in California shows that rehabilitation is not a trivial matter. When rehabilitation is mandated with few statutory constraints, as in California, costs can mount rapidly. Apparently simple changes in the wording of the objectives of rehabilitation can have significant cost consequences, as the experience in Washington seems to show. Yet the data we do have for 13 states' rehabilitation expenditures do not show very obvious and dramatic differences among the states. These data merit careful watching in future years when we may be able to detect differences that may come about as the result of recent legislative activity in this area.

Although the idea of rehabilitation has always enjoyed strong emotional support, the sad truth is that we have almost no information about its efficacy and its cost-effectiveness. The joint state–federal program of vocational rehabilitation enjoys strong public support amidst growing realization that its cost-effectiveness has never been brought to the test.

But clearly the cost-effectiveness of rehabilitation in general is not the issue. The questions are much more complex. When should services be provided? What kind of services should be offered? Probably most important, how many? The quantum of services is most controversial and is involved with the larger notion of the appropriate objectives of the process, the question that the state of Washington struggled with and that all newer programs are quick to specify. If private rehabilitationists are to be the primary providers, the issues of licensing, certification, and fee schedules come to the fore.

Are state workers' compensation agencies prepared to take on the burdens of supervision and control of the rehabilitation process? Obviously, making rehabilitation mandatory will impose costs on the system. If nothing else, reporting or having to evaluate all cases in a certain class of cases will be expensive. The question is whether sufficient benefits can be derived to justify the increased costs.

What seems to be clear from the limited experience with compulsory rehabilitation is that problems may arise if the system is merely grafted onto the existing workers' compensation scheme without due attention to the incentive structure faced by both parties. Regulation of the rehabilitation process with its necessity to specify fine details of the system is inherently difficult. When the incentives are perverse, it becomes almost impossible.

Reduced to its simplest terms, rehabilitation means getting the worker back to the job—preferably his old job, but at least to a job that he can perform with his residual functioning capacities. We have learned a lot over the years about how this can be accomplished, but only in a tiny minority of cases will an extensive range of services be required. What is needed first is the type of benefit structure that will motivate the worker to return to the job and the employer to take him back. It is at this point where rehabilitation in its real sense takes place.

This author holds no particular brief for the Minnesota system and can foresee difficulties in administering some of its complicated benefit provisions, but the intent of the law deserves plaudits. The idea of differential benefits depending upon the worker's willingness to take a job and the employer's willingness to offer him one is probably a good one. It remains to be seen if the difference in these benefits can be made sufficiently large so as to stimulate the optimal amount of rehabilitation activity. Obviously, Minnesota did not think so, for it accompanied its latest amendments with provisions mandating rehabilitation-services and has plunged itself into the area of policing rehabilitation providers and monitoring the rehabilitation process.

The crucial issues are the determinations of when, to whom, and how many services should be offered, and in an ideal world, these decisions would be left to the parties to resolve. In our less than ideal world, there will always be functions to be entrusted to the active administrative agency. Here possibly is the real challenge of rehabilitation for workers' compensation. If state agencies are serious about assuring that all workers who are out of work for more than a specified number of days be considered for rehabilitation, then it is necessary for them to be active administrators in the sense of having some record-keeping system and monitoring the progress of cases. If the agency's sole administrative functions are concerned with administering contested cases, then the agency probably will not be able to discharge all of the monitoring and supervisory functions required in a system of mandatory rehabilitation. If the agency abandons its supervisory functions, the it would seem quite natural that the injured worker will turn to litigation to enforce his rights. The result may well be that the clinically based system of rehabilitation becomes legalistically oriented, as seems to the trend in California.

The question posed at the outset of this chapter was whether rehabilitation and workers' compensation are incompatible or inseparable. At one time they were inseparable, but that is no longer true. This author has grave doubts about the compatibility of a workers' compensation system and a mandatory system of rehabilitation. It would be encouraging to see rehabilitation extended to all workers where the benefits outweigh the costs, but the ability of agencies largely concerned with adjudicating cases to monitor such processes seems doubtful. Rehabilitation as we have known probably cannot survive long in an adversarial situation where essentially clinical decisions are made only after some adjudicatory process. Under such conditions, the parties might well consider leaving the details of the rehabilitation process to the parties and concentrating instead on devising a system that affords optimal incentives for the return to work of injured workers to jobs that are within their residual functioning capacities.

## Notes

1. An explanation of the different systems in use in the state programs is found in Berkowitz, Monroe, and John F. Burton, Jr. *Permanent Disability in Workers' Compensation*. Kalamazoo, MI: W. E. Upjohn Institute, 1987.

2. The author is conscious of the fact that this description of the process is of some ideal type—the way the process is supposed to operate. Such thinking is greatly influenced by some comparatively recent developments in the field, most notably the professionalization of the rehabilitation counselor. As Edward Berkowitz notes, much of this trend toward professionalization is due to Mary Switzer, who became head of the federal vocational rehabilitation program in 1950. "Switzer cajoled the Eisenhower administration into sponsoring major new vocational rehabilitation legislation in 1954 to put the program on a professional basis." (*Disability Policy*. New York: Cambridge University Press, 1987, 171.) She succeeded far beyond anyone's expectations. "By 1965, about forty colleges or universities offered graduate degrees in rehabilitation counseling; by 1980, the number approached one hundred....By 1976, the profession contained as many as 19,000 members, nearly three-quarters of whom worked for the state–federal vocational rehabilitation program" (p. 172). Although we have no exact figures, it is likely that today the number of counselors in the private sector may be as many as half or more of all persons in the profession.

3. A more detailed explanation of the relationships between workers' compensation and the public rehabilitation program can be found in *Disabled Policy* cited in note 2, Chapter 5

4. Donoghue, Francis D. "Restoring the Injured Employee to Work." In IAIABC *Proceedings*, 1916 United States Department of Labor, Bureau of Labor Statistics, Bulletin 210, 1917, p. 212.

5. The rise and fall of the close collaborative efforts in New Jersey are detailed in Berkowitz, Monroe. *Workmen's Compensation*. New Brunswick, NJ: Rutgers University Press, 1960, chapter 8.

6. Berkowitz, Edward and Kim McQuaid. *Creating the Welfare State*. New York: Praeger Publishers, 1980, p. 64.

7. The author is indebted to Mark Wozny of Ecosometrics, Inc. for providing information from the RSA-300 1984 statistics as to the number of cases referred to the several state vocational rehabilitation agencies.

John Anderson, State Standards Adviser, Division of State Workers' Compensation Programs, Employment Standards Administration of the U.S. Department of Labor has been exceedingly helpful in supplying detailed information as to the practices in individual states.

8. The changes in the program occurred gradually over the years and can be traced to developments in medicine, to the interests of the Chief Executive, and to a host of other factors. Kennedy's interest in mental retardation, for example, and Johnson's emphasis on the disadvantaged all had their impact on the clientele served by the program. The major change occurred in the Rehabilitation amendments of 1973, when Congress mandated that the program give priority to the "severely handicapped."

9. For the most part, rehabilitation services are being provided by the private sector, which has moved into this field in ever increasing numbers. Private providers are most active in those states that have adopted some form of mandatory law providing for compulsory employer-financed rehabilitation. In these states, the employer becomes responsible for referral of workers to rehabilitation, and for financing a rehabilitation plan if one is indicated. The employer becomes liable for the expenses, including the fees paid to the rehabilitation counselor. The enactment of the California law was followed by a sharp increase in the number of rehabilitation providers in the private sector, a pattern duplicated in Florida when that state amended its compensation law to provide for mandatory rehabilitation. Mandatory rehabilitation does not necessarily mean that the public program abdicates the field. In California, for a time, the public vocational rehabilitation agency took on cases when cases were referred to it and billed carriers for the time of the counselors, in much the same way and at about the same rates as the private providers. The state vocational rehabilitation program in Michigan is participating in that state's non-mandatory workers' compensation rehabilitation program in direct competition with the private sector.

10. The R form procedure was instituted by the Chairman of the Workers' Compensation Board in 1959 in accordance with his rule-making authority but without specific legislative action. Under this procedure, the insurance carrier, or employer if self-insured, is to file a one-page case finding form (the R form) within 20 days after the worker has lost eight weeks time due to his work injury. The form asks whether a medical or vocational rehabilitation program has been arranged. If it has not, the respondent is asked to explain. The forms are reviewed by counselors in the Board's rehabilitation bureau who may investigate the case and may try to persuade the carrier to provide services if they seem indicated. The program is voluntary and the carrier is usually not obligated to pay for vocational rehabilitation services.

11. The rehabilitation section cooperates with the public rehabilitation program, which has streamlined its procedures to provide counseling and job placement services without the necessity of going through formal acceptance procedures. A more detailed explanation of New York's procedures can be found in Berkowitz, Monroe. "Rehabilitation and Workers' Compensation in New York." In *Research Papers of the Temporary State Commission on Workers' Compensation and Disability Benefits.* Albany, NY: 1986.

12. "Workers' Compensation Costs Moderate." WCRI Research Brief, Vol. 2, No. 6. Cambridge, MA: Workers' Compensation Research Institute, June, 1986. The evidence about moderation of the increases is from Burton, John F. Jr., H. Allan Hunt, and Alan B. Kreuger. "The Recent Moderation in Workers' Compensation Costs in Michigan and the Nation." In *The Economic Outlook for 1986*, Proceedings of the Thirty-third Annual Conference on the Economic Outlook, Department of Economics, University of Michigan, 1986.

13. Galvin, Donald E. "Health Promotion, Disability Management, and Rehabilitation in the Workplace." In *Rehabilitation Literature* (1986): 218–223. See also Carbine, Michael E., and Gail E. Schwartz. *Strategies for Managing Disability Costs.* Washington, D.C.: Washington Business Group on Health/Institute for Rehabilitation and Disability Management, 1987.

14. The evidence seems to be that the relatively small number of long-term disability cases

take up a more than proportionate share of medical care costs. Persons with long-term disability are only 10% of the population, but they account for almost 34% of total medical care costs according to information from the 1980 National Medical Care Utilization and Expenditure Survey.

15. Worrall, John D., and Richard J. Butler. "Some Lessons in Workers' Compensation." In Monroe Berkowitz and M. Anne Hill (eds.), *Disability and the Labor Market: Economic Problems, Policies and Programs*. Ithaca, NY: ILR Press, 1986.

16. We will use the term *employer* for sake of simplicity, but recognize that the agent of decision making may be the employer, the insurance carrier, or even an adjustment agency.

17. Compare the model formulated on the basis of individual behavior in a non-workers'-compensation situation. Mann, Duncan. "Models Based on Individual Behavior." In Monroe Berkowitz (ed.), *Measuring the Efficiency of Public Programs*. Philadelphia: Temple University Press, 1988.

18. The socially desirable optimum may differ from the private optimum if there are social benefits to be derived from rehabilitation that are not completely captured in the private assessment, or if the private costs do not encompass all of the social costs. In the workers' compensation system, the indemnity benefits may overstate or understate the actual losses, or the parties may lack information about the technology of rehabilitation. Neither of these conditions necessarily justifies mandatory rehabilitation, although they may argue for revisions in the benefit scales and for easing the channel of communications about the rehabilitation process.

19. The California system is examined and evaluated in Berkowitz, Monroe, and John F. Burton, Jr. *Permanent Disability Benefits in Workers' Compensation*. Kalamazoo, MI: W. E. Upjohn Institute, 1987, chapter 7.

20. "A Report to the Industry—Vocational Rehabilitation." California Workers' Compensation Institute, San Francisco, November, 1983.

21. See note 20 above.

22. *Controlling Workers' Compensation Costs: A Guide for Employers*. Minnesota Department of Labor and Industry, May, 1984, p. 23.

23. Rules to Implement M.S. 176.102, Rehabilitation of Work Related Injuries and Diseases, Including Rules Necessary to be a Qualified Rehabilitation Consultant or Registered Rehabilitation Vendor, 5220.0100 Definitions, Subp. 13.

24. Chicago: American Medical Association, 1971.

25. *Labor and Industry Compact*. St. Paul, MN: Department of Labor and Industry, August, 1987, issue 16, p. 15.

26. Keefe, Steve, Jay Benanav, Joan Volz, and Wayne Simoneau. "1983 Amendments to the Minnesota Workers Compensation Act." Draft, mimeo, 1985.

27. "Effects of the 1983 Workers' Compensation Reforms: Business Size Open Claim Study, Permanent Partial Disability Open Claim Study." Prepared by the Research and Education Division, Minnesota Department of Labor and Industry. Mimeo, March, 1985.

28. Chapter 51.31, Laws of 1985.

# 5 MOSTLY ON MONDAY: IS WORKERS' COMPENSATION COVERING OFF-THE-JOB INJURIES?

Robert S. Smith

Social insurance programs that compensate individuals for loss of earnings create incentive problems of three kinds. First, because they receive income support when not working, and lose such support upon returning to work, individuals often face diminished labor supply incentives. Thus, workers receiving more generous social insurance payments as compensation for some economic calamity can be expected to take longer to recover from that calamity. Second, offering insurance payments to those suffering losses can raise the probabilities that such losses will occur. People insured against losses frequently face diminished incentives to avoid risky outcomes, and in cases of overinsurance they can even find it in their best interests to deliberately cause the loss to occur (the problem of moral hazard). The third problem inherent in social insurance programs involves false reporting. Insurance payments are triggered by the occurrence of some contingency, and the temptation to falsely report an occurrence can be quite strong—especially if penalties for misrepresentation are weak and/or the benefits are high.

The author wishes to thank Bonnie Rabin, Paula Coleman, and Eileen Driscoll for their help in analyzing the data set used in this chapter.

This chapter attempts to assemble circumstantial evidence related to a particular form of false reporting in the workers' compensation system. In particular, the research reported upon here sets out to gather data on an assertion, which is part of the oral tradition of workers' compensation, that workers injured in off-the-job activities frequently report these injuries as having occurred at work so that they qualify for medical and indemnity payments.

Evaluating this assertion can proceed in two ways. One way would involve inspecting injury reports and gathering corroborating evidence on what allegedly happened. This method may be the only way to build a thoroughly convincing case, one way or the other, concerning the assertion that workers' compensation is paying for some off-the-job injuries; however, this method would be an expensive undertaking that is called for only if a case of probable cause can be established.

The method used in this chapter seeks to discover whether the observed *patterns* of injury reporting can reveal circumstantial evidence that the workers' compensation system is being asked to pay for injuries that occur off the job. Put differently, the fact that not all injuries are equally susceptible of misrepresentation will be exploited in establishing whether a measurable amount of false reporting is likely to exist.

## Expected Patterns If Misrepresentation Exists

The alleged misreporting, if it occurs, involves two essential characteristics: *delay* in treatment and *concealment* of the injury. If an injury that occurs on Sunday is to be reported on Monday as having happened at work, it must be of a type for which treatment can be delayed. Thus, it must not be life-threatening, involve extreme discomfort, or entail known and significant deterioration of one's physical well-being if treatment is not immediate. Moreover, the injury must be one that is not readily apparent to supervisors or colleagues when the worker first reports for work.

For the moment, then, let us suppose that injuries of type F can be feasibly misrepresented as having occurred at work, even if they occurred earlier and away from the work environment. Those of type N cannot be falsely reported if they occurred elsewhere, because treatment cannot be delayed or the injuries cannot be concealed. What can be hypothesized about the relative patterns of reporting if some type F injuries are being falsely reported as work-related?

In considering the patterns one might expect, it is important to stress that we are focusing on injuries that have *truly* occurred; the alleged fraud involved is that they have occurred *away* from one's job. Since all injuries produce some amount of pain or discomfort, it is reasonable to presume that a worker intending to misrepresent the environment in which the injury took place would have incentives to report it *as soon as possible* after reporting for work.

From the simple considerations above, one could reasonably conjecture that type F injuries will be overreported on Mondays or on days following a holiday weekend (representing three or four days off). Further, since a worker intending to misreport an injury will want to do it soon enough after the beginning of the workday to receive prompt relief, yet late enough to generate plausibility of work-relatedness, one might further suppose that type F injuries would be overrepresented in the group of injuries reported during the first two or three hours of work. Finally, because the possibilities for falsely reporting are directly proportional to the potential number of off-the-job injuries, we would expect to observe the most evidence of false reporting after a three-day weekend, lesser evidence after a standard two-day weekend, and much less on ordinary workdays (which may exhibit *some* evidence of false reporting, because off-the-job injuries do not occur *only* on weekends or holidays).

The above suppositions can be distilled into two testable hypotheses. Thus, if some type F injuries are being reported as job-related even though they occurred in off-the-job activities, and if type N injuries are not feasibly misreported, then the following hypotheses should be empirically supportable:

*Hypothesis 1*: A higher proportion of type F than type N injuries will be reported on Mondays and on the days after a holiday weekend, with a greater discrepancy in proportions after a holiday weekend.

*Hypothesis 2*: Type F injuries will tend to be reported earlier in the work shift than will type N injuries, with their relative earliness more pronounced on Mondays and most pronounced on the first workday following a holiday weekend.

## Data Used in Testing These Hypotheses

To test the hypotheses above, one clearly needs data on the day and time that injuries are reported to have occurred. Also required is the nature of the injuries, so that they can be categorized as type F or type N. Fortunately, the Bureau of Labor Statistics (BLS) prepares for public use the Supplemental Data System (SDS), which contains a wealth of information on several thousand individual cases of injury for which workers' compensation was paid. Among the variables in this data set are the nature of the injury and the day and time that the injury was reported. The data set analyzed here is a 1979 SDS tape that contains information on injuries in 1978 and 1979 for the states of Colorado, Delaware, Montana, New York, North Carolina, Virginia, and Wisconsin.

The SDS data are reported by state to the BLS, which accepts the data on any basis that they are reported. For many items, including day of the week and the nature of the injury, reporting is uniformly complete in the above states. However, not all these states report the time of the day that injuries were reported. The data analyzed here pertain only to those states recording the time of day that injuries were reported: Colorado, Delaware, North Carolina, and Virginia.[1]

One weakness of the SDS data is that states differ in their criteria for inclusion in the sample. North Carolina and Virginia, for example, report cases involving eight or more days or disability—although North Carolina will also report a case if it involves over $100 in medical costs. Colorado reports injuries involving three or more lost workdays, while in Delaware the inclusion criterion is four or more lost workdays. The above inclusion criteria suggest that very minor injuries are excluded from our analysis, which may not be troubling because the incentives to misreport them are comparatively small anyway.

Most of the injuries reported in the data set analyzed here fall into one of three categories: cuts and lacerations (19%), fractures (16%), and sprains and strains (35%). The remaining 30% are spread around such categories as burns, dislocations, poisonings, pneumoconiosis, dermatitis, and so forth. It was decided to focus the analysis on just the three most common types of injuries, because when injuries of a given type are categorized by day and time of reporting, cell sizes can become rather thin unless injuries of that type are relatively numerous.

Finally, it should be noted that testing of the above hypotheses involves distinguishing among days that follow holiday weekends, ordinary Mondays, and workdays that do not immediately follow nonworkdays. To this end, the celebration days of federal holidays[2] were identified for 1978 and 1979, along with the day immediately following the holiday weekend. All holidays were excluded from the sample because they were clearly not ordinary workdays, and for the same reasons all days in Christmas week were also excluded. July fifth, a return-to-work day following an unusual one-day holiday break, was analyzed separately; the results, however, were inconclusive due to the paucity of observations on any one day. The remaining days were thus categorized as days after a holiday weekend, ordinary Mondays, and ordinary Tuesdays through Fridays.

## Tests of Hypothesis 1

Of the three common types of injury, cuts and lacerations are most clearly type N; bleeding must be immediately attended to and is difficult to conceal. In contrast, sprains and strains are much more likely to be type F, because they do not always require immediate attention and, if the worker is not observed too closely, are relatively easy to conceal. Fractures represent something of an intermediate case, with the more serious cases compelling immediate attention and the less serious cases closer in nature to sprains.

In testing hypotheses 1 and 2, therefore, it will be especially instructive to compare the patterns of injury-reporting for cuts and lacerations with those for sprains and strains. If off-the-job injuries are being falsely reported as having occurred at work, the misrepresentation is expected to be centered largely in the sprains and strains category, with fractures involved to a lesser extent; cuts and lacerations are assumed to be unaffected.

Empirically, then, hypothesis 1 implies that, of all reported sprains and strains, and percentage reported on the workdays immediately following a weekend—Mondays or the Tuesdays following holiday weekends—will be higher than the corresponding percentage for cuts and lacerations. The percentage of fractures reported on the days after a weekend might be expected to lie between those of cuts and sprains.

Table 5–1 reports evidence supportive of hypothesis 1. In both 1978 and 1979, the percentage of sprains reported on the day after a weekend is higher than the percentage of cuts reported on those days; the corresponding percentage for fractures lies in between the other two. The differences between the percentage for sprains and the percentage for cuts within each year are statistically significant at the .05 level (applying a one-tail test). Thus, it is clear that a higher proportion of sprains are reported on days after a weekend than is the case for cuts and lacerations.

Another test of hypothesis 1 is shown in table 5–2. The data in this table indicate that the mix of injuries reported on the days following a weekend is more oriented toward sprains than on other workdays—and the mix is even more heavily weighted toward sprains on days after a holiday weekend than on ordinary Mondays. In both years, the percentages of sprains on days after a long weekend and on Mondays are significantly higher than the percentages reported on Tuesdays through Fridays.[3]

Conversely, cuts and lacerations (type N injuries) are a significantly higher percentage of all injuries reported on ordinary Tuesdays through Fridays than they are on days following a weekend; their proportion among all injuries reported is lowest following a holiday weekend. Fractures

Table 5–1. The Percentage of Injuries of Each Type Reported on Days After a Weekend, 1978 and 1979 (Colorado, Delaware, North Carolina, Virginia)

| Type of Injury (and Total Number Reported in Each Year) | Reported on Days After a Weekend | | | |
| --- | --- | --- | --- | --- |
| | 1978 | | 1979 | |
| | Number | Percentage | Number | Percentage |
| Cuts and Lacerations (1978: 7549) (1979: 8031) | 1501 | 19.88[a] | 1483 | 18.47[b,c] |
| Fractures (1978: 6512) (1979: 6657) | 1305 | 20.04 | 1316 | 19.77[c,d] |
| Sprains and Strains (1978: 11,417) (1979: 17,566) | 2394 | 20.97[a] | 3755 | 21.38[b,d] |

*Note:* Sample excludes holidays and Christmas week.

Each pair of percentages denoted by "a", "b", "c", and "d" are significantly different from each other at the .05 significance level (one-tail test).

do not vary significantly as a proportion of injuries reported by day of the week.

## Tests of Hypothesis 2

We have been from the data in tables 5–1 and 5–2 that sprains and strains, the injuries that are more susceptible of delayed treatment and concealment, are more likely to be reported on Mondays and days after holiday weekends than cuts and lacerations are. Put differently, sprains and strains are more likely to be reported on the first day of a work week than cuts and lacerations are. Is it also the case, as suggested by hypothesis 2, that they are more likely than cuts to be reported early in the workday? Further, are sprains and strains reported relatively earlier on the days following a weekend?

Table 5–3 contains data on the time of day injuries were reported. In considering these data, it must be noted that it was not generally possible to find out when each worker's shift began; therefore the times of 8–10 a.m. were selected as representative of the early hours of the most common workday, which begins in the time span of 7–8:30 a.m. for most workers. The recorded time was rounded to the nearest hour when

Table 5–2. Mix of Injuries Reported on Various Days of the Week, 1978 and 1979

| | 1978 | | | 1979 | | |
|---|---|---|---|---|---|---|
| Day | Cuts | Fractures | Sprains | Cuts | Fractures | Sprains |
| Day After Holiday Weekend | 27.27[e] | 24.61 | 48.12[a] | 20.51[g,i] | 20.64 | 58.85[b] |
| Monday After Two-Day Weekend | 29.17[f] | 25.19 | 45.65[d] | 22.93[h,i] | 19.95 | 57.12[c] |
| Tuesday Through Friday, Excluding Holidays and Days After Holiday Weekend | 30.19[e,f] | 25.56 | 44.25[a,d] | 25.78[g,h] | 20.80 | 53.42[b,c] |

*Note:* Percentages in each row sum to 100% for both years (except for rounding error).

[a,b,c] Each pair of percentages denoted by "a," "b," "c," "e," "f," "g," and "h" are significantly different from each other at the .05 [e,f,g,h] significance level (one-tail test).

[d,i] Each pair of percentages denoted by "d" and "i" are significantly different from each other at the .10 significance level (one-tail test).

Table 5–3.  Percentage of Injuries of Each Type Reported Between 7:30 a.m. and 10:30 a.m., by Workday, 1978 and 1979

| | % of Each Type of Injury Reported 7:30–10:30 a.m. | | | | | |
| | 1978 | | | 1979 | | |
| | *Cuts* | *Fractures* | *Sprains* | *Cuts* | *Fractures* | *Sprains* |
|---|---|---|---|---|---|---|
| Day Following Holiday Weekend | 27.56 | 25.62 | 30.23 | 28.75 | 33.54 | 33.55 |
| Monday Following Two-Day Weekend | 25.71 | 29.76[a] | 33.00[a] | 27.14 | 29.45[a] | 33.25[a] |
| Tuesday Through Friday, Excluding Holidays and Days After Holiday Weekend | 25.32 | 24.72 | 26.20 | 24.39 | 25.02 | 26.77[a] |

[a] There is a statistically significant difference between this percentage and the corresponding percentage for cuts, .05 level (one-tail test).

creating the SDS data set, so that injuries reported as happening between 8 a.m. and 10 a.m. were in fact reported between 7:30 a.m. and 10:30 a.m.

From the data in table 5–3, one can note three patterns of interest. First, sprains and strains are apparently reported earlier on all days of the work week than are cuts and lacerations, with fractures and cuts not showing much difference except on Mondays. Second, all three kinds of injuries are reported earlier on the days following a weekend. Third, the differentials between the early reporting of sprains and the early reporting of cuts are larger on days following a weekend than for other workdays (although larger on ordinary Mondays than on days following a holiday weekend).

These patterns lend themselves to the following interpretation. Injuries reported on the day following a weekend tend to be reported earlier in the workday, and because this is true for cuts as well as other types of injuries, one must conclude that workers are more prone to injury early on the first day of the work week. However, whatever the proneness to early injury on any given day of the week, it is difficult to argue that sprains would be expected to occur earlier than fractures, and fractures earlier than cuts. Moreover, whatever the *increase* in proneness to early injury on the first workday of the week, it is hard to maintain that the increases are truly larger for sprains than fractures and cuts. The most reasonable explanation for these patterns is the one under consideration here: that some off-the-job injuries are being reported as having occurred at work.

Thus, hypothesis 2 and the related inferences one can draw from it receive reasonably strong support from the data in table 5–3. The only soft spot in this support is the data on days following a holiday weekend. In the 1978 data, there are indications that sprains and fractures were reported earlier on ordinary Mondays than on the days following a holiday weekend; however, the expected pattern appears in 1979 (although, in the case of sprains, not strongly). Further, while the differences between the percentage of sprains reported early and the percentage of cuts reported early are larger on the days after a holiday weekend than on ordinary Tuesdays through Fridays, the differences are larger still on ordinary Mondays in both years. However, the number of injuries reported in a three-hour period on days following a holiday weekend (there are only seven such days) is relatively small, so perhaps not too much can be made of observed patterns on those few days.

## Estimating the Extent of False Reporting

Let us assume that cuts and lacerations are not susceptible of concealment and delayed treatment, and that off-the-job cuts are thus impossible to claim as having occurred at work. Let us assume, further, that the distribution (across hours of the workday) of sprains that *actually* happen at work is the same as the distribution for cuts. Finally, let us assume that all injuries reported later than 10:30 a.m. actually happened at work. If these assumptions are approximately correct, then the *excess early reporting* that has been observed for sprains and fractures, most notably on Mondays, can be attributed to the filing of claims for off-the-job injury.

Panel A of table 5–4 contains the calculation, for sprains and fractures, of excess early reporting for ordinary Mondays and ordinary Tuesdays through Fridays (the days after holiday weekends were excluded from these calculations owing to the problems caused by small sample sizes). The steps in creating this table were as follows:

1.  Calculate, for each day, the ratio (from table 5–3) of cuts reported at times other than 7:30–10:30 a.m. to the cuts reported between 7:30 a.m. and 10:30 a.m. On Mondays in 1979, for example, 27.1% of all cuts were reported between 7:30 a.m. and 10:30 a.m. Thus, the appropriate ratio is 72.9/27.1 = 2.66.
2.  Calculate the expected number of sprains or fractures reported between 7:30 a.m. and 10:30 a.m. by dividing the ratio in step 1 into the number of sprains or fractures reported on the relevant day. On Mondays in 1979, for example, 2200 sprains were reported at times other than 7:30–10:30 a.m.; dividing 2200 by 2.66 yields 827, the number of sprains one might expect to have *actually occurred* at work between 7:30 a.m. and 10:30 a.m.
3.  Subtract the expected number of sprains or fractures calculated in step 2 from the actual numbers reported between 7:30 a.m. and 10:30 a.m., and calculate this excess as a percentage of actual. For sprains in 1979, for example, the excess comes to 24.5% (269/1096)—suggesting that 24.5% of sprains reported early on Monday in 1979 had actually occurred off-the-job.
4.  The excess number of injuries is also calculated as a percentage of all injuries reported on given days. Thus, the excess early sprains reported on Mondays in 1979 comprised 8.3% of all sprains reported on Mondays.

Table 5–4 quantifies the patterns of reporting already observed. As expected, the highest proportions of excess early reporting are on Mondays among sprains and strains. Overall, for both years combined, it appears that about 9% of sprains and strains reported on Monday could be attributed to off-the-job injuries being falsely reported. On Tuesdays

Table 5–4. Estimates of Excess Early Reporting for Sprains and Fractures, by Day of Week, 1978 and 1979

| Day of Week | Reported 7:30–10:30 a.m. | | | | Total All Times of Day | |
|---|---|---|---|---|---|---|
| | Actual Number Reported | Expected Number Reported | Excess | Excess as % of Total | Total Injuries Reported | Excess as % of Total |
| **A. SPRAINS AND STRAINS** | | | | | | |
| Mondays After Two-Day Weekend | | | | | | |
| 1978 | 659 | 463 | 196 | 29.7 | 1,997 | 9.8 |
| 1979 | 1096 | 827 | 269 | 24.5 | 3,223 | 8.3 |
| Total | 1755 | 1290 | 465 | 26.5 | 5,220 | 8.9 |
| Tuesday–Friday, Exclusive of Holiday and Days After Holiday Weekend | | | | | | |
| 1978 | 2066 | 1972 | 94 | 4.5 | 7,884 | 1.2 |
| 1979 | 3223 | 2844 | 379 | 11.8 | 12,039 | 3.1 |
| Total | 5289 | 4816 | 473 | 8.9 | 19,923 | 2.4 |
| **B. FRACTURES** | | | | | | |
| Mondays After Two-Day Weekend | | | | | | |
| 1978 | 328 | 268 | 60 | 18.3 | 1,102 | 5.4 |
| 1979 | 339 | 305 | 34 | 10.0 | 1,151 | 3.0 |
| Total | 667 | 573 | 94 | 14.1 | 2,253 | 4.2 |
| Tuesday–Friday, Exclusive of Holidays and Days After Holiday Weekend | | | | | | |
| 1978 | 1126 | 1126[a] | 0 | 0 | 4,555 | .0 |
| 1979 | 1173 | 1134 | 39 | 3.3 | 4,688 | .8 |
| Total | 2299 | 2260 | 39 | 1.7 | 9,243 | .4 |

[a] The percentage of fractures reported from 7:30–10:30 a.m. on Tuesdays through Fridays was less than the percentage for cuts.

through Fridays, falsely reported sprains and strains represent a considerably smaller percentage of the total: about 2%. Overall, for all workdays other than those after a holiday weekend, it is conceivable that some 4% of the sprains in our sample were misrepresented.

There is modest evidence of excess early reporting of fractures, but only on Mondays. Overall, only about 1% of all fractures are likely to be falsely reported.

What can be said about the total cost of the false reporting that apparently exists? In our sample, the 1979–1980 average cost (indemnity plus medical) for the three types of injuries studied was as follows:

Cuts and lacerations:     $870

Fractures:                $1850

Sprains and strains:      $919

Assuming these values, using the sample's total cases of each injury type (table 5–3), and assuming that 4% of all sprains/strains and 1% of all fractures represent off-the-job injury, it was estimated that some 2% of the total costs of cuts, fractures, and sprains probably represented compensation for off-the-job injury in 1978–1979.


## Conclusions

This study has found circumstantial evidence that injuries susceptible of concealment and delayed treatment are reported earlier in the workday than are other injuries. Moreover, the most pronounced differences in the time of reporting are on Mondays and the days following holiday weekends; these are days on which the mix of reported injuries are more heavily weighted than usual toward those injuries that are prone to concealment and delayed treatment.

The patterns just outlined are exactly what one would expect if employees injured in off-the-job activities sometimes report their injuries as having occurred at work. It was estimated, if misrepresentation is accepted as the explanation for these patterns, that some 4% of the cases involving sprains and strains in 1978–1979, and 1% of those involving fractures, represented off-the-job injuries. These cases accounted for some 2% of the total compensation paid for the most common types of injuries: cuts, lacerations, fractures, sprains and strains. (This chapter did not attempt to analyze the reporting patterns for less common injuries, some of which are much more costly.)

While the bad news is that there is strong circumstantial evidence to support the contention that workers' compensation is paying for some off-the-job injuries, the good news is that the extent of misrepresentation appears relatively small—at least among the common, less expensive types of injuries. Still, it may well pay insurance companies to more carefully scrutinize sprains and strains (or other similar injuries) reported early in the workday on days following a weekend.

## Notes

1. Economic theory suggests that the level and structure of benefits in a state will affect incentives to misreport. Preliminary attempts to ascertain the effects of a state's benefits were frustrated by the small number of states in the sample.

2. These holidays are New Year's Day, Washington's Birthday, Memorial Day, Independence Day, Labor Day, Columbus Day, Veteran's Day, Thanksgiving, and Christmas.

3. It is conceivable that injured employees often try to "work through" sprains or strains and, realizing that the injury persists, report them a couple of days after they occur. If so, Thursday and Friday sprains would be reported on Mondays, and one might argue that delayed reporting is what elevates Monday's totals.

There are three reasons to believe that delayed reporting is not what is causing the patterns noted in this section. First, the SDS data indicate the day of *occurrence*, not the day reported. Second, delayed reporting of sprains actually incurred at work cannot explain why there are more sprains reported after a three-day than a two-day weekend. Third, reporting with a two-day delay would imply below-average reporting of sprains on Tuesdays relative to Wednesdays, Thursdays and Fridays. The SDS data show no such dip in Tuesday's report.

# 6 PREMIUM AND LOSS CYCLES IN WORKERS' COMPENSATION

Richard J. Butler
John D. Worrall

## Cycles Within and Between States

Cycles in workers' compensation are, like any recurrent economic pheno-menon, interesting either because they ultimately reflect some underlying social process or because they have the potential for significantly altering the way that economic agents allocate scarce resources. The underwriting cycle is nominally interesting for the latter reason: to the extent that the combined ratio (losses plus expenses to premiums) reflects the profitability of an insurance enterprise, systematic movements in the combined ratio should signal arbitrage opportunities. In an insurance market like workers' compensation, with relatively easy entrance and exit, stable profit cycles ought to be accompanied by concomitant cycles of capital flowing in and out of the industry or at least by a systematic change in the value of in-

We wish to thank the National Council on Compensation Insurance for generous research support and David Durbin for especially competent help in setting up the data files for analysis. Comments from Professors Neil Doherty and Emilio Venezian were appreciated, and the suggestions of a referee were especially helpful.

surance stock over the cycle. The fact that there are neither capital flows nor changes in the value of the insurance firm over these profitability cycles (Doherty and Kang (1984) note that such profit cycles should be reflected in the market price of insurance stock) seems to indicate that combined ratio is not a useful indicator of profits. At least we are not convinced that it is.

In this chapter, our interest lies in examining the nature of these cycles, and in finding out what generates these cycles, rather than what the cycles imply for resource allocation. In order to keep the discussion readable, we will initially employ some tools introduced into the insurance cycle literature by Venezian (1985), though in spirit our approach to modeling the cycle is much closer to that of Doherty and Kang (1984). Venezian suggests that the uncertainty of future costs can generate statistical underwriting cycles. The model is innovative, but he implicitly treats the combined ratio as a index of profitability. His model begins appropriately focused on the prediction of average costs, but ends with conclusions about profit margins based on the combined ratio—a leap that would seem to require that firms be in long-run equilibrium over these profitability cycles. But in a long-run competitive equilibrium, the combined ratio is probably a better measure of insurance price than it is of insurance profit. Indeed, Doherty and Kang argue that it is a good proxy for price, embed it in a simultaneous equation system with lags, and explain the profitability cycle as simple price movements responding to cyclical economic phenomena, especially the movement of interest rates.

But while the combined ratio is more closely a price than a profit, it is an imperfect proxy. In our analysis of the combined ratio, we focus on models that determine its two principal elements: premiums and losses. We ignore expenses in the analysis for two reasons. By accepted actuarial practices, expenses are either assumed to be a fractional part of losses (loss-adjustment expenses) or of premiums (other operating expenses). Since our analysis below is given in logarithms, these multiplicative factors of proportionality are readily assumed into the constant term in the regressions that are specified below. If these proportionality factors are relatively constant over time, the inclusion of expenses in our analysis would not significantly alter any of our conclusions. Secondly, reported expenses based on accounting practices are certainly a poor proxy for economic expenses, while accounting premiums and losses are relatively cleaner measures of total sales and manufacturing costs (or output).

We follow the standard convention of empirical economic research in that we transform the data into natural logarithms and deflate it by the 1967 consumer price index. And because the log of the loss/premium ratio is just the difference in the logs, we focus on cycles in the logarithm of each of these variables separately. That is, our focus implicitly is on the cycles in the log of the loss-to-premium ratio, which can be written as

$$-\ln(\text{losses/premiums}) = \ln(\text{premiums}) - \ln(\text{losses}). \qquad (6.1)$$

By understanding the cycles in the components (namely premiums and losses separately) of the ratio, we can isolate the source of the cycle: are losses steadily increasing in the face of cyclical premiums, or do losses themselves exhibit cycles?

This is the first systematic analysis of cycles in workers' compensation by state, and so our analysis will be largely descriptive. In the remainder of this section we provide descriptions of the loss and premium cycles by state. In the second and third section we see how well economic models of premiums and losses capture cyclical movements, and then we conclude in the final section with a description of what remains of the cycles after the effects of the economic variables have been removed from losses and premiums.

We employ a second-order autoregressive process to examine each of the terms in equation (6.1), following the technique suggested by Venezian. (Higher-order autoregressive processes were fit to these and the models below, but almost inevitably the second-order process was sufficient to model the changes. Hence only the second-order specifications will be presented and discussed in this chapter.) Venezian summarizes his technique as follows (1985, p. 492; we paraphrase slightly to conform with our model):

> [...Consider the following equation for a second-order process (explicitly including "time" for detrending purposes)....]
>
> $$\ln\text{Loss}_t = a + b \text{ time} + c \ln\text{Loss}_{t-1} + d \ln\text{Loss}_{t-2} + e_t \qquad (6.2)$$
>
> in which $a$, $b$, $c$ and $d$ are constants, and $e_t$ is a random element. If the absolute value of $d$ is less than unity and $d < 1 - c$, series $\ln\text{Loss}_t$ is stationary. Stationary series with $c + 4d > 0$ are damped but not oscillatory. If, however, $c + 4d < 0$, the series, suitably translated, is a damped since wave with noise and is characterized (Box and Jenkins, 1976) as displaying "pseudo periodic behavior" with period:
>
> $$\text{Period} = 2\pi \;/\; \text{arc } \cos(c/2\sqrt{-d}) \qquad (6.3)$$

Throughout this chapter we will use specifications like that in equation (6.2) to summarize the cycles in our data. Our data derive from a cross section–time series of workers' compensation data covering 37 states from 1954 to 1983, and include typical economic variables in addition to earned premiums and incurred losses. All data are state- and year-specific (except the interest rates, which are year- but not state-specific). All pecuniary variables are measured in real 1967 dollars. To apply the Venezian technique and introduce our analysis, consider fitting equation (6.2) to the variables in equation (6.1) for our data. These estimated functions (with the absolute value of the $t$-statistic in parentheses) are

$$\ln(P/L)_t = .078 + .001t + .685 \ln(P/L)_{t-1} + .152 \ln(P/L)_{t-2}$$
$$\quad\quad (4.22) \quad (1.88) \quad (21.03) \quad\quad\quad\quad (4.35)$$
$$R^2 = .56$$

$$\ln L_t = .475 + .002t + .736 \ln L_{t-1} + .239 \ln L_{t-2}$$
$$\quad\quad (5.72) \quad (2.15) \quad (23.17) \quad\quad (7.60)$$
$$\quad\quad\quad\quad\quad\quad\quad\quad\quad\quad\quad\quad (6.4)$$
$$R^2 = .98$$

$$\ln P_t = .196 + .001t + 1.149 \ln P_{t-1} + -.159 \ln P_{t-2}$$
$$\quad\quad (4.34) \quad (2.16) \quad (34.66) \quad\quad (4.81)$$
$$R^2 = .99$$

Since the effect of time is removed by the inclusion of the second regressor (like Venezian, we focus on the cyclical rather than the secular component of change), cycles are captured by the sign and magnitude of the lagged values of the dependent variables. As indicated above, all three detrended time series are stationary, but none of them show any cycling.

The absence of cycles in the pooled data is not because there are no cycles in workers' compensation time series, but because the estimation has imposed the same autoregressive structure over administrative units (namely the states) that have, in fact, significantly varying cycles. (Inclusion of state fixed effects in the models in equation (6.4) does not change the estimated $c$ and $d$ coefficients there). Table 6–1 records those state-specific loss and premium cycles by fitting the same specification that we given in equation (6.4) for the pooled data. Specifications with four lags generally fit the time series no better than those with two lags: in the loss autoregressive models, the fourth lag was never significant at the 5% level, while the third lag was significant only twice; and for premiums, significane was only achieved twice and once respectively for the fourth and third lags. In almost every case, the first lag was significant, and the second was statistically significant in about half of the states. Only the coefficients from the models that just included the first two lags are included in the table, with the accompanying $R^2$ measure of fit and the period of the cycle implied by the coefficients using equation (6.3) above. The NA recorded in the period column indicates that there is no cyclical behavior in that particular series.

Table 6–1.  Autoregressive Trends in Losses and Premiums by State

| State id | Parameters of Loss Model | | | | | Parameters of Premium Model | | | | |
|---|---|---|---|---|---|---|---|---|---|---|
| | lag1 | lag2 | time | $R^2$ | period | lag1 | lag2 | time | $R^2$ | period |
| AL | .724 | −.256 | .041 | .98 | 8.12 | 1.058 | −.329 | .021 | .99 | 15.83 |
| AR | .890 | −.338 | .026 | .97 | 8.99 | .844 | .086 | .002 | .98 | NA |
| CO | .869 | −.017 | .015 | .95 | NA | .589 | −.265 | .054 | .98 | 6.53 |
| CT | .650 | −.234 | .022 | .96 | 7.53 | 1.137 | −.370 | .014 | .98 | 17.28 |
| DC | 1.156 | −.374 | .011 | .93 | 18.88 | 1.329 | −.592 | .016 | .95 | 11.89 |
| FL | 1.168 | −.308 | .006 | .97 | NA | 1.400 | −.700 | .022 | .98 | 10.84 |
| GA | .932 | −.295 | .029 | .99 | 11.65 | 1.011 | −.516 | .040 | .99 | 7.95 |
| HI | −.028 | −.050 | .074 | .84 | 3.85 | .284 | −.024 | .065 | .98 | NA |
| IA | 1.135 | −.386 | .017 | .98 | 14.99 | 1.289 | −.515 | .017 | .99 | 13.80 |
| ID | 1.182 | −.543 | .024 | .97 | 9.82 | .882 | −.223 | .023 | .96 | 17.18 |
| IL | .872 | −.290 | .024 | .95 | 10.02 | 1.156 | −.584 | .024 | .96 | 8.81 |
| IN | .949 | −.382 | .014 | .94 | 9.03 | 1.474 | −.734 | .007 | .95 | 11.74 |
| KS | 1.326 | −.455 | .007 | .98 | 33.92 | 1.074 | −.315 | .012 | .97 | 21.30 |
| KY | 1.327 | −.609 | .022 | .98 | 11.34 | 1.410 | −.532 | .008 | .97 | 24.23 |
| LA | .517 | −.087 | .026 | .86 | NA | 1.062 | −.429 | .019 | .96 | 10.05 |
| MD | 1.162 | −.535 | .020 | .98 | 9.62 | .570 | −.175 | .039 | .99 | 7.65 |
| ME | .920 | −.371 | .047 | .99 | 8.79 | .754 | −.148 | .040 | .99 | NA |
| MI | 1.386 | −.492 | .002 | .96 | 40.49 | 1.441 | −.670 | .014 | .96 | 12.71 |
| MN | .624 | −.084 | .022 | .86 | NA | 1.565 | −.831 | .019 | .99 | 11.66 |

Table 6-1. (continued).

| State id | Parameters of Loss Model | | | | | Parameters of Premium Model | | | | |
|---|---|---|---|---|---|---|---|---|---|---|
| | lag1 | lag2 | time | $R^2$ | period | lag1 | lag2 | time | $R^2$ | period |
| MO | .437 | −.475 | .045 | .95 | 5.03 | .477 | −.017 | .017 | .91 | NA |
| MS | .781 | −.492 | .026 | .91 | 6.41 | .718 | −.091 | .014 | .96 | NA |
| MT | .808 | −.078 | .029 | .91 | NA | .963 | −.270 | .022 | .95 | 16.30 |
| NC | 1.055 | −.687 | .034 | .99 | 7.13 | 1.183 | −.576 | .022 | .99 | 9.28 |
| NE | 1.150 | −.587 | .026 | .99 | 8.70 | 1.075 | −.317 | .013 | .98 | 20.79 |
| NH | 1.317 | −.531 | .015 | .98 | 14.20 | .984 | −.324 | .029 | .98 | 11.92 |
| NJ | .648 | .320 | −.005 | .89 | NA | 1.289 | −.438 | .005 | .98 | 27.41 |
| NM | 1.061 | .016 | .007 | .93 | NA | 1.381 | −.478 | .007 | .99 | 124.8 |
| NY | .535 | −.309 | .004 | .39 | 5.88 | 1.321 | −.811 | .014 | .97 | 8.41 |
| OK | .775 | .103 | .012 | .95 | NA | 1.368 | −.576 | .012 | .97 | 14.02 |
| RI | .968 | −.103 | .011 | .97 | NA | .677 | −.071 | .021 | .95 | NA |
| SC | .401 | .105 | .029 | .96 | NA | .870 | −.275 | .025 | .98 | 10.60 |
| SD | .832 | −.262 | .037 | .97 | 10.10 | .945 | −.307 | .023 | .97 | 11.43 |
| TN | 1.094 | −.681 | .033 | .99 | 7.43 | 1.240 | −.410 | .009 | .98 | 24.88 |
| TX | .949 | −.285 | .025 | .98 | 13.20 | 1.340 | −.531 | .014 | .99 | 15.55 |
| VA | .693 | .052 | .022 | .98 | NA | 1.287 | −.600 | .026 | .99 | 10.64 |
| VT | .664 | .094 | .047 | .89 | NA | .961 | −.433 | .025 | .97 | 8.35 |
| WI | −.047 | −.015 | .029 | .07 | 3.56 | .991 | −.550 | .028 | .99 | 7.49 |

Excepting Wisconsin's losses, the fit of the autoregressive specification seems to be quite good on an individual state by individual state basis. The coefficients on the time-trend variable indicate the average annual percentage growth rate in premiums and losses for each state. The largest real (recall that these are inflation-adjusted) secular growth rate in losses, for example, is 7.4 in Hawaii, which also exhibited the largest growth rate in premiums—about 6.5% over the sample period. Losses actually fell slightly on average in New Mexico, and Arkansas had the slowest growth rate in premiums, with an average of only .2% per year. Since these are annual average growth rates, the implied differences in secular growth over say a 10- or 20-year period would be astronomical. Note that the annual percentage increase in losses seems to be greather on average than that in premiums. There are a number of interpretations of these trends. Our own is that competition in the insurance market for compensation effectively returns investment income to firms in the form of lower premiums.

But in this chapter our interest is not in the secular growth rate, but in deviations (i.e., cycles) in real losses and premiums around that long-run growth rate. And the implied cycles in workers' compensation insurance are just as diverse as the secular growth rates, as indicated both by the magnitude of the coefficients and the period of the implied cycle (calculated as indicated in equation (6.2) above). Loss cycles fall largely into two groups: a group of states with loss cycles of 3 to 6 years (five states), and a larger group consisting of cycles ranging from 7 to 10 years (12 states). Premium cycles are much longer on average, with virtually all states exhibiting cycles greater than seven years, and a number with 11- to 14-year cycles (eight states) and 15- to 17-year cycles (five states). It is interesting to note that Venezian's model (1985) suggests periods of from 4 to 9 years, which is truer of the loss cycles (recall that Venezian's model is based on average losses) than of the longer premium cycles. A close look at table 6–1 also reveals that there are no systematic region-specific periods in the cycles.

The diversity of cycles across states suggests that explanations of cyclical behavior must principally rely on state-specific phenomenon rather than on processes that would be common to all states. For workers' compensation insurance, at least, an explanation that relies on state-specific administrative features (such as Venezian's cost-projection model) would be more plausible than one that assumed a common driving force across all states (such as Doherty and Kang's model, in which interest rates ultimately generate changes in the combined ratio).

The hypothesis that cycles are state-specific (relative to the alternative explanation that they are generated by a common country-wide cyclical process) implies interstate differences in the turning points of the cycles, as well as differences in their length. Hence we would expect that interstate correlations would be low as well. To examine such interstate correlations, we regressed losses and premiums on an intercept and time-trend variable for each state, and looked at the pairwise correlations between the residuals of these regressions (which capture the cyclical component of losses or premiums) when they are partitioned according to the length of the cycle. Comparisons of states with cycles of vastly varying lengths would not be appropriate, both because we want to look at correlations between states whose cycles have the same length, and because in small samples like ours there are likely to be spurious correlations when comparing, for example, a 12-year and an 8-year cycle.

These correlations, which are given in tables 6–2A, and 6–2B for losses and premiums, lend further support to the state-specific origin of workers' compensation cycles. If there were different country-wide processes of varying lengths, then the residuals across those states with cycles of similar length ought to be highly correlated. Hence we would expect to see significant and positive correlations within those states of similar cyclical length. In the first row of the loss cycles, containing correlations of states with 3- to 6-year cycles, Hawaii is significantly, correlated (as indicated by a value in parentheses of less than .05) only with Mississippi in the cyclical phase, with a correlation coefficient of .664 (though the relationship may be partially spurious, since Mississippi's period is over 1.5 times longer than Hawaii's cyclical period). Hawaii is inversely correlated in phase with both Missouri and Wisconsin, both of which have periods more nearly equal to Hawaii's than does Mississippi, though the relationship is not significant. Except for the 11- to 14-year loss cycles, the cyclical patterns for either premiums or losses appear not only to vary by length across states but also to be out of phase with each other. It appears that whatever model is offered as a description of these cycles ought to be able to explain why they appear to be state-specific.

## The Simple Economics of Losses

In a world of competitive markets and rational agents, profitable activities will always be expanded to the point where there is just a normal return to capital at the margin. The persistence of regular and predictable premium and loss cycles, which would seem to allow for such profit-taking, means that either agents—in this case, firms and insurance carriers—are not

Table 6–2A.  Interstate Comparisons in Trends in Compensation Losses*

**Three- to Six-Year Loss Cycles**

|      | HI            | MO            | MS            | NY            | WI            |
|------|---------------|---------------|---------------|---------------|---------------|
| HI   | 1.000 (.00)   | -.022 (.91)   | .664 (.00)    | .107 (.59)    | -.146 (.48)   |
| MO   |               | 1.000 (.00)   | -.042 (.84)   | .451 (.02)    | -.502 (.01)   |
| MS   |               |               | 1.000 (.00)   | -.034 (.87)   | .332 (.11)    |
| NY   |               |               |               | 1.000 (.00)   | -.085 (.68)   |

**Seven- to Ten-Year Loss Cycles (Selected States)**

|      | AR          | CT           | ID           | IL          | IN          | MD          | ME          | NC          | NE          | SD          |
|------|-------------|--------------|--------------|-------------|-------------|-------------|-------------|-------------|-------------|-------------|
| AR   | 1.00 (.00)  | -.189 (.33)  | .284 (.14)   | -.019 (.92) | .481 (.01)  | -.150 (.45) | -.290 (.13) | .082 (.68)  | -.288 (.14) | -.327 (.10) |
| CT   |             | 1.000 (.00)  | -.253 (.19)  | -.043 (.83) | .054 (.79)  | -.283 (.14) | .470 (.01)  | .427 (.02)  | .410 (.03)  | -.124 (.54) |
| ID   |             |              | 1.000 (.00)  | .181 (.36)  | .117 (.55)  | .556 (.00)  | -.130 (.51) | .183 (.35)  | .109 (.58)  | .310 (.12)  |
| IL   |             |              |              | 1.000 (.00) | .483 (.01)  | .398 (.04)  | .386 (.04)  | .509 (.01)  | .357 (.06)  | .334 (.09)  |
| IN   |             |              |              |             | 1.000 (.00) | -.059 (.76) | -.040 (.84) | .339 (.08)  | -.186 (.34) | -.276 (.16) |

Table 6–2A.   (continued).

**Seven- to Ten-Year Loss Cycles (Selected States)**

|     | AR | CT | ID | IL | IN | MD | ME | NC | NE | SD |
|-----|----|----|----|----|----|--------|--------|--------|--------|--------|
| MD  |    |    |    |    |    | 1.000  | .238   | .068   | .374   | .628   |
|     |    |    |    |    |    | (.00)  | (.22)  | (.73)  | (.05)  | (.00)  |
| ME  |    |    |    |    |    |        | 1.000  | .268   | .821   | .232   |
|     |    |    |    |    |    |        | (.00)  | (.17)  | (.00)  | (.25)  |
| NC  |    |    |    |    |    |        |        | 1.000  | .478   | .353   |
|     |    |    |    |    |    |        |        | (.00)  | (.01)  | (.07)  |
| NE  |    |    |    |    |    |        |        |        | 1.000  | .608   |
|     |    |    |    |    |    |        |        |        | (.00)  | (.00)  |

**Eleven- to Fourteen-Year Loss Cycles**

|     | GA    | IA    | KY    | NH    | TX    |
|-----|-------|-------|-------|-------|-------|
| GA  | 1.000 | .675  | .855  | .795  | .499  |
|     | (.00) | (.00) | (.00) | (.00) | (.01) |
| IA  |       | 1.000 | .583  | .762  | .472  |
|     |       | (.00) | (.00) | (.00) | (.01) |
| KY  |       |       | 1.000 | .825  | .588  |
|     |       |       | (.00) | (.00) | (.00) |
| NH  |       |       |       | 1.000 | .685  |
|     |       |       |       | (.00) | (.00) |

* Residual ($e$) comparisons using OLS: In Losses $= a + b$ Time $+ e$; states by length of cycles (significance level in parentheses).

Table 6–2B. Interstate Comparisons in Trends in Compensation Premiums*

**Seven- to Ten-Year Premium Cycles**

|     | CO     | DC     | GA     | IL     | LA     | MD     | NC     | NY     | VT     | WI     |
|-----|--------|--------|--------|--------|--------|--------|--------|--------|--------|--------|
| CO  | 1.00   | -.208  | .500   | -.051  | -.231  | .365   | .135   | -.148  | .531   | .101   |
|     | (.00)  | (.30)  | (.01)  | (.80)  | (.24)  | (.06)  | (.49)  | (.45)  | (.00)  | (.62)  |
| DC  |        | 1.000  | .292   | -.022  | .119   | .549   | -.443  | .325   | -.499  | .038   |
|     |        | (.00)  | (.14)  | (.91)  | (.55)  | (.00)  | (.02)  | (.10)  | (.01)  | (.86)  |
| GA  |        |        | 1.000  | -.662  | -.324  | .692   | .412   | .229   | .540   | .353   |
|     |        |        | (.00)  | (.00)  | (.10)  | (.00)  | (.03)  | (.25)  | (.00)  | (.08)  |
| IL  |        |        |        | 1.000  | -.529  | .398   | .509   | .368   | .497   | .291   |
|     |        |        |        | (.00)  | (.00)  | (.04)  | (.00)  | (.05)  | (.00)  | (.15)  |
| LA  |        |        |        |        | 1.000  | -.393  | -.124  | -.182  | -.396  | -.323  |
|     |        |        |        |        | (.00)  | (.04)  | (.53)  | (.35)  | (.04)  | (.11)  |
| MD  |        |        |        |        |        | 1.000  | .068   | .358   | .180   | .420   |
|     |        |        |        |        |        | (.00)  | (.73)  | (.06)  | (.36)  | (.03)  |
| NC  |        |        |        |        |        |        | 1.000  | .121   | .588   | .226   |
|     |        |        |        |        |        |        | (.00)  | (.54)  | (.00)  | (.27)  |
| NY  |        |        |        |        |        |        |        | 1.000  | -.183  | -.085  |
|     |        |        |        |        |        |        |        | (.00)  | (.35)  | (.68)  |
| VT  |        |        |        |        |        |        |        |        | 1.000  | .192   |
|     |        |        |        |        |        |        |        |        | (.00)  | (.35)  |

Table 6–2B. (continued).

**Eleven- to Fourteen-Year Premium Cycles**

|     | DC | IA | IN | MI | MN | NH | OK | SD |
|-----|-----|-----|-----|-----|-----|-----|-----|-----|
| DC  | 1.000<br>(.00) | .468<br>(.01) | -.085<br>(.66) | -.303<br>(.12) | .563<br>(.00) | .559<br>(.00) | .231<br>(.24) | .745<br>(.00) |
| IA  |     | 1.000<br>(.00) | .239<br>(.22) | -.295<br>(.13) | .671<br>(.00) | .762<br>(.00) | .230<br>(.24) | .417<br>(.03) |
| IN  |     |     | 1.000<br>(.00) | .637<br>(.00) | .021<br>(.92) | -.060<br>(.76) | -.477<br>(.01) | -.276<br>(.16) |
| MI  |     |     |     | 1.000<br>(.00) | -.297<br>(.16) | -.281<br>(.15) | -.727<br>(.00) | -.572<br>(.00) |
| MN  |     |     |     |     | 1.000<br>(.00) | .494<br>(.01) | .383<br>(.06) | .395<br>(.06) |
| NH  |     |     |     |     |     | 1.000<br>(.00) | .314<br>(.10) | .491<br>(.01) |
| OK  |     |     |     |     |     |     | 1.000<br>(.00) | .348<br>(.08) |

**Fifteen- to Seventh-Year Premium Cycles**

|     | AL | CT | ID | MT | TX |
|-----|-----|-----|-----|-----|-----|
| AL  | 1.000<br>(.00) | -.132<br>(.50) | .519<br>(.00) | -.216<br>(.27) | -.042<br>(.83) |
| CT  |     | 1.000<br>(.00) | -.253<br>(.19) | .250<br>(.20) | .086<br>(.66) |
| ID  |     |     | 1.000<br>(.00) | .065<br>(.74) | .088<br>(.65) |
| MT  |     |     |     | 1.000<br>(.00) | .512<br>(.01) |

* Residual ($e$) comparisons using OLS: ln Premiums $= a + b$ Time $+ e$; states by length of cycles (significance level in parentheses).

rational, or that such cycles merely reflect the rational behavior of agents who live in a world of either imperfect information or imperfect markets (including markets in which prices adjust slowly). The insurance market for workers' compensation exhibits a little of both types of imperfections: prices are regulated and will not always reflect market conditions, and costs are uncertain both because the economic incentives of firms and workers depend on economic conditions that are frequently cyclical (wages and output, for example) and because the legislated nominal changes in benefits have not matched the changes in nominal wages.

We capture these underlying determinants of the premium/loss cycle in workers' compensation by modeling the economic incentives of those in the market, and then linking the market cycles to one of three exogenous sources: legislated changes (in the benefit structure and insurance alternatives available to the firm), economy-wide cyclical changes, and the regulatory process. As is indicated in table 6–3, our model of this market is recursive. We take legislated changes in the benefit structure (and the alternative means facing the firm of insuring their risks) as exogenously determined. These changes, along with current economic conditions, determine an equilibrium level of losses in which wages are the principal mechanism by which the supply and demand of lost work time is equilibrated. A model for this process is developed and its parameters estimated in this section. In the next section we take up the determination of premium levels, integrating the behaviors of the firm, the insurance carrier, and the regulator.

### The Economic Determinants of Compensation Losses in Theory

Participation in the workers' compensation program is by definition conditional on being employed. Hence at the aggregate level we are concerned with the indemnity losses generated only by the employed workforce, and we only model and employ estimation procedures appropriate for the sample of employed workers. We will not consider those not in the labor force or the currently unemployed—for example, we will not examine the impact that a change in the level of workers' compensation benefits may have no new entrants to the workforce, and the decision of the currently employed to leave the labor force should they be injured. Such considerations would unnecessarily complicate the analysis and clearly lie beyond the scope of this study. The relevant decisions for the representative employee are how much risk he or she will taken on the job (given the safety

Table 6–3. A Recursive Model of cycles in Workers' Compensation

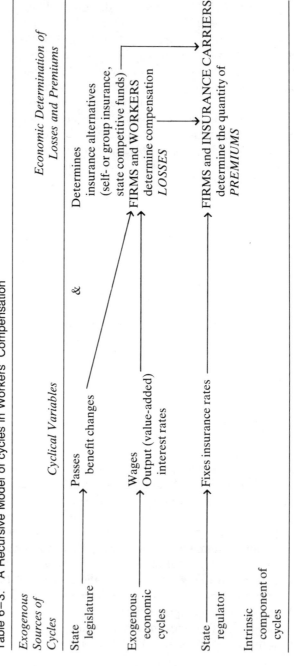

| *Exogenous Sources of Cycles* | *Cyclical Variables* | & | *Economic Determination of Losses and Premiums* |
|---|---|---|---|
| State legislature | Passes benefit changes | | Determines insurance alternatives (self- or group insurance, state competitive funds) |
| Exogenous economic cycles | Wages Output (value-added) interest rates | | FIRMS and WORKERS determine compensation *LOSSES* |
| State regulator | Fixes insurance rates | | FIRMS and INSURANCE CARRIERS determine the quantity of *PREMIUMS* |
| Intrinsic component of cycles | | | |

environment generated by the firm) in a given unit of time, and if he or she is injured, whether to file for a claim and how long to remain in claimant status. In terms of a week, the employee's time constraint is

$$1 = N + L, \tag{6.5}$$

where $N$ = proportion of week spent working, and $L$ = proportion of week spent on claim.

It follows that the average cost is

$$E(C) = L \cdot B, \tag{6.6}$$

where $C$ = average cost per employee as predicted by economic theory, and $B$ = weekly benefit amount.

Note that the expected proportion (recall that we are modeling behavior in the aggregate) of time that a worker will spend on a claim, $L$, is just the probability of starting a claim multiplied by the average duration once it starts. We do not observe $L$ directly in our data, but we can model its economic determinants, and hence the determinants of the expected costs.

We take natural logarithms of equation (6.6) to get

$$\ln C = \ln L + \ln B. \tag{6.7}$$

Assuming that the compensation time is endogenously determined with the wage rate (and that both are functions of exogenously determined compensation benefits), we solve for the reduced determinants of $L$, substitute that into equation (6.7), and then substitute equation (6.8) into equation (6.9) to achieve the final estimation form. To see what the implied signs on the reduced form coefficients would be in such a model, we examine the economic incentives of the workers and firms.

### Incentives of the Workers

The time constraint of the employee is given in equation (6.5). The budget constraint is simply that empenditures on goods (or simply expenditures) be equal to all sources of income

$$X = W \cdot N + B \cdot L + A, \tag{6.8}$$

where $B$ = weekly compensation benefits,
  $X$ = the quantity of goods,
  $W$ = the weekly wage rate, and
  $A$ = nonlabor income,

where the price of goods $X$ has been normalized to 1 (all pecuniary variables are in real terms). Constrained utility maximization implicitly yields of supply-of-compensation-time function (i.e., the optimal amount of time that the representative worker spends on a workers' compensation claim), which we approximate by

$$\ln L = \alpha_0 + \alpha_1 \ln W + \alpha_2 \ln B + \alpha_3 \ln A + \alpha_4 \ln AGE + \varepsilon_s. \quad (6.9)$$
$$\quad\quad\quad\quad\quad - \quad\quad\quad + \quad\quad\quad + \quad\quad\quad +$$

If for the marginal worker (eligible for a workers' compensation claim) the income elasticity is small and positive, so that all substitution effects outweigh the income effects of price changes, then each of the unknown parameters of the analysis will have the sign pattern indicated underneath the respective variables. Note that $\varepsilon_s$ represents measurement uncertainty. In order to capture differences across individuals in their labor-supply incentives associated with different amounts of firm-specific and safety-specific human capital, we have also included an age variable (AGE), the proportion of young workers in the sample. New, younger workers in the workforce are more likely to be unfamiliar with the working environment and hence more likely to experience injuries, which we expect to dominate the more severe (but fewer) injuries of the older workers.

### The Firms' Incentives in Workers' Compensation

Consider the economic incentives facing the firm. Given the level of output (pace of industrial activity) and production technology, the firm tries to minimize the costs of production, given the following prices: the cost of labor or wage, $W$; the price of capital, $S$, as captured here by the interest rates; the price of time lost to a workers' compensation claim—namely, the level of compensation benefits, $B$; and the medical price of a unit of compensation time, HOSP. Given relative prices, we view injuries as the unavoidable consequence of increased levels of production, holding technology constant. This *joint-production* view of output and injuries was originally advanced by Oi (1974).

The firm's minimization process yields a demand-for-compensation-*time* function (which is just one minus the demand-for-work function), which depends on the level of output and the prices that the firm faces, and which we approximate in logarithmic form and solve for wages to get

$$\ln W = \beta_0 + \beta_1 \ln Y + \beta_2 \ln S + \beta_3 \ln L + \beta_4 \ln B + \beta_5 \ln HOSP \quad (6.10)$$
$$+ \varepsilon_d.$$

Equations (6.9) and (6.10) are the structural equations of our economic model. Equation (6.9) represents the supply of compensation time (absence from work) given level of wages and other prices including compensation benefits, and equation (6.10) can be viewed from an aggregate perspective as the highest wages that the demanders of *compensation* time, namely the firms, are willing to pay workers as the expected length of claimant status changes for the representative worker. Since measures of compensation time, $L$, are not available in the aggregate, these structural equations cannot be estimated separately, although the components of $L$—frequency and severity of claims—have been examined for different data sets in limited time periods (see for example Worrall and Appel, 1982; Worrall and Butler, 1985; Chelius, 1974; and Butler and Worrall, 1983, 1985). However, by solving for the reduced form equation for the log of $L$ (compensation time), and then using equation (6.7), we can see what the reduced-form effect of the exogenous variables is on total indemnity costs. We are assuming that wages equilibrate the amount of compensation time supplied by the worker so that it equals the amount of compensation time allowed by the firm, where compensation benefits are viewed as exogenously shifting these functions up or down.

From equations (6.9) and (6.10), we have to solve for compensation time, $L$, to get

$$\ln L = (\alpha_0 + \alpha_1\beta)^o + \alpha_1\beta_1 {}^o\ln Y + \alpha_1\beta_2 {}^o\ln S +$$
$$(\alpha_1\beta_4 + \alpha_2)^o\ln B + \alpha_3{}^o\ln A + \alpha_4{}^o\ln AGE +$$
$$(\varepsilon_s + \alpha_1\varepsilon_d)^o, \tag{6.11}$$

where $(---)^o = (---)/(1 - \alpha_1\beta_3)$, which when plugged into equation (6.7) yields

$$\ln C = (\text{r.h.s. of } 6.11) + \ln B \tag{6.12}$$

This represents the per-employee total losses (costs) of workers' compensation expected on the basis of observable exogenous variables.

Our empirical results for our aggregated sample of 37 states for the years 1954 to 1982 are found in table 6–4. The model that we developed in the previous section has as the dependent variable the indemnity plus medical costs per worker. The dependent variable used in our analysis, total indemnity losses, was kindly made available to us from the National Council on Compensation Insurance. Since our model is specified in terms of losses per worker, we must either divide total losses by total employment or simply include (the log of) total employment as a right-hand-side regressor in our analysis. We report results using the latter approach, though results using the former approach (normalizing losses by employ-

Table 6–4.   Empirical Model for Workers' Compensation (Medical and Indemnity) Losses: Time Series/Cross Section (Absolute *t*-statistics)

| Independent Variables | Dependent Variable: Total WC Losses | |
|---|---|---|
| | State Effects | State & Lags |
| Intercept | 6.702 | .349 |
| | (12.06) | (.93) |
| lnVALAD | .027 | .083 |
| | (.35) | (1.86) |
| lnTbill | −.007 | −.085 |
| | (.25) | (4.80) |
| lnAGE | .667 | .080 |
| | (5.01) | (1.03) |
| lnOTHINC | .632 | .013 |
| | (6.77) | (.23) |
| lnHOSP | .278 | .151 |
| | (.36) | (3.53) |
| LnMaxBen | .568 | .020 |
| | (11.59) | (.64) |
| LnAllemp | .491 | −.041 |
| | (4.290) | (.59) |
| Lag1Loss | | .852 |
| | | (27.08) |
| Lag2Loss | | .038 |
| | | (1.24) |
| F-fixed effects | 55.609 | 1.417 |
| $R^2$ | .960 | .987 |
| Nobs | .952 | .890 |

ment on the left-hand side of the equation) yielded estimates that were very similar to those reported here. All pecuniary variables have been put into real 1967 dollars by using the Consumer Price Index deflator for all items (1967 = 100). Since all the independent and the dependent variables are entered in logarithmic form, the estimated coefficients are elasticities—they indicate the percent change in losses given a 1% change in the value of the independent variables. Hence, a 1% change in employment will be accompanied by a .49% increase in total losses. this means that a 10% upswing in employment over the employment cycle will induce a roughly 5% increase in losses that, holding all other influences constant, will follow the employment cycle. All of the coefficients here can be similarly interpreted. In order to know which variables determine the cycle of losses, we would need to know cycles of the exogenous variables (in each state) in addition to their estimated coefficient.

The pattern of coefficients in table 6–4 generally conforms with our model, though the effects are not always significant. One concern of aggregating observations from different states and different years is that there may be significant effects, specific to each year or to each state, that are not being captured by our model. To test this hypothesis and examine the potential effects that such fixed effects may have on our empirical specification, we have included dummy variables for each state (the state fixed effect). We have not included year-specific effects, since these are obviously a part of the cycle that we want to explain. As might be expected in data that have strong cyclical components, the inclusion of year-specific effects does alter the coefficients of those regressors with strong cyclical components: notably, in the loss regressions reported here, in the presence of the year fixed effects, the coefficients of the interest rate, real benefit, and hospital cost variables sometimes changed sign. F-statistics for the test of joint significance of the state fixed effects are given at the bottom of each specification. The state effects (though not reported in table 6–4) are significant, as can be seen by the F-value of 55.6 in our basic specification in the left-hand column.

The other specification of interest is given in the right-hand column, which supplements the basic model with the inclusion of the first two lags of the dependent variable. This specification allows for the cyclical influence of the exogenous variables in the model, as well as for intrinsic or otherwise unexplained cyclical behavior in the pattern of losses over time. The previous values of losses are quite significant in determining the current level of losses, and even though equation (6.4) and table 6–1 jointly suggest that the autoregressive process is not similar across states (we have more to say about this below), this specification is probably the best summary of the influence of external economic cycles in the presence of some inherent cyclicality. We focus our discussion on this specification.

### Demand-Side Determinants of Workers' Compensation Claims

The coefficients of the output and interest-rate variables conform to those predicted by the model once the effect of the intrinsic cycle is taken into account. The VALAD (real value added by manufacturers) coefficient indicates that for a 1% change in output there will be a .08% change (from table 6–4, row 2, column 2) in the of workers' compensation losses as the VALAD coefficient changes over its cycle. As interest rates rise, the cost of capital (nonlabor input) increases, and the profit-maximizing firm has an incentive to substitute away from capital and towards able-bodied laborers. One way to accomplish this is by encouraging (possibly through wage and fringe-benefit adjustments) greater workplace safety, so that fewer accidents will occur. Costs should fall as such substitution is made. This effect may be offset if the increase in interest rates causes a sufficient substitution away from safety capital, but such an effect appears to be small: a 1% increase in the interest rate results in a .081% decrease in indemnity losses. Hence the cyclical impact of synchronized output and interest-rate patterns would be neutral on losses, since they roughly offset each other. LnHOSP costs affect losses both directly, since they form part of measured total losses (this is a one-to-one effect on the level of medical losses), and indirectly, through the firm's demand function as given above. Since the direct and indirect effects act in opposing directions, the net impact on total losses is theoretically ambiguous, though we find that the empirical effect is to increase real losses.

### Supply-Side Determinants of Workers' Compensation Claims

In both specifications in table 6–4, the assets and age variables have positive elasticities, although they are statistically insignificant when previous losses are included in the specification. The income elasticity for compensation time, as given by the OTHINC (transfers and asset income) variable, decreases from about .63 to about .01 when the previous costs are included in the analysis. A similar decrease in the AGE coefficient is observed—increasing the proportion of young workers (AGE) apparently has little impact when inherent cyclicality is allowed in the model.

### The Benefit Effect

The ambiguous benefit effect is not statistically significant in right-hand specification. Since AGE, OTHINC, and RMAX (real maximum weekly benefit level for temporary total workers' compensation claims) are all supply-side variables, significant without the lagged values and insignificant with them, perhaps a large part of the inherent nature of the cycles is correlated with changes in the supply responses of workers over the last few years, particularly since benefits have increased so dramatically.

As a further check for specification of the model, we performed statistical tests on the benefit variable to see if we could really treat it as an exogenous influence in our specification. If benefits were not exogenous but rather jointly determined by the interaction with claims weeks, then our recursive model would be misspecified. However, in Hausman endogeneity (1978) type tests,[1] the hypothesis that benefits are indeed exogenous could not be rejected for either of the specifications.

## Regulation and Premiums in Workers' Compensation

Rates that individual insurance companies can charge their insureds are regulated in each state by a governmental body.[2] Since decisions regarding those rates often involve protracted hearings and considerable expense on the part of the various parties concerned with the workers' compensation system, it follows that government agencies must have the potential to significantly affect either the allocation of resources in this market or the distribution of incomes. Since future costs associated with indemnity losses are uncertain, one of the areas of frequent contention in these hearings is the cost consequences of any given change in the institutional structure (especially rates or benefits) of workers' compensation. In this section, as can be seen in the recursive model shown in table 6–3, we take the rate-fixing process as exogenously determined, and given the level of losses, benefits, and relevant economic factors, we assume that the level of premiums is determined by the interaction of firms and insurance carriers.

Elsewhere (Butler and Worrall, 1986), we develop a model in which the regulator balances the costs of having inefficient market rates against the costs of changing those rates in a world of uncertain future costs. This results in a simple model of experience rating that includes lagged values in a cost specification. Hence what we here call *inherent cyclicality* is treated as part of the regulatory behavior there. Though developed from a different perspective, this model (Butler and Worrall, 1986) is similar in spirit to Venezian (1985). However, while that specification is appropriate when our concern is with modeling the level of losses and premiums, here our focus is on premium and loss cycles; consequently, we consciously steer clear of a specification that explicitly includes lagged values of the dependent variable in the model. We want to explain the cycles before including lagged values of the dependent variable in the regression. Otherwise we would be assuming that we already knew the causes of cycles (at least partially) by the way we specified the model. Hence in this chapter we take an alternative approach to modeling premiums and losses.

## The Demand for Insurance Coverage by the Firm

The maximum amount that a firm is willing to pay for insurance is a decreasing function of the quantity of insurance offered per unit of time and an increasing function of the price of substitutes. Unfortunately, we have not measured alternative prices, though we do have measures of the availability of alternative sources of insurance coverage: the possibility of group self-insurance for smaller companies (SELF = 1 if group self-insurance is possible and 0 otherwise), and the availability of a state fund that competes for business with private insurance carriers in the market COMPFD = 1 if there is a competitive state fund, 0 if there is not).[3] Hence demand specification is as follows:

$$\ln P = d_0 \ln Q + d_1 \text{SELF} + d_2 \text{COMPFD} + \mu_d \qquad (6.13)$$

with the expected signs for the variables given below.

## The Supply of Coverage by Insurance Carriers

The carrier supplies more insurance as the price increases, but is also willing to increase the quantity supplied at given prices as interest rates rise. As the interest rate increases, gains from the higher investment yields can be realized only as the quantity of insurance increases. (Note, however, that the effect of interest rates on premiums, which is the price of insurance times its quantity, is indeterminate since an increase in the quantity demanded depends on a fall in the price, and the net outcome on premiums depends on the elasticity of demand.) In addition, we include losses per employee as a proxy for the costs of other supply-side prices. The specification for supply then becomes

$$\ln Q = s_0 + s_1 \ln P + s_2 \ln S + s_3 \ln (\text{TC/EE}) + \mu_s, \qquad (6.14)$$

with the expected signs for the coefficients indicated underneath the model, and (TC/EE) is the proportion of total losses per employee.

If the market is competitive and adjusted instantaneously to shifts in the demand and supply functions, then equations (6.13) and (6.14) would be sufficient to characterize the equilibrium. Prices are nominally set by the regulator, though competition in this market has led to the development of a myriad of schemes that collectively lead, we believe, to the *nearly* competitive level of prices. These mechanisms to achieve competition include discounts, deviations from the fixed rates, cross-subsidization of price (the prices of other nonregulated lines of insurance are adjusted), dividend policies of carriers, cost plus insurance including retroactive rating, etc. However, real resources are spent to overcome the effects of price regulation, and so the size of these expenditures should shift the supply and demand curve for insurance up and down. Hence, even though the effect of price regulation is overcome, the nearly competitive price (the real-market price in the presence of regulation) will tend to deviate from the price that would be obtained without regulation, because the supply and demand curves have been shifted as real resources were spent to achieve the nearly competitive price. (We expect that the difference between the nearly competitive price and the competitive price will be greatest when insurance rates are set too low, since it is relatively easy for the insurance carrier to return premiums to the firm, but more difficult for the firm to pay more than the regulated price.)

In order to incorporate some of this process into our analysis, in an admittedly imperfect way, consider what happens when the regulated rate for workers' compensation insurance is below the market clearing price. Then to the supply specification given in equation (6.14) we need to add another term indicating that the supply curve will shift up (the quantity will fall for any given level of prices) the greater the divergence between the competitive price $(P)$ and the regulated price $(P^*)$. We model this effect by modifying the supply specification as follows:

$$\ln Q = s_0 + s_1\ln P + s_2\ln S + s_3\ln (\text{TC/EE}) + s_4 \ (\ln P - \ln P^*)*D$$
$$\quad\ \ + \quad\quad + \quad\quad + \quad\quad\quad\quad\quad -$$
$$+ \mu_s, \tag{6.15}$$

where the $(\ln P - \ln P^*)*D$ term captures the effect of overcoming the regulated price, and the $(\ln P - \ln P^*)$ term is interacted with a dummy variable that is 1 when competitive price is greater than or equal to the regulated price $(P^*)$.

In the empirical specification, the dependent variable is the actual (logarithm of) premium, which is the sum of $\ln P$ and $\ln Q$. So to get the reduced-form specification for premiums, we need to solve equations (6.13) and (6.14) for the reduced-form specification, which can be readily seen to involve not only all the variables specified in those equations, but also those variables interacted with the dummy variable $(D)$ (which is 1 when the regulated price is set too low, and 0 otherwise). The reduced-form signs are indeterminate unless we make stricter assumptions about the coefficients in the structural equations. We proxy $P^*$ by the target loss ratio (an actuarially determined ratio of losses to premiums),[4] and code the dummy variable as 1 when $P^*$ is less than the actual ratio of losses to premiums. Solving for the reduced-form equations for $\ln P + \ln Q$ yields a reduced-form specification, which we present in tables 6–5 whose coefficients and general structure can be interpreted analogously to table 6–4. Again, the overall fit is quite good with or without the lagged values of the dependent variables, and there is no cycle indicated when all states are restricted to have the same autoregressive process that this pooled specification assumes.

Although the model corresponds to our theoretical expectations in terms of the structural specification for the supply (carrier) side of the market, the demand shifters (SELF and COMPFD) have perverse (from the standpoint of the structural expectations given in equation (6.13)) positive coefficients. We suspect that these may be the result of misspecification in the sense that state competitive funds, and group self-insurance, seem to be established in states with relatively higher prices for workers' compensation insurance. In this case, the positive coefficients are understood as indicating that competitive state funds and group self-insurance are not exogeneous influences, with the recursive structure indicated in table 6–3, but that in fact alternative financial possibilities are jointly determined with the level of premiums in the model. If this is the case, then at least one more regression function (in addition to those for losses and premiums) would need to be added to the specification, and our analysis would be complicated considerably. Clearly this is an interesting question that moves beyond the scope of the descriptive analysis attempted here.

We did, however, also perform a Hausman (1978) type test to check the endogeneity of the loss variables in the premiums regression. Although we rejected the null hypothesis of no endogeneity at the 5% level, when we reestimated the model using the predicted values of the loss variables in the analysis (rather than the actual values), the coefficients of the parameters were virtually unaffected, and none of our analysis or conclusions were substantially altered.

## The Cycles Revisited

Note the qualitatively similar coefficients on the lagged values of the dependent variables between the models given in equation (6.4) at beginning of this chapter without other regressors in the specification, and those given in table 6–4 and 6–5. This similarity raises the interesting question of whether or not we have removed much of the cycle from premiums and losses by employing standard autoregressive/econometric techniques. To address this question, we repeated much of the analysis we undertook in

Table 6−5. Empirical Model for Workers' Compensation Premiums: Time Series/Cross Section (Absolute *t*-statistics)

| Independent Variables | Dependent Variable: Total WC Premiums | | | |
|---|---|---|---|---|
| | *State Effects* | *Year Effects* | *State/Year* | *State & Lags* |
| Intercept | −.039 | −1.995 | 4.725 | 1.068 |
| | (.03) | (1.21) | (2.85) | (1.11) |
| InPremLR | .357 | .936 | −.292 | −.211 |
| | (1.00) | (2.92) | (.76) | (.89) |
| InTbill | .090 | −.015 | .045 | .044 |
| | (4.86) | (.47) | (1.72) | (2.61) |
| SELF | .255 | .281 | .219 | .029 |
| | (6.15) | (6.06) | (5.56) | (1.08) |
| COMPFD | .444 | .122 | .377 | .120 |
| | (10.16) | (5.76) | (9.12) | (3.95) |
| InTotloss | .656 | .883 | .612 | .229 |
| | (24.76) | (40.39) | (22.97) | (10.63) |
| LnAllemp | .684 | .104 | .479 | .190 |
| | (13.60) | (4.06) | (8.81) | (4.91) |
| Ineff.Dummy | 2.623 | 5.616 | 1.037 | .045 |
| | (1.75) | (3.35) | (.68) | (.05) |
| Dum*PremLR | −.739 | −1.432 | −.332 | −.060 |
| | (1.99) | (3.35) | (.87) | (.25) |
| Dum*Tbill | −.002 | −.019 | −.032 | −.026 |
| | (.12) | (.79) | (1.54) | (1.55) |
| Dum*SELF | −.204 | −.239 | −.162 | −.022 |
| | (4.42) | (4.58) | (3.75) | (.76) |
| Dum*COMPDF | −.061 | −.026 | −.046 | −.035 |
| | (2.67) | (.97) | (2.11) | (2.40) |
| Dum*Totloss | .025 | −.010 | .019 | .014 |
| | (1.05) | (.38) | (.86) | (.87) |
| Dum*Allemp | −.017 | .043 | −.009 | −.001 |
| | (.61) | (1.38) | (.33) | (.09) |
| Lag1Prem | | | | .893 |
| | | | | (25.36) |
| Lag2Prem | | | | −.205 |
| | | | | (6.36) |
| F-fixed effects | 15.586 | 4.993 | 12.968 | 2.553 |
| $R^2$ | .989 | .982 | .991 | .996 |
| Nobs | .899 | .899 | .899 | .827 |

tables 6–1 and tables 6–2A and 6–2B for the detrended residuals (i.e., by examining the residuals from premium and loss regressions where time was the only dependent variable) for the residuals from the regressions in the far right-hand side of tables 6–4 and 6–5. (That is, we used the models without the lagged values of the dependent variable in the model, for reasons given at the beginning of the last section.)

These cycles, with the economic components removed from them, are given in table 6–6. Note that since these are the residuals from the models in tables 6–4, and 6–5, the time-trend variable is solely a detrending factor, and cannot be interpreted as it was in table 6–1. Note also that we have imposed the same economic responses across all states by pooling the data (although we do allow the intercept for each state to vary, since we have included the state dummy variables), and so have made it probably more difficult for the economic variables to remove cycles compared to an analysis where these effects were estimated on a state-by-state basis. Future studies may want to examine whether (and why) states' loss and premium regressions vary from state to state and what effect this may have no explaining variations in cycles between states, but clearly such an effort is beyond the scope of our analysis. Finally, because these are residuals with a lot of communality removed from them by means of the regression, they have systematically lower $R^2$ than the losses and premiums did before we removed the economic factors (table 6–4 and –5).

The most notable difference between table 6–1 (the *before* modeling cycles) and table 6–6 (the *after* modeling cycles) is that the periods are much shorter, the length of the premium period being nearly the same as the loss period on average. We do not understand why this should be the case, and especially why the premium cycles are differentially affected, but one thing is clear: the cycles with the economic components removed are considerably different than they were before we modeled changes in premiums and losses. Comparing tables 6–7A and 6–7B with tables 6–2A and 6–2B also suggests that modeling has not at all synchronized the cycles between states. So with or without consideration of the observable factors included in our study (i.e., with or without the analysis of tables 6–4 or 6–5), each state seems to have its own individuals cycle. We believe that the state-specific mechanisms outlined in Venezian (1985) and Butler and Worrall (1986) may prove to be useful explanations of the cycles that remain.

We find evidence in this chapter that the mechanisms outlined in table 6–3 are at least part of the explanation for the state-specific cycles that we observe for workers' compensation. But cyclical components still remain even after we control for such factors as interest rates, benefits, employment, etc. It seems to us that future research might further reduce

Table 6–6. Autoregressive Trends in Losses and Premiums by State After Modeling Components Have Been Removed

| State id | Parameters of Loss Model | | | | | Parameters of Premium Model | | | | |
|---|---|---|---|---|---|---|---|---|---|---|
| | lag1 | lag2 | time | $R^2$ | period | lag1 | lag2 | time | $R^2$ | period |
| AL | .144 | −.264 | .026 | .82 | 4.49 | .702 | −.353 | −.022 | .48 | 6.70 |
| AR | .433 | −.404 | .001 | .15 | 5.14 | — | — | — | — | — |
| CO | .777 | −.295 | −.027 | .41 | 8.11 | −.014 | −.520 | .037 | .27 | 3.98 |
| CT | 1.005 | −.788 | −.024 | .54 | 6.49 | .898 | −.539 | −.011 | .66 | 6.88 |
| DC | .321 | −.119 | −.027 | .63 | 5.78 | .614 | −.164 | −.009 | .74 | 8.82 |
| FL | 1.245 | −.418 | −.056 | .57 | 22.91 | .127 | −.299 | .005 | .53 | 4.32 |
| GA | .696 | .206 | −.060 | .35 | NA | .426 | −.035 | −.030 | .34 | NA |
| HI | −.084 | −.108 | .037 | .22 | 4.15 | .192 | −.317 | .023 | .25 | 4.49 |
| IA | 1.046 | −.682 | −.026 | .49 | 7.10 | .640 | −.298 | −.021 | .64 | 6.66 |
| ID | .367 | −.344 | −.014 | .60 | 5.01 | .276 | .195 | −.037 | .50 | NA |
| IL | .469 | −.242 | −.016 | .17 | 6.01 | .600 | −.095 | −.024 | .54 | NA |
| IN | .465 | −.094 | −.026 | .81 | NA | .435 | −.307 | −.009 | .40 | 5.38 |
| KS | .959 | −.344 | −.033 | .79 | 10.25 | .322 | .052 | −.018 | .34 | NA |
| KY | .866 | −.246 | −.029 | .90 | 12.31 | −.424 | .355 | .023 | .71 | NA |
| LA | .622 | .173 | −.044 | .31 | NA | 1.000 | −.610 | −.026 | .31 | 7.17 |
| MD | 1.231 | −.705 | −.035 | .61 | 8.40 | .244 | −.312 | .008 | .19 | 4.65 |
| ME | .679 | −.287 | −.005 | .89 | 7.11 | .308 | −.063 | −.012 | .66 | NA |
| MI | .859 | −.876 | −.034 | .91 | 5.74 | .090 | −.770 | .066 | .71 | 4.36 |
| MN | .552 | −.148 | −.029 | .45 | 8.15 | −.321 | .247 | .014 | .48 | NA |

Table 6–6. (continued).

| State id | Parameters of Loss Model | | | | | Parameters of Premium Model | | | | |
|---|---|---|---|---|---|---|---|---|---|---|
| | lag1 | lag2 | time | $R^2$ | period | lag1 | lag2 | time | $R^2$ | period |
| MO | .618 | -.411 | -.014 | .35 | 5.89 | .096 | .313 | -.017 | .17 | NA |
| MS | .700 | -.520 | -.030 | .79 | 5.91 | .479 | .018 | -.032 | .42 | NA |
| MT | .876 | -.521 | -.004 | .61 | 6.84 | .860 | -.417 | -.034 | .24 | 7.47 |
| NC | .032 | .196 | -.025 | .60 | NA | .503 | -.084 | -.035 | .81 | NA |
| NE | .834 | -.270 | -.030 | .49 | 9.84 | — | — | — | — | — |
| NH | .855 | -.293 | -.030 | .81 | 9.51 | .942 | -.585 | -.027 | .52 | 6.93 |
| NJ | .279 | -.152 | -.028 | .78 | 5.22 | .277 | -.235 | .004 | .39 | 4.90 |
| NM | .754 | .027 | -.048 | .74 | NA | .308 | -.422 | -.005 | .45 | 4.72 |
| NY | .088 | .025 | -.038 | .85 | NA | .894 | -.799 | .006 | .62 | 6.00 |
| OK | .486 | .208 | -.034 | .53 | NA | .614 | -.281 | -.023 | .50 | 6.60 |
| RI | .508 | .318 | -.042 | .82 | NA | .294 | -.266 | -.005 | .14 | 4.90 |
| SC | .152 | .311 | -.037 | .36 | NA | .783 | -.063 | -.051 | .63 | NA |
| SD | .716 | -.417 | .001 | .80 | 6.39 | .177 | -.107 | -.019 | .77 | 4.85 |
| TN | .337 | -.250 | -.004 | .11 | 5.12 | .489 | -.194 | -.019 | .40 | 6.39 |
| TX | .862 | -.423 | -.017 | .68 | 7.43 | .729 | -.438 | -.027 | .34 | 6.36 |
| VA | 1.041 | -.889 | -.022 | .73 | 6.37 | 1.275 | -.746 | -.035 | .65 | 8.48 |
| VT | .662 | .095 | -.023 | .76 | NA | .986 | .108 | -.089 | .27 | NA |
| WI | .217 | .069 | -.024 | .48 | NA | — | — | — | — | — |

Table 6–7A. Interstate Comparisons in Trends in Compensation Losses*

**Four- to Six-Year Loss Cycles (Selected States)**

| | AL | AR | CT | DC | HI | ID | IL | MI | MO | MS |
|---|---|---|---|---|---|---|---|---|---|---|
| AL | 1.00 (.00) | .025 (.90) | -.148 (.46) | .122 (.54) | -.173 (.49) | .346 (.11) | .244 (.22) | .494 (.18) | .007 (.97) | .347 (.09) |
| AR | | 1.000 (.00) | -.043 (.83) | -.026 (.90) | -.385 (.10) | -.295 (.16) | -.204 (.30) | -.345 (.33) | -.058 (.77) | -.205 (.32) |
| CT | | | 1.000 (.00) | .163 (.41) | -.034 (.89) | .140 (.51) | -.147 (.46) | .428 (.22) | .283 (.15) | .364 (.07) |
| DC | | | | 1.000 (.00) | .094 (.70) | .375 (.07) | .013 (.95) | .429 (.22) | .302 (.13) | .452 (.02) |
| HI | | | | | 1.000 (.00) | -.055 (.82) | -.185 (.45) | -.618 (.06) | .088 (.73) | .571 (.01) |
| ID | | | | | | 1.000 (.00) | .254 (.23) | .747 (.01) | .215 (.32) | .250 (.25) |
| IL | | | | | | | 1.000 (.00) | .544 (.10) | .353 (.07) | -.316 (.12) |
| MI | | | | | | | | 1.000 (.00) | .486 (.18) | .418 (.26) |
| MS | | | | | | | | | 1.000 (.00) | .001 (.96) |

Table 6–7A. (continued).

**Seven- to Ten-Year Loss Cycles**

|     | CO     | IA     | KS     | MD     | ME     | MN     | NE     | NH     |
|-----|--------|--------|--------|--------|--------|--------|--------|--------|
| CO  | 1.000  | −.216  | .518   | .416   | .183   | .215   | .153   | .220   |
|     | (.00)  | (.27)  | (.01)  | (.03)  | (.35)  | (.31)  | (.44)  | (.26)  |
| IA  |        | 1.000  | .400   | −.045  | .605   | .490   | .592   | .699   |
|     |        | (.00)  | (.04)  | (.83)  | (.00)  | (.02)  | (.00)  | (.00)  |
| KS  |        |        | 1.000  | .249   | .404   | .651   | .559   | .495   |
|     |        |        | (.00)  | (.24)  | (.04)  | (.00)  | (.00)  | (.01)  |
| MD  |        |        |        | 1.000  | .244   | .177   | −.053  | .379   |
|     |        |        |        | (.00)  | (.23)  | (.43)  | (.80)  | (.06)  |
| ME  |        |        |        |        | 1.000  | .357   | .797   | .637   |
|     |        |        |        |        | (.00)  | (.09)  | (.00)  | (.00)  |
| MN  |        |        |        |        |        | 1.000  | .470   | .468   |
|     |        |        |        |        |        | (.00)  | (.02)  | (.02)  |
| NE  |        |        |        |        |        |        | 1.000  | .631   |
|     |        |        |        |        |        |        | (.00)  | (.00)  |

* Residual (e) comparisons using OLS: lnLosses = $a + b$ Time $+ e$; states by length of cycles (significance level in parentheses).

Table 6–7B. Interstate Comparisons in Trends in Compensation Premiums*

**Three- to Six-Year Premium Cycles (Selected States)**

|      | AL   | CO    | CT    | EL    | HI    | IA    | IL    | KY    | MD    | ME    |
|------|------|-------|-------|-------|-------|-------|-------|-------|-------|-------|
| AL   | 1.00 | .324  | .211  | .329  | -.143 | .353  | .297  | .124  | .419  | .149  |
|      | (.00)| (.09) | (.28) | (.09) | (.51) | (.07) | (.13) | (.54) | (.03) | (.45) |
| CO   |      | 1.000 | -.119 | .445  | .406  | .024  | .195  | .282  | .115  | -.027 |
|      |      | (.00) | (.55) | (.02) | (.05) | (.91) | (.32) | (.15) | (.56) | (.89) |
| CT   |      |       | 1.000 | .097  | .180  | .697  | .658  | .181  | .634  | .534  |
|      |      |       | (.00) | (.63) | (.40) | (.00) | (.00) | (.36) | (.00) | (.00) |
| FL   |      |       |       | 1.000 | .105  | .185  | .417  | .693  | .193  | .288  |
|      |      |       |       | (.00) | (.63) | (.36) | (.03) | (.00) | (.33) | (.14) |
| HI   |      |       |       |       | 1.000 | .027  | .125  | .126  | -.033 | .116  |
|      |      |       |       |       | (.00) | (.90) | (.56) | (.57) | (.88) | (.59) |
| IA   |      |       |       |       |       | 1.000 | .595  | .126  | .598  | .576  |
|      |      |       |       |       |       | (.00) | (.00) | (.53) | (.00) | (.00) |
| IL   |      |       |       |       |       |       | 1.000 | .141  | .595  | .528  |
|      |      |       |       |       |       |       | (.00) | (.48) | (.00) | (.00) |
| KY   |      |       |       |       |       |       |       | 1.000 | .022  | .432  |
|      |      |       |       |       |       |       |       | (.00) | (.91) | (.02) |
| MD   |      |       |       |       |       |       |       |       | 1.000 | .364  |
|      |      |       |       |       |       |       |       |       | (.00) | (.06) |

Table 6–7B.　(continued).

**Seven- to Ten-Year Premium Cycles**

|     | DC | LA | MT | VA |
|-----|-----|-----|-----|-----|
| DC | 1.000<br>(.00) | .336<br>(.08) | -.482<br>(.01) | .746<br>(.00) |
| LA |     | 1.000<br>(.00) | .034<br>(.86) | .366<br>(.06) |
| MT |     |     | 1.000<br>(.00) | -.430<br>(.02) |

* Residual ($e$) comparisons using OLS: lnPremiums = $a + b$ Time + $e$; states by length of cycles (significance level in parentheses).

the cyclical components by getting good empirical proxies for the working of the workers' compensation administration in each state. More exact cyclical decompositions can be made by the use of finite Fourier transformations. And more theoretical work should be directed to the interesting question of what, if any, meaning can be given to the cycles that yet remain.

## Notes

1. The test for endogeneity is simple: an instrumental-variable estimator is always unbiased in large samples, regardless of whether the benefit variable is endogeneous or not, whereas the OLS estimator will be biased if the assumption of endogeneity does not hold. The test simply compares the OLS estimated coefficients with the instrumental-variable estimated coefficients.

2. Actually, this is the case for most but not all states. Rates in a few states are administered on a *file and use* basis. In the six states with monopolistic state funds, insurance companies write a minimal amount of coverage.

3. As pointed out to us by a referee, the simple binary control for a competitive state fund may not be sufficient to capture the heterogeneity within the state fund category. The Arizona and Oklahoma state funds use NCCI rates, and are generally regarded as having sufficient reserves to pay outstanding claims. By way of contrast, Maryland and Montana do not use NCCI rates and so may be underreserved. This heterogeneity among the state funds may help explain the unexpected results in table 6–5.

4. The target loss ratio is just one minus and expense allowance: that is, given the expected production and acquisition costs, premium taxes and assessments, and an underwriting profit and contingency factor, the residual of the premium dollar (usually 65% to 80%) is the target loss ratio.

## References

Box, G. E. P., and G. M. Jenkins. *Time Series analysis—Forecasting and Control*. Oakland, CA: Holden-Day, 1976.

Butler, Richard, J., and John D. Worrall, "Workers Compensation: Benefit and Injury Claims Rates in the 1970s." *Review of Economics and Statistics* 65 (1983): 580–589.

Butler, Richard J., and John D. Worrall. "Work Injury Compensation and the Duration of Nonwork Spells." *Economic Journal* 95 (1985): 714–724.

Chelius, James R. "The Control of Industrial Accidents: Economic Theory and Empirical Evidence." *Law and Contemporary Problems* 38 (1974): 700–729.

Doherty, Neil A., and Han Bin Kang. "Underwriting Cycles: A Partial Adjustment Model." Paper delivered at the Novemeber 1984 NCCI conference on Workers' Compensation, New York.

Hausman, Jerry A. "Specification Tests in Econometrics." *Econometrica* 49

(1984): 1251–1272.

Venezian, Emilio C. "Ratemaking Methods and Profit Cycles in Property and Liability Insurance." *Journal of Risk and Insurance* 52 (1985): 464–476.

Worrall, John D., and David Appel. "The Wage Replacement Rate and Benefit Utilization in Workers' Compensation Insurance." *Journal of Risk and Insurance* 49 (1982): 361–371.

Worrall, John D., and Richard J. Butler. "Benefits and Claim Duration." In John D. Worrall and David Appel (eds.), *Workers Compensation Benefits: Adequacy, Equity and Efficiency.* Ithaca, NY: ILR Press, 1985, pp. 57–70.

# 7 DISCOUNTED CASH-FLOW RATEMAKING MODELS IN PROPERTY–LIABILITY INSURANCE

## J. David Cummins

Property–liability insurance contracts are characterized by a time lag between the premium payment and loss settlement dates. During this time lag, the insurance company earns investment income on the unexpended component of the premium. Given this timing difference, it is surprising that the recognition of investment income in ratemaking is a relatively recent phenomenon. Prior to the late 1960s, property–liability ratemaking formulas reflected a profit margin that was a flat percentage of the gross premium (usually 5%). The timing difference between premiums and claims and the resulting investment income were ignored in formal ratemaking procedures.

During the late 1960s, rising claim costs and higher interest rates began to motivate regulators to scrutinize ratemaking formulas more carefully. The result was that states such as New Jersey and Taxes began to require insurers to give explicit consideration to investment income in ratemaking.

Since property–liability insurance transactions involve cash flows occurring at different points in time, it would seem that the models developed in corporate finance would have been the logical starting point for the incorporation of investment income in insurance rates. However, property–liability insurance is heavily mired in statutory accounting. As a result, the earliest models were primarily based on accounting concepts.

The accounting models have been extremely influential and are still proposed from time to time by insurers and their rating bureaus, e.g., the Insurance Services Office (ISO). Descriptions and analyses of accounting models can be found in the National Association of Insurance Commissioners (NAIC) (1983), Cummins and Chang (1983), and Williams (1983). The most serious defects of the accounting models are 1) they are retrospective rather than prospective and 2) they use *embedded yields* to measure the rate of return on policyholder funds. Both of these characteristics are contrary to well-known principles of corporate finance.

Instead of looking forward to estimate the cash flows that will result from any given insurance policy, the accounting models look backward. That is, they typically measure policyholder funds as a proportion of unearned premiums and loss reserves. Policyholder funds are multiplied by the rate of return on the company's investment portfolio (the embedded yield) to obtain the investment income credit to be used in ratemaking.

Reserves are an imperfect proxy, at best, for the amount and timing of future cash flows (see Cummins and Chang, 1983, for an analysis of this problem). Reserves represent *sunk costs*, which should be irrelevant in setting rates for policies issued in the future. Researves are an ex post rather than ex ante measure of cash-flow relationships. Current book reserves reflect past realized losses rather than the expected future losses that are relevant for cash-flow analysis. Reserves do contain valuable information on the time lag between the premium and loss payment dates, but this information is accurate only to the extent that payout patterns are stationary. The relevant information on payout patterns can be extracted using paid claim development triangles, provided that the potential nonstationary problem is recognized (see Taylor, 1986). It is the paid claim development patterns that are relevant for cash-flow ratemaking.

The embedded yield is also irrelevant for ratemaking. The correct rate of investment return is the rate that will be earned on the funds received under any given policy. This has nothing to do with the past investment yields. When the company receives the premium under a newly issued policy, these funds (net of expenses) will be invested at current market rates, not at the embedded yield. Ratemaking should always reflect the best possible estimate of the yields that will be attainable when the cash flows are received.

The accounting methodologies also attempt to provide the insurer with a reward for risk-bearing based on a more rational foundation than the traditional flat percentage. Usually, the approach is to compare the mean and variance of book returns across industries. Insurance usually plots below the market line derived from these statistics. The usual inference is that insurance is underearning for an industry in its risk class (see NAIC, 1983; Arthur D. Little 1967).

Like the accounting methodologies, interindustry book-return comparisons are invalid. Book-return comparisons rest on the assumption that there should be a positive relationship between book return and book variance. This assumption is wrong on at least two counts—it is well established that market values rather than book values represent the correct basis of comparison and equally well established that the systematic component(s) of total variance will be priced differently than the unsystematic component, if the latter is priced at all. Indeed, a regression line fitted to the interindustry book-return data presented in NAIC (1983) reveals an inverse relationship between book return and book variance across industries (see Venezian, 1984).

Even if book figures were appropriate for evaluating insurance risk and return, the interindustry method would be invalidated due to differences in accounting procedures across industries. For example, the book values of assets for most industrial firms tend to be far below their market values. Insurers, on the other hand, invest primarily in marketable securities, which have book values much closer to their market values. Thus, other things being equal, an industrial firm will show a higher book return on equity than an insurance company.[1] Fisher and McGowan (1983) have shown that even *intraindustry* comparisons can be misleading if firms utilize different depreciation methods.

The recognition of these defects has led to the development of more appropriate financial pricing models for property–liability insurance contracts. The earliest of these were based on the capital-asset pricing model (CAPM) (see, for example, Biger and Kahane, 1978; Fairley, 1979). These authors obtained the following formula for underwriting profits as a proportion of premiums:

$$R_u = -kR_f + \beta_u [R_m - R_f), \tag{7.1}$$

where

$R_u$ = underwriting profits as a proportion of gross premiums,

$R_f$ = risk-free rate of interest,

$R_m$ = rate of return on the market portfolio,

$\beta_u$ = the underwriting beta = Cov $(R_u, R_m)/\text{Var}(R_m)$, and

$k$ = the average holding period (reserve/premium ratio).[2]

The reasoning behind this formula is simple: The company gives the policyholder credit for the use of his funds at the risk-free rate (the credit is $-kR_f$) and is given a reward for risk-bearing based on the covariability of underwriting profits with the market portfolio.

Although the CAPM underwriting profit formula represented a major advance in insurance pricing, it has a number of potentially serious limitations. A complete analysis of this formula is beyond the scope of this chapter. However, it is relevant to note that the $k$ factor is a carry-over from the accounting methodologies. This factor is a poor proxy for the cash-flow pattern inherent in the insurance transaction.

Since the actual cash-flow pattern is now readily available, there is no justification for the continued use of a proxy variable. This was pointed out by Myers and Cohn (1987), who developed one of the most influential discounted cash-flow models for insurance ratemaking. This model is utilized in regulating automobile and workers' compensation insurance rates in Massachusetts and has been proposed in other states. Other models have been proposed by various insurance organizations and regulators. The model that has achieved the most prominence is the one utilized by the National Council on Compensation Insurance (NCCI), the rating bureau for workers' compensation insurance. Workers' compensation is the most important commercial line of insurance in terms of premium volume. Voluntary-market workers' compensation premiums are regulated in all but ten states. The NCCI represents the insurance industry in approximately 40 states.[3]

On the surface, the Myers–Cohn and NCCI models differ significantly, and the latter model appears to violate many of the underlying principles of capital budgeting. On closer inspection, however, the two models are not entirely dissimilar, and the NCCI approach is in fact consistent with financial principles. However, there are some important differences between the two models, which must be recognized if rates are to be set correctly. The purpose of this chapter is to review and critique these two models, to make recommendations for improvement, and to provide numerical examples of their use.

Before proceeding, it is important to point out that other methods for pricing property–liability insurance contracts are currently being developed. These are based on options pricing models (Doherty and Garven, 1986) and on more general models of continuous time finance (Kraus and Ross, 1982; Cummins, 1988b). These models, or models that evolve from them, may eventually supplant discrete-time discounted cash-flow models in insurance ratemaking. These models are not yet fully operational, and a number of problems must be solved before they can be used in a real-world context. In addition, their technical nature may pose a barrier to their use in some regulatory jurisdictions. Consequently, it is likely that more conventional discounted cash-flow models will continue to be used for the foreseeable future. Discounted cash-flow models may appear to be straight-forward, but a number of unresolved issues exist, which annually consume thousands of hours of professional time in insurance-rate hearings. It is to these models and issues that we now turn.[4]

## Principles of Discounted Cash-Flow (DCF) Models

The Myers–Cohn (hereafter referred to as MC) model and the NCCI model are based on concepts of capital budgeting. Essentially, the in-surance policy is viewed as a project that is being considered by the firm. The methods attempt to arrive at a price (the premium) for the project that will provide a fair rate of return to the insurance company, considering the timing and risk of the cash flows arising under the policy as well as the market rate of interest.

Considering the parallels with capital budgeting, it is tempting simply to adopt an off-the-shelf model from one of the leading corporate finance text-books. This approach would overlook critically important subtleties of the insurance transaction and could lead to serious errors in computing insurance premiums. Such errors are rather common in rate-regulatory proceedings.

Most of the common errors can easily be avoided by following a few basic principles, which are variants of the principles of capital budgeting set forth in finance texts (e.g., Ross and Westerfield, 1988; Brealey and Myers, 1988). The DCF principles that are most important in insurance are the following:

1. *Value additivity.* Each policy (or block of policies, in the case of ratemaking for a state) should stand on its own. In particular, policies should not be priced to reflect the insurer's past experience, such as embedded yields and sunk costs.

2. *Irrelevance of accounting (both statutory and GAAP).* Accounting numbers generally are not relevant in a DCF analysis except as they directly impact cash flows. In most instances, a firm's accounting numbers do not affect its cash flows. An important exception is the firm's federal tax payments, which to some extent are based on accounting results. It is important to recognize, however, that it is the flow (the tax payment) and not the accounting numbers that enter the DCF formula. The irrelevance of accounting also implies that loss reserves and loss development factors

are irrelevant in DCF analysis. Instead, the analysis should focus on the loss *payout* pattern, so a paid loss rather than an incurred loss triangle should be used. The use of paid rather than incurred losses is consistent not only with principles of corporate finance but with the international actuarial literature (Taylor, 1986).

A possible exception to the accounting irrelevance rule would be a binding regulatory constraint that affects cash flows. For example, if regulation effectively constrains firm growth due to the application of the 3:1 premiums-to-surplus rule, this would have to be taken into account in pricing. In normal periods, regulatory constraints probably are not binding. However, rigorous empirical evidence on this issue presently does not exist.

3. *Avoidance of double counting.* Double counting is always a potential problem in capital budgeting but seems to be particularly significant in insurance. The way to avoid double counting is to *adopt a perspective.* Two perspectives are available, both of which can lead to correct results: the policy can be priced from the point of view of the policyholder, or from the point of view of the company (or the equity provider). Flows from one are flows to the other. Thus, if appropriately defined, the two perspectives lead to models that are mirror images of one another. Mixing the perspectives can lead to double counting.

## Insurance Cash-Flow Perspectives

This section provides an intuitive overview of flow definition in insurance. The precise details of the models are discussed in subsequent sections. In defining flows, the Myers–Cohn model adopts the policyholder perspect-ive, while the NCCI model utilizes the perspective of the equity provider. The relevant flows are the following:

| *Policyholder Perspective (MC)* | *Equity-Provider Perspective (NCCI)* |
|---|---|
| Premium payments (net of expenses) | Surplus commitment |
| | Investment income |
| Loss payments | Underwriting profit |
| Corporate taxes | Corporate taxes |
| | Release of surplus commitment |

The MC approach counts all flows that the policyholder either pays or receives. Thus, the policyholder pays premiums (a cash outflow) and receives loss payments (cash inflow). The policyholder is also responsible for paying the corporate taxes that resuslt from the insurance transaction. These include both taxes on underwriting profits and taxes on investment income received on funds backing the policy. Funds backing the policy include the unexpended premium balance (which exists because premiums are paid early in the policy period and losses are paid later) and the surplus committed to the policy.

Under MC, surplus is assumed to be committed in proportion to premiums when the policy is initiated and to be released to the company as losses are paid. The investment income tax on this surplus must be paid by the policyholder in order for the firm to receive a fair rate of return. The rationale is that the owners of the firm could invest directly in financial assets and not have to pay the corporate income tax. They will not subject themselves to an additional layer of taxation by investing in an insurance company. Therefore, the policyholder must pay the corporate tax. This is the only direct compensation the company receives for its surplus commitment under the MC model. Because surplus is committed when the policy is written (an outflow for the company) and released as the losses are paid (an inflow), the MC model is also sometimes called the *surplus flow* model, although this term could as easily be applied to the NCCI model.[5]

The NCCI model also recognizes the company's surplus commitment. The company is assumed to commit surplus as premiums are earned (i.e., as losses are incurred), and the surplus is released as losses are paid. The pattern of surplus release is slightly different from that in the MC model, and this difference is discussed in more detail below. In the NCCI model, it is noteworthy that it is the surplus flow itself, not just the taxes on the flow, that is incorporated in the model. This distinction is important, as discussed below. The NCCI model assumes that the company receives the investment income (net of taxes) on the surplus commitment and premium balance and that the company receives the underwriting profit (again, net of tax). In the NCCI model, taxes affect the investment balance, which throws off investment income.[6] The investment income is treated as a discounted flow. At first glance, the use of investment income as a flow seems to be contrary to capital budgeting principles. However, as shown below, this is not a problem if done correctly.

An issue in both models is the appropriate level of surplus commitment. Usually, this commitment is selected rather arbitrarily based on industry-wide ratios of premiums-to-surplus (MC) or reserves-to-surplus (NCCI). The reason for this is that no widely accepted theoretical rationale for surplus commitment in insurance presently exists. Ultimately, the level of surplus is determined by supply and demand considerations and perhaps by regulation. For example, prices set in a competitive insurance market can be expected to lead to an equilibrium *demand for safety*, which would imply a level of surplus commitment. The capital costs required to maintain this surplus commitment would be included in the price of insurance. The more advanced financial pricing models mentioned above (e.g., Doherty–Garven, 1986; Cummins, 1988b) provide the foundations for a theory of surplus commitment. However, until the details of this theory have been worked out, a market premiums-to-surplus or reserves-to-surplus ratio will continue to be used. The following analysis assumes the existence of such a ratio, imposed by regulatory fiat. This assumption is consistent with the realities of insurance ratemaking in a regulatory environment.

## Internal Rate of Return (IRR) versus Net Present Value (NPV)

As in conventional capital budgeting, an important issue in insurance DCF analysis is whether to utilize an internal rate of return (IRR) or net present value (NPV) approach. The NCCI model uses IRR, while Myers–Cohn use NPV.

The problems with the IRR method are well known (see, for example, Brealy and Myers, 1988, pp. 77–85). Two of the IRR pitfalls are especially important in insurance. These are briefly discussed here because they so often lead to errors in insurance applications.

Consider the formula for the net present value (NPV) of a cash flow stream:

$$NPV = C_0 + C_1/(1 + R) + C_2/(1 + R)^2 + C_3/(1 + R)^3 + \ldots, \qquad (7.2)$$

where

$C_i =$ cash flow at time $i$, and

$R =$ the discount rate.

The IRR is defined as the discount rate that results in NPV $= 0$. In the usual corporate capital budgeting problem, $C_0$ is negative (the cost of the project) and the later cash flows are positive (net returns from the project). In this case, the firm is *lending* $C_0$ and receiving returns from the loan in later years. The firm would like the rate of return on a loan to be as *large* as possible; hence, the decision rule is: Accept if IRR $> R_c$, where $R_c =$ the cost of capital appropriate for the project.

The insurance problem does not fall into the standard framework. The reason is that insurance cash flows (from the company perspective) are positive initially and negative later on.[7] The intuitive interpretation is that the firm is *borrowing* rather than lending. Thus, it would like the cost of borrowing to be as *small* as possible. The decision rule here is: Accept if IRR $< R_c$.

Similar difficulties arise in interpreting changes in the cash-flow stream. Thus, an increase in the premium ($C_0$) leads to a *reduction* in the IRR, while a proportionate increase in every loss flow leads to an *increase* in IRR. While the IRR can still lead to correct decisions in this context if interpreted appropriately, the seemingly counterintuitive nature of the relationships can present significant problems in a regulatory setting.

Insurance cash flows also tend to run afoul of two other IRR pitfalls: multiple rates of return problem and the term-structure of interest rates. By Descartes' *rule of signs*, there can be as many solutions of equation (7.2) as there are changes in sign. Thus, if the cash-flow stream changes from positive (at time 0) to negative and then back to positive, there may be two values of $R$ that solve equation (7.2). In most cases, only one solution has a meaningful economic interpretation, but regulators may be skeptical of a method that can yield meaningless solutions. Finally, in long-tail lines it may be desirable to use different interest rates for different durations. This too can lead to serious problems in interpreting the IRR (see Brealey and Myers, 1988, p. 85).

One rationale that is given for using the IRR in insurance is that it is difficult to estimate the cost of capital for an insurance project. At first glance, the IRR seems to finesse the cost of capital problem by making no assumptions regarding the discount rate. This advantage is illusory, however, because the IRR decision rule requires a comparison with the cost of capital. Thus, ultimately, one must deal with the estimation problem.

Considering the potential problems that can arise in using the IRR for insurance pricing, the NPV method is the better choice. While the IRR method does give correct results if interpreted correctly, it is simpler and less ambiguous to use the NPV approach. The NCCI method can easily be recast in the NPV framework, simply by using the cost of capital as the discount rate and applying the usual decision rule: Accept if NPV $> 0$.

## The Models: Two-Period Case

The distinctions between the models can be seen most easily by considering a simple two-period case. The multiperiod formulas and examples are presented elsewhere (Cummins, 1988c).

In the two-period case, the premium is received at time 0 and losses are paid at time 1. Taxes are assumed to be paid at time 1. Surplus is assumed to be committed at time 0 at surplus-to-premium ratio $\delta$ (MC) or reserves-to-premium ratio $\phi$ (NCCI). For example, if $\delta = .5$, $.50$ of surplus is committed for each dollar of premium. Initially, it is assumed that assets are invested at the risk-free rate. The importance of this assumption is analyzed in a subsequent section.

### The Myers–Cohn (MC) Model

The Myers–Cohn model solves the following formula for $P$, the premium:

$$PV(P) = PV(L) + PV(\text{Tax}), \qquad (7.3)$$

where

PV($'$) = the present value operator,

$P$ = the premium,

$L$ = expected losses, loss-adjustment expenses, and underwriting expense payments (this flow is referred to hereafter as the *loss flow*), and

Tax = corporate taxes on underwriting and investment income associated with this policy or policy block.

The method is an application of Myers' *adjusted present value* method (see Brealey and Myers, 1988, pp. 443–446). The project is evaluated as if it were totally equity-financed, and each component of the cash-flow stream is evaluated at the risk-adjusted discount rate appropriate for that flow.

The cash flows for the two-period Myers–Cohn model are presented in table 7–1. The risk-adjusted discount rate for loss flows is $R_L$. Although any theoretically defensible risk-adjusted discount rate could be used, the model is usually applied using the CAPM: $R_L = R_f + \beta_L[R_m - R_f]$, where $\beta_L$ has the obvious definition.

Using the cash flows in table 7–1, equation (7.3) becomes

$$P = L/(1 + R_L) + \tau R_f P(1 + \delta)/(1 + R_f) + \tau P/(1 + R_f) - \tau L/(1 + R_L). \qquad (7.4)$$

Notice that the premium component of the underwriting profit tax is discounted at the risk-free rate, while the loss component is discounted at

Table 7-1. Cash Flows In Two-Period Myers–Cohn Model

| Flow | Time 0 | 1 | Discount Rate |
|------|--------|---|---------------|
| Premium | $P$ | 0 | $R_f$ |
| Loss | 0 | $L$ | $R_L$ |
| Underwriting Profits Tax | 0 | $\tau(P-L)$ | $R_f, R_L$ |
| Investment Balance (IB) | $P(1+\delta)$ | 0 | |
| IB Tax | 0 | $\tau R_f P(1+\delta)$ | $R_f$ |

Key: $P$ = premiums, $L$ = expected losses, $R_f$ = risk-free rate of interest, $R_L$ = risk-adjusted discount rate for losses, $\tau$ = corporate income tax rate, $\delta$ = surplus-to-premiums ratio.

the RADR for losses. Solving equation (6.4) for P and conducting some algebraic manipulations yields

$$P = \frac{L}{(1 + R_L)\,(1 - \tau R_f \delta/[(1 + R_f)\,(1 - \tau)])} . \qquad (7.5)$$

The comparative statics are as follows: $P_{R_L} < O, P_t > O, P\delta > 0$, and $P_{R_f} < 0$, where subscripts indicate partial derivatives with respect to the subscripted variable or parameter.[8] The denominator of equation (7.5) is a tax-adjusted RADR analogous to Fairley's (1979) tax-adjusted underwriting margin. The tax-adjustment term is exactly the same as Fairley's. However, his result gives an underwriting profit margin with a $k$ factor to represent the payout tail, while our discount rate is applied directly, to the loss cash flow.

## The NCCI Model

The cash flows for the NCCI model are shown in table 7–2. As mentioned above, this is usually applied as an IRR model. Hence, one would solve for $R$ such that the present valud of all cash flows is zero, the result is then compared with the cost of capital $R_c$. The fair premium is the value for which IRR $= R_c$. Alternatively, the cost of capital could be used as the discount rate and the premium set so that NPV $= 0$. As discussed above, this would be the more appropriate procedure in view of the potential ambiguities of the IRR.

Table 7–2.  Cash Flows in Two-Period NCCI Model

|  | Time | | |
| --- | --- | --- | --- |
| Flow | 0 | 1 | Discount Rate |
| Surplus Investment | $-\phi D$ | $\phi D$ | R |
| Income Underwriting | 0 | $(1-\tau)(P+\phi D)R_f$ | R |
| Profit | 0 | $(1-\tau)(P-L)$ | R |

Key: $P$ = premiums, $L$ = expected losses, $R_f$ = risk-free rate of interest, $\tau$ = corporate income tax rate, $\phi$ = surplus-to-reserves ratio.

For comparison with the MC model, it is helpful to set the NCCI cash flows equal to zero and solve for $P$, given $R_c$. The result is the following equation:

$$P = \frac{L + \phi D[\tau R_f + (R_c - R_f)]/(1 - \tau)}{(1 + R_f)}, \tag{7.6}$$

where $D$ = reserves and $\phi$ = the surplus-to-reserves ratio. In general, the two formulas (7.5) and (7.6) do not give the same results. Two conditions under which the results are the same are the following: 1) if all flows are discounted at the same rate, i.e., if $R_f = R_c = R_L$, or 2) if, in the NCCI model, losses are discounted at $R_L$ and other flows at $R_f$. This essentially means that duality is present in the flows but not necessarily in the discount rates.

## Evaluation

Myers and Cohn are applying orthodox capital budgeting theory. Their model implies that the cost of insurance is the present value of losses, discounted to reflect systematic risk, plus the present value of the corporate taxes incurred as a result of pooling risks through a corporate insurance entity. Although the NCCI model does not appear to be a conventional capital budgeting model, it is in fact quite similar in concept to the MC model. The premium in the NCCI model is the present value of expected losses plus an amount sufficient, after-tax, to pay the taxes on investment income on committed surplus plus a risk charge $(R_c - R_f)$, which also is proportional to the surplus commitment.

Since the models are usually applied using CAPM risk-adjusted discount rates or costs of capital, no loading usually is present for unsystematic risk, i.e., the probability of ruin is not priced. However, neither model is specifically linked to the CAPM. Any defensible cost of capital or RADR formula could be used.

The MC model compensates the policyholder at the risk-free rate for the loss of use of his funds between the premium and loss payment dates. To facilitate comparability, the NCCI model was derived above on the assumption that investments are in risk-free assets. However, in actual applications of this model, the anticipated market rate of investment return usually is used.

The use of the risk-free rate is based on Fairley's (1979) argument that the policyholder does not buy insurance to take investment risk. Consequently, if the company chooses to invest premiums and surplus in riskier assets, it should bear the risk and receive the return (or loss) from the riskier strategy. According to Fairley, the policyholder would be insulated from the company's investment risk-taking behavior through the regulatory requirement that investment income credits follow the risk-free rate.

Recent work by Cummins (1988a) reveals that Fairley's argument is incorrect and that the investment income credit should be at the company's anticipated market return, not at the risk-free rate. If policyholders are credited with investment income at $R_f$ and if guaranty fund premiums are not risk-based, the insurer has an incentive to pursue risky investment strategies, which increase the probability of bankruptcy. There is no market penalty for doing this, since the existence of the guaranty fund renders all policies free of default risk. If the guaranty fund premiums are flat, there is no penalty from the guaranty fund either, so that all gains from risky investing accrue to the company. If the company must credit the policyholder with investment income based on its anticipated portfolio mix, however, the problem is lessened because part of the gain from risky investing accrues to the policyholder.

In a recent paper, Cummins (1988a) develops risk-adjusted discount rates for risky insurance policies, i.e., policies issued by firms that can become bankrupt. Under these circumstances, the following risk-adjusted discount rate would be used:

$$R_L = R_f + [(D_A A/D) \beta_A + (D_L L/D) \beta_L] [R_m - R_f] \qquad (7.7)$$

where

$A$ = assets,

$L$ = liabilities,

$D$ = the value of debt, i.e., $L[\exp(-R_f T) - B(x,T)]$,

$B(x,T)$ = a Black–Scholes put option on the firms asset-to-liability ratio, $x = A/L$, with exercise price 1 and time to expiration $T$.

In this formula, the risk-adjustment would be a function of the firm's capital structure and its asset risk, as well as the liability risk. The additional risk charge would either reduce the policyholder's premium, if no guaranty fund were present, or would be paid to the guaranty fund. This would eliminate the firm's incentive to take unnecessary investment risk.

It is revealing to compare the rate of return on shareholders' equity under the two premium formulas. In each case, the year-end values for the two models are defined as

$$MC: V_1 = P(1 + R_f) + \delta P(1 + R_f) - L - \tau(P - L) - \tau R_f P(1 + \delta), \quad (7.8a)$$

$$NCCI: V_1 = P(1 + R_f) + \phi D(1 + R_f) - L - \tau(P - L) - \tau R_f(P + \phi D). \quad (7.8b)$$

Equations (7.8a) and (7.8b) can be thought of as the value of the stockholders' equity if the company wrote only this policy and was dissolved at time 1. The return to stockholders' equity is defined as $V_1/S - 1$, where $S$ is initial surplus commitment. After some algebra, we find the following rates of return on the company's surplus commitment:[9]

$$MC: R = R_f + (L/S)(1 - \tau)(R_f - R_L)/(1 + R_L), \quad (7.9a)$$

$$NCCI: R = R_c. \quad (7.9b)$$

The MC result has a clear intuitive interpretation. Capital is rewarded at the profit margin $(R_f - R_L)$ on the basis of the present value of the losses assumed by the company, $L/(1 + R_L)$. The value of losses is after-tax, reflecting the federal tax shield for loss payments. The intuitive interpretation of the NCCI model is also quite clear: the company is compensated for its surplus commitment at the cost of capital.

To see the relationship between the two models, consider the formula for the cost of capital of a levered firm:

$$R_c = R_A + (D/S)(R_A - R_L) \quad (7.10)$$

where

$D$ = the market value of liabilities,

$S$ = the market value of surplus, and

$R_A$ = the rate of return on the firm's assets.

Using equation (7.10) with $R_f$ substituted for $R_A$, it is clear that equations (7.9a) and (7.9b) will be equivalent if $D$, the market value of liabilities, is equal to $L(1 - \tau)/(1 + R_L)$. We argue that the latter expression is the market value of liabilities for the insurer under the assumption that losses generate a tax shield that can be immediately recovered at full value.

These results indicate that both the MC and NCCI models give correct results if interpreted correctly. However, the results imply that the present market value, not the book value of liabilities, must be used in the NCCI approach. Thus, if a market-surplus commitment ratio is used, the ratio should be based on the estimated market value of liabilities, not on the book value. Other things being equal, the adjustment of liabilities to present market value also will affect surplus. If the market value of liabilities is less than the nominal value, the market value of surplus will be higher than the book value and the market value of $D/S$ will be lower than the book ratio.

The NCCI model has a possible advantage over MC in terms of parameter estimation. This is the case because the cost of capital $R_c$ is much easier to estimate than the liability $\beta_L$, at least for traded firms (see Cummins and Harrington, 1985). However, it is important to emphaszie that the use of a company-wide cost of capital implicitly assumes that the new policy has the same risk-return characteristics as the firm as a whole. Although this assumption may be questionable in multiple-line companies, the error involved by assuming equivalent risk may be less than the error that would be introduced by using a liability beta.

## Conclusions

Discounted cash-flow methods are rapidly becoming the prevailing ratemaking methodology in property-liability insurance. The two most prominent models are the Myers–Cohn (MC) and NCCI models. The former is utilized in ratemaking in Massachusetts, while the latter is used in workers' compensation insurance ratemaking in several jurisdictions. The MC model is a net present-value model, while the NCCI model uses the IRR approach.

This chapter has analyzed and evaluated the MC and NCCI models. Among the conclusions are the following:

1. It is important to be very careful in defining cash flows. Accounting numbers are irrelevant, and double counting should be avoided. The latter problem can be obviated by adopting a perspective, i.e., the

policy should be valued either from the policyholder perspective or the equity-provider perspective.

2. Due to potential ambiguities with the IRR methodology, care must be taken in interpreting IRR results in insurance ratemaking. To avoid ambiguities, it is preferable to utilize the NPV approach. The NCCI model can easily be recast as an NPV model.

3. The Myers–Cohn model uses the risk-free rate of interest to derive the investment income credit to policyholders for the loss of use of their funds between the premium and loss payment dates. In order to avoid undue risk-taking by the insurer, the actual rate of investment income expected to be earned on funds invested under the policy should be used, rather than the risk-free rate. This should not be an embedded yield, but rather the best estimate of the rate that will be earned on the funds invested in support of the policy being priced.

4. In spite of their apparent differences, the MC and NCCI models are both consistent with the principles of corporate finance and will give correct results if applied correctly. To achieve correct results with the NCCI model, reserves must be measured at market values in estimating the surplus-to-reserves ratio.

5. Ideally, the costs of capital should reflect firm capital structure and bankruptcy risk. Even if this procedure is not followed, crediting policyholders with the company's actual anticipated investment return will help to accomplish the same objective.

Significant progress will be made in the financial pricing of property–liability insurance during the coming years. Options pricing and more general models of continuous time finance will become available in operational versions. An emerging area of research is pricing models for interest-sensitive cash flows. These models will build upon the existing DCF models to establish more sophisticated criteria for insurance ratemaking.

## Notes

1. The net effect of accounting practices on the market/book value ratio of insurers has never been subjected to a comprehensive empirical analysis. The major valuation practices that should be analyzed are the valuation of bonds and reserves. Bonds are stated at amortized values, which will be above (below) market values during periods when interest rates have been rising (falling). Reserves, on the other hand, are stated at nominal (undiscounted) values. The net effect of expressing both bonds and reserves at market value is uncertain. However, it is unlikely that the difference between the market and book values of equity is as large for insurers as for industrial firms. The complexity of the isue reinforces the conclusion that interindustry book-return comparisons convey little useful information.

2. Fairley's definition of $k$ is "the average amount of investable funds created by the cash flow per dollar of annual premium" (Fairley, 1979, p.6; the page number refers to the Fairley chapter in the cited Cummins–Harrington book.) While he recognizes $k$ as being generated by the difference between premiums and expense and loss cash flows, his estimates of $k$ are based on ratios of reserves to premiums (1979, p. 7). Even if Fairley had estimated $k$ on the basis of cash flows, his use of $r_f k$ as the investment income credit would still not yield an accurate approximation to a true discounted cash flow price. See Myers and Cohn (1987) for further discussion of this issue.

3. Even in states with competitive rating laws for workers' compensation, rates for residual markets typically are subject to regulation. The NCCI represents insurers in about 40 states and directly makes rates in 32.

4. The term *discounted cash-flow model* is used here to refer to insurance pricing models that obtain prices by discounting the cash flows involved in the insurance transaction. In some finance texts, this term is used to refer to the model developed by Myron Gordon and J. B. Williams for the valuation of common stocks. For a discussion of the Gordon–Williams model, see Francis (1986, chapter 14).

5. Another version of the Myers–Cohn model, sometimes called the *surplus block* or *surplus stock* model, releases all surplus at the end of the policy year. This approach was not proposed by Myers and Cohn. It is difficult to justify the surplus block model theoretically, since it implies that no surplus is needed to back policy obligations after all premiums have been earned. There is a substantial amount of uncertainty regarding loss obligations that persists as long as any losses remain unpaid. Thus, the Myers–Cohn surplus flow approach is superior to the surplus block approach.

6. Thus, the present value of the tax effect is considered in this model, even though taxes do not appear as a separate flow as in MC.

7. In the NCCI model, as usually applied in practice, the perspective is strictly speaking that of the equity provider rather than the company. The NCCI views the equity provider's perspective as follows: a block of policies is sold, resulting in the collection of premiums and the establishment of loss reserves. Capital and surplus are committed in proportion to loss reserves. Since the premium is exhausted after the establishment of loss reserves and the payment of expenses, and initial cash flows to the equity holder and negative, consisting primarily of the surplus that is committed proportional to reserves. Thus, in the NCCI view the cash-flows pattern is analogous to the usual capital budgeting problem. This approach assumes that regulatory constraints are present such that accounting conventions are relevant for cash-flow analysis. The issue is whether or not the underwriting loss should be funded for cash-flow purposes when the policy is written or when the negative cash flow actually occurs (i.e., when the cash leaves the company rather than when it is transferred from the company's surplus account to its liability accounts). The issue can be resolved only by determining whether regulatory constraints are actually binding. As mentioned above, rigorous empirical evidence on this issue presently does not exist.

8. It would be possible to construct a set of parameter values such that $P_{Rf}$ would be $> 0$. However, such a combination of parameter values would not be economically meaningful.

9. The derivation utilizes equation (7.8) with $R_A$ set equal to $R_f$.

# References

Arthur D. Little, Inc. *Prices and Profits in Property and Liability Insurance: A Report to American Insurance Association.* Boston: Arthur D. Little, 1967.

Biger, Nihum, and Yehuda Kahane. "Risk Considerations In Insurance Ratemaking." *Journal of Risk and Insurance* 45 (1978): 121–132.

Brealey, Richard A., and Stewart C. Myers. *Principles of Corporate Finance.* 3rd ed. New York: McGraw-Hill Book Co, 1988.

Cummins, J. David. "Capital Structure and Fair Profits In Property–Liability Insurance." Working paper, University of Pennsylvania, 1988a.

Cummins, J. David. "Risk-Based Premiums for Insurance Guaranty Funds." *Journal of Finance* 43 (1988b).

Cummins, J. David, "Multi-Period Discounted Cash Flow Ratemaking In Property–Liability Insurance." Working paper, University of Pennsylvania, 1988c.

Cummins, J. David, and Lena Chang. "An Analysis of the New Jersey Formula for Including Investment Income In Property–Liability Insurance Ratemaking." *Journal of Insurance Regulation* 1 (1983): 555–573.

Cummins, J. David, and Scott E. Harrington. "Property–Liability Insurance Rate Regulation: Estimation of Underwriting Betas Using Quarterly Profit Data." *Journal of Risk and Insurance* 52 (1985): 16–43.

Cummins, J. David, and David J. Nye. "The Stochastic Characteristics of Property–Liability Insurance Profits." *Journal of Risk and Insurance* 47(1980): 61–80.

D'Arcy, Stephen, and Neil A. Doherty. *Financial Theory of Insurance Pricing.* Philadelphia: S. S. Huebner Foundation, 1988.

Doherty, Neil A., and James R. Garven. "Price Regulation in Property–Liability Insurance: A Contingent Claims Approach." *Journal of Finance* 41 (1986): 1031–1050.

Fairley, William. "Investment Income and Profit Margins in Property–Liability Insurance: Theory and Empirical Tests." *Bell Journal* 10 (1979): 192–210. Reprinted in J. D. Cummins and S. E. Harrington (eds.), *Fair Rate of Return In Property–Liability Insurance.* Norwell, MA: Kluwer Academic Publishers, 1987.

Fisher, F. M., and McGowan, J. J. "On the Misuse of Accounting Rates of Return to Infer Monopoly Profits." *American Economic Review* 65 (1983): 82–97.

Francis, Jack Clark. *Investment: Analysis and Management.* 4th ed. New York: McGraw-Hill, 1986.

Hill, Raymond, and Franco Modigliani. "The Massachusetts Model of Profit Regulation in Non-Life Insurance." In J. D. Cummins and S. E. Harrington (eds.), *Fair Rate of Return in Property–Liability Insurance.* Norwell, MA: Kluwer Academic Publishers, 1987.

Kraus, Alan, and Stephen Ross. "The Determination of Fair Profits for the Property –Liability Insurance Firm." *Journal of Finance* 33 (1982): 1015–1028.

Myers, Stewart and Richard Cohn. "Insurance Rate Regulation and the Capital Asset Pricing Model." In J. D. Cummins and S. E. Harrington (eds.), *Fair Rate of Return in Property–Liability Insurance.* Norwell, MA: Kluwer Academic Publishers, 1987.

National Association of Insurance Commissioners. *Report of the Advisory*

*Committee To the NAIC Task Force on Profitability and Investment Income.*
Kansas City, MO: National Association of Insurance Commissioners, 1983.
Ross, Stephen A., and Randolph Westerfield. *Corporate Finance.* St. Louis, MO:
Times Mirror/Mosby College Publishing, 1988.
Taylor, Gregory C. *Claim Reserving In Non-Life Insurance.* New York: North-
Holland, 1986.
Venezian, Emilio C. "Are Insurers Underearning?" *Journal of Risk and Insurance*
51 (1984): 150–156.
Williams, C. Arthur Jr. "Regulating Property Liability Insurance Rates Through
Excess Profits Statutes." *Journal of Risk and Insurance* 50 (1983): 445–472.

# Index